Clarinets, Pipelines and Unforeseen Places
The Evolution of an Engineer

Grahame Campbell

Copyright 2016 © Grahame Campbell
All rights reserved

No part of this book may be copied, reproduced, adapted, stored in a retrieval system, communicated or transmitted in any form or by any means without prior written permission. All inquiries should be made to the author at the address below.

Contact the author:
grahame.campbell@gmail.com

Production by Hourigan & Co.
http://hourigan.co

Set in Linux Libertine

**National Library of Australia
Cataloguing-in-Publication entry**

Creator: Campbell, Grahame, author.
Title: Clarinets, pipelines and unforeseen places : the evolution of
an engineer / Grahame Campbell.

ISBN: 9780994525406 (paperback)
Campbell, Grahame.
Engineers–Australia–Biography.
Clarinetists–Australia–Biography.
Saxophonists–Australia–Biography.
620.0092

About the author

Grahame Campbell was born in 1943, and grew up in the Sydney suburb of Kyeemagh. He studied engineering at the University of New South Wales while also fostering a love of music, and went on to work for the NSW Railways before joining CMPS, a consultancy where he would eventually rise to become CEO. His later career has involved directorships at CMPS&F, Anaconda Nickel, ACEA, SWR, USC and Iluka Resources. Today he travels extensively, and still plays jazz.

Contents

Acknowledgements ix

Prologue. xi

I Roots and wings: 1942   1

    1. Callithumpian roots 3

    2. Falling into engineering 21

    3. On the road 33

    4. Learning curve 51

    5. My love of music 59

II Learning about projects: 1965   75

    6. I join the workforce. 77

    7. I stop the Southern Aurora. 85

    8. The harsh reality of private enterprise   105

    9. Southern discomfort 117

    10. Master's thesis. 131

    11. Indonesia: Into the deep end 137

III	The oil and gas industry: 1972	155
	12. Moomba to Sydney Pipeline	157
	13. Tulsa Oil	185
	14. Trial by fire in Iraq	201
	15. My career takes a turn	249
	16. Project manager blues	251
IV	Reflections and choices: 1977	265
	17. World trip	267
	18. Wollongong or bust	287
	19. Building a business	293
V	Around the world: 1979	305
	20. On island time	307
	21. Helping Huffco	335
	22. The USA gas bubble bursts	347
	23. The good oil in Bakersfield	353
VI	Pipelines in Australia: 1982	365
	24. Home turf: 1982	367
	25. Oil from western Queensland	377

	26. Gas from the Red Centre: 1984	395
	27. The PNG Highlands: 1985	421
VII	**THE ENGINEERING BUSINESS: 1987**	435
	28. CMPS	437
	29. The private road business: 1988	451
	30. CMPS grows in different ways: 1991	459
VIII	**POLITICS AND BOARDS: 1996**	467
	31. I spread my political wings	469
	32. The board years	481
	33. Reflections	523

Acknowledgements

Many people contributed to the final manuscript of this memoir by correcting my imperfect memory and contributing ideas. Chris Linnegar, Tony Shepherd, John Green, John Grill, Jim McDonald, Michael Folie and Steve Harrison took the time to read and respond.

Tricia Dearborn, Ian Heads and Larry Writer provided editorial skill and advice.

A special thanks to Geoff Lehmann for suggesting the title and to Steve Clisby for the portrait image on the back cover.

Julie Hibberd encouraged me to 'put it down on paper' and finish the job.

My sincere thanks to you all.

Prologue

North Iraq, 1974

We were sitting in the lounge of the Kirkuk oil camp in north Iraq, trying to gather data for a new natural gas project to use the associated gas from the oil production – 'putting out the flares', as the Western press described it. From somewhere nearby came the sound of a field gun firing. I turned to Ali and asked what damage the Kurds had done to the oil fields. He replied 'Grahame, we have no reliable records, but production is only down 10% – new wells are commissioned regularly.'

'Ali, I can't do my job if I don't know where the production is coming from and what the plans are for the next twelve months.'

I was working for an American oil and gas engineering company, managing a project for the Iraqi government, who were supported by the Russians in their war effort. Ali stared at me wearily and replied, 'We are at war and every day is new.' he said 'Our field operators are under pressure, and the bureaucrats in Baghdad are insensitive to the local problems.'

Ali Parlak was the liaison officer for the ministry of

oil charged with helping me access the files and plans for the northern oil fields. He was of Turkish descent and had spent many years working for the Iraq Petroleum Company under British management. I had left the USA with a clear plan and led a team comprising Salim Jarrah, a plant specialist, and geologist Robert Blake to gather the required information to design the system. A billion cubic feet of natural gas containing 100,000 barrels per day of liquid petroleum gas (LPG) was being burned in the flare to keep the oil production on track. Our job was to design a scheme to collect the gas and LPG and transport them to places where they could be productively used.

On our arrival in Baghdad, we learned that a major war was being waged in the north, in the area of our project. Ostensibly it was an uprising of Kurdish nationalists trying to establish a homeland for the Kurdish people. In reality, it was a proxy Iran-Iraq war ultimately supported by US and Russian military hardware. None of this was reported in the Western press; if mentioned at all, it was described as 'mountain skirmishes'. I had accepted this project management role after studying Mid-East recent history, and was aware of the Yom Kippur War the prior year. I was shocked to discover 150,000 fighters were involved – 'skirmishes' did not really cover it. The Shah of Iran was flexing his muscles and threatening to invade Iraq to protect the Shia Muslims, who were oppressed by Saddam Hussein.

We were potentially in the middle of it.

Ali excused himself and left me nursing a beer and wondering how I had arrived at this point in my life. I had discovered that Robert, the geologist, was an alcoholic and that Salim, the plant expert, was a rabid supporter of Palestinian terrorism. My family was living in Tulsa, Oklahoma, and Christmas was only weeks away. It was 1974, and I had no way of communicating with my wife, as it was impossible to make international phone calls and telex was unavailable. The dull thud of field guns firing into the darkness reminded me of my situation.

The previous evening, Robert had laid out a map of the region to show me our escape route in the event that Iran formally invaded Iraq. He had been to Iraq several times, advising the government on oil-field management, and had become friendly with senior managers of Turkish background. 'Grahame, we will need to drive to Mosul and then on to the Turkish border to safety. My friends will help.' I looked at him quizzically. 'Aren't the Iranians supported by the Americans?' I asked. His eyes lit up, 'Yes, but the locals won't look kindly on people helping the Iraq government.' I shook my head. 'I won't be going; I'll take my chances here.'

Now Robert approached with a bottle of scotch and three glasses. 'Where's Ali?' he said looking around. 'He's gone to bed.' Robert set the bottle down carefully,

'He was going to explain the production plans.' 'I don't think he knows anything about the production,' I said. 'I have a feeling that there *are* no plans and they're just responding to the attacks on the facilities by the Kurds.' Robert stared at the bottle and replied, 'My friends told me they're trying to do a water flood on the Jambur field. If it's true, they must be having production problems, and they don't have the technology to do a water flood.'

A flash through the window followed by a *krump* announced another shell winging its way into the darkness. Robert caught my eye and remarked, 'It's practice for the coming invasion.'

* * *

When I finished my university studies in civil engineering ten years earlier, I never anticipated, much less imagined, that I would find myself in these far-flung outposts of the world, sometimes in the middle of a war zone, trying to make sense of the brief and complete the project. Bizarre events I assumed were a one-off seemed to happen all the time. And wild, unpredictable characters who were technically unemployable seemed to be in charge. It was never like this in the texts I studied.

This book tells the story of that journey—not so much a baptism by fire as an entire career with a blowtorch to the belly—where I survived and prospered by evolving from an engineer-on-paper to the fully informed, adaptable, multifunctional engineer I became.

Part I
Roots and wings
1942

1. Callithumpian roots

Don't expect too much...

I grew up in Kyeemagh, a suburb of Sydney, next to the airport. Jacobson Avenue to be exact. It was a street of nondescript brick houses, with a grass verge and a footpath on each side of the bitumen strip. It hasn't changed today, except for the demographic, which morphed from Anglo-Celtic to Greek over the decades. It was wide enough to play football, cricket and other games, and so was where all the neighbourhood kids gathered. We were a group of about twenty on our block, with about a five-year age spread. The Spooners next door were the focus, as they had the older boys, John and Barry, who kept the peace and made sure we were safe. They also had two younger sisters, Janet and Judy, about the age of my sister Andrea and me. The tennis court in the Spooners' backyard became an important location in my childhood.

From age five I walked to school by myself. The buildings were demountable wooden structures, built as an emergency war effort. They survive today. Bushland surrounded the school and became our extended playground and the battle line for the kids who lived on the next block. The bush was home to snakes, goannas and lizards, with birds swirling above them.

After I was six, my mother each week gave me a shopping list to take to the Chinese lady in the market gardens for vegetables. I was nervous on my first visits. I had to cross down into a grassy area outside a group of old wooden sheds which were in front of the fields of vegetables that grew in long rows, seeming to stretch a mile. A dark open area with a rough concrete floor served as a truck parking zone. On my first visit, no one seemed to be there. I called out tentatively and noticed some movement to the left. A lady who looked to be a hundred years old grasping a machete emerged from the side room of a gloomy old shed wearing a conical hat and long fawn gown. Mind you, everyone over thirty looks a hundred to a six-year-old. The shed, I learned, was where the vegetables were prepared. I stood transfixed as she approached, and gingerly handed her my mother's list. She glanced at it and, without a word, turned and shuffled away. The place smelt different from anything I'd experienced, earthy with overtones of chilli. I glanced around but saw only a dirty lamp hanging against the wall. The lady disappeared into the field and returned fifteen minutes later with an armful of harvest. Once she'd chopped and wrapped the vegetables, I gave her some money and then ran home without looking back. I had survived. It was all a mysterious experience for a boy who gorged on blood-curdling stories of foreign intrigue. After a time I enjoyed my trips to the gardens and would follow the lady – I never knew her name – into the fields and watch her gather the listed items. Nothing was pre-cut, it came straight from the field. The gardens are still there today.

Only local traffic passed our house, mainly vendors like the milkman, coke delivery and the 'sanny man'. Not many people had cars, and the local private bus to Rockdale served as a feeder for the Illawarra train to the city. The 302 bus on General Holmes Drive wound its way to the city through the sand hills that surrounded the airport. It was a government service, with green double-deckers. Things changed when I was about seven years old; my father drove up in an Austin A40. The dream of holidays away became a reality.

We had no sewerage pipes, just a council service which took the pans and left empties. Door-to-door salesmen plied their wares, and Seventh Day Adventists and the Avon Lady came calling. A couple of times the milkman let me accompany him on his run delivering milk in pots and pans. His route incorporated a gypsy camp in the sandhills around the airport. A sand track wound around the low hills to the encampment set on a flat area. The Romany had caravans and swarthy skin. The appearance of our truck stirred them as they found jugs to receive their milk. Breakfast fires were set up in a circle, with makeshift chairs and tables among them.

I was appalled when a pigeon was killed for breakfast in front of me. This was my first 'multicultural' exposure, but my parents didn't think it extraordinary when I brought it up at tea in the evening. 'They have different ways,' my mother explained. 'Why do they live in caravans?' met with the same response. In reality, I grew up in a multicultural semi-rural place by the sea.

The primary school was in Brighton-Le-Sands on Crawford Road, about two kilometres away to the south. I could take the bus to school, but sometimes I walked to save the fare for lollies. The school backed onto a dairy and had a rural feel to it. Cows sometimes strayed across the playground.

Life was simple, and we made our own fun in the street outside the house. Nobody seemed disadvantaged. Billy carts were constructed in the Spooners' garage and raced in the street. I had a vivid imagination and followed explorers' adventures across the world in books, comics and magazines.

On weekends, I played tennis next door when the court was free. Barry Spooner had taught me to play, and when the court was occupied, I made do with hitting the ball that I kept in my pocket against the house wall. Barry would quiz me about the future,' What are you going to be? Do you like school?' I had no idea. The world hardly extended a few miles. Barry was very important in my life as he would answer my questions and discuss any subject I raised. These generally came from books that I was reading. When I was given a bike for my birthday, my horizons expanded. I rode to school. Junior branch tennis in the St George district where I lived was a phenomenon. More than 6,000 kids aged from 10–15 played on Saturday mornings, and, as a member of a team of two girls and two boys, we managed without parental involvement.

Summers were always hot. Back then, scorchers generally ended with a thunderstorm or a southerly buster. In school holidays, we went to Palm Beach in the new Austin A40. Dad bought a tent, and we'd camp next to the golf course. There was a religious group that organised kids' games and studies on the beach. I joined in because of the competition and the prizes. It was probably my only religious training.

The end of school year break meant camping. Our range extended to Burrill Lake on the south coast as my parents became more sophisticated, with a larger tent and a small caravan. Around Christmas bushfires were always a threat. We would monitor fires in the area on the local radio and watch for smoke. The radio also gave us the Davis Cup tennis broadcasts when we barracked for Australia against the USA.

We also ventured north to Mullumbimby on the far north coast, where several of Dad's cousins had dairy farms. The trip was endless for us kids: two days of driving. Our car was stacked with bags and camping equipment, so we were jammed in the back, almost hidden by gear. The tent was pitched in the yard next to the farmhouse, and we ate our meals in the house with our relatives. 'Uncle' DD Campbell, my father's uncle, the patriarch, had the longest neck and when he ate his Adam's apple seemed to travel a foot up and down. I couldn't take my eyes off it. Sunday morning meant attending the Presbyterian church in the morning and then the vicar joining us for lunch; suits and ties for the men and Sunday best for the ladies.

I was always interested in the world at large, and books were a window on the cultural diversity that intrigued me. *Chums* magazine was my favourite, with its tales of Africa and the Middle East. The pen drawings of crusaders fighting evil Arabs are still in my memory. In second class, I topped social studies, and my teacher earmarked me as a potential contestant for the radio show *The Quiz Kids*, hosted by John Dease. I was selected and donned a mortarboard in the Macquarie studios in the city. I was very nervous as there was a large studio audience. My first question, 'Who wrote *The Scarlet Pimpernel*?' seemed easy. I replied that I was reading it at the moment, and John laughed. 'Well, some of us get lucky. For the record, what is it?' I said, 'I don't know,' and the audience erupted in laughter. It was a great experience, and I earned my first real money, appearance money ... there was no prize money.

High school beckoned in 1956, a momentous year. Melbourne hosted the Olympic Games, the first time the games had been held outside the USA and Europe, and television came into our lives.

My first day at Sydney Boys' High was terrifying. Barry Spooner, my neighbour, who was four years older, was a student at the school and took me on the bus and got me inside the gate. He asked, 'Why have you got a hat?' 'My mother said it was compulsory.' 'Well, it won't last long.' Barry waved goodbye and disappeared into the throng. Within seconds, the hat was snatched off my head and disappeared for good. I stood startled. Aggressive eyes watched for my next move, but I just walked away.

I don't remember much more – classes were assigned, instructions issued and the day swirled by till I found myself on the bus home. 'Where's your hat?' was Mum's first question. 'I left it in my locker at school. You don't have to have it on the bus.' In fact, hats weren't an essential part of the Sydney High uniform, but mothers worry about these things.

At primary school, I generally ranked in the top couple of places in exams. Things were very different at Sydney Boys' High where in my first year I took up residence in the bottom 10% of my class. My father was scathing. 'Why did you take German?' he demanded. 'Don't know,' was my answer. I couldn't tell him that

I had been told it was easier than French. They had neglected to say that it only became easier after the first three years. Over my five years at High, I clawed my way into the top 10% in my year, but my father had lost interest by then. I had always wanted my parents to be proud of me, and I think they secretly were, but my father never showed emotion. Sport dominated my thoughts. Tennis was my sporting love, and I made High's top team. We won the state championships with Ray Wilson our star. Ray went on to great success on the pro tennis tour.

When I was thirteen, I was despatched for the summer holidays to stay with my father's second cousins at Mooball, a village on the far north coast in a largely dairy farming district. Mary was a niece of Uncle DD in Main Arm, west of Mullumbimby. I would be only a few kilometres north of there. I took the train, with detailed instructions to make sure I was on the right end of the train as it split in half at Casino and a section went to Brisbane. I alighted at Burringbar, just north of Mooball, alone, and looked about for Adam, Mary's husband. Ten minutes later, an old pickup pulled up, and he threw my bag in the back without a greeting. I walked to the other side and the door handle fell off. 'Bloody thing!' he exclaimed, and leaned over to open the door. I put the handle on the seat between us, glancing up at Adam to see if he thought I had broken it.

We drove to a small house on the side of a hill, and I retrieved my bag as Mary came out to welcome me. I recognised her from our earlier visit to Mullumbimby. Adam went off to milk the cows, and I found my bed. Tea was early, and grace was said before we ate. Adam hardly spoke but Mary, in an old print dress covered in flowers, peppered me with questions. She explained the daily routine: up at 5am to eat some cereal, milk the cows and come in for a full breakfast about 8.30am. After that, up in the hills spraying Lantana with a metal spray stick attached to a large backpack of Lantana poison. The humidity was stifling, and it was 95 degrees F on her thermometer. At 1pm, we broke for a sandwich lunch and continued trying not to step on snakes or get tangled in the blackberries. At three, we headed back to the house to recommence the milking.

After a week I was in the swing and enjoying the farm. I was amazed to find they didn't sell any milk; they were not part of the quota system. The government limited the sale of milk to the public to keep the price up and only farms with a licence could sell. The cream was separated and sold, and their pigs dined on the skimmed milk. They also had a vegetable patch, which Mary tended.

After three weeks, Mary announced that we would camp at the beach at Brunswick Heads; it was the last week of January, and she felt I needed a break. Other relatives were already there. The pickup was loaded and arrived at the camping area adjacent to the river. I linked up with the other kids to explore it. Towards the end of the week, there was a terrible event. Three children had released a dinghy and were carried down the stream with the outgoing tide. Initially, there was no panic, as they seemed safe. As they neared the surf and the current quickened, two men dived in to swim to the boat, but it accelerated away from them. People began running and shouting for another boat, but none was available. Everybody stood on the shore and watched the dinghy race onto the bar and disappear into a swirl of spray as the children screamed I stood stunned. Some men fetched the lifeboat from the surf club, but it took ten minutes to reach the scene. By then, the children were gone. Their bodies were found the next day. We packed the sodden bedding and headed for the farm. No one spoke. I was afraid to say anything.

Two days later I was on the train home, reflecting on my month away. I'll always remember how hard Mary and Adam worked. In their married life of fifteen years, they had never spent a day apart. Their Christian beliefs were their bedrock.

The following Christmas holidays, I got a job selling ice cream, a Peters peddler. I went to West Botany Street to collect my rig, which was basically a large box mounted on wheels with a bicycle attached to the back. We were given a route and told the prices of the products. As I set off, my contraption was quite heavy and difficult to steer in the hot January sun. I had a big bell that I rang hoping people would come out of their houses and buy ice creams as I passed by. My most profitable product was the brick of ice cream, literally a brick-sized slab of ice cream, but I didn't sell many. After six hours on the blazing road, I pushed the rig up the hill and signed in. The manager checked stock and the money in the till. 'You're short! What happened?' he asked. I shrugged. 'Did you eat some?' he asked. 'Well, maybe a couple,' I replied. 'It was hot.' 'I can only pay you two shillings, in that case. Keep track of what you eat,' he said.

After a week of this, I had made very little money. One reason for that was I was often cheated. I would hand someone an ice block and they'd bolt without paying. As much as I wanted to, I couldn't chase them as I couldn't leave the rig unattended. I was learning a hard lesson in commerce. It was a cruel world out there. Why would they pick on a young kid, I thought.

By the second week, I discovered that the best spot to sell was by the beach at Ramsgate, several kilometres south of Kyeemagh. Ramsgate wasn't on my route, but I was desperate to sell something. Once I started riding there and selling to the hot and hungry beachgoers, it made the whole run worthwhile. My first business lesson had been learned; Know your territory.

My first commercial venture, as a Peters peddler

One day I sold out and had to ask for more stock. Loaded with a full box of ice creams, the rig was heavy, but I figured that it was all downhill and hoped I'd be empty when I returned to the depot. As I approached The Esplanade, the road to the seawall was very steep, and the rig started sliding towards the water. I jumped off and ran to the front to stop it before it went over. It was too heavy. I jumped aside just before my bike and store of ice creams plunged into Botany Bay. Only the back wheel was visible out of the sand and water. A couple came over and stared at the wreckage with me. 'What happened?' they asked. 'It's gone,' I sighed.

I wondered what to do as I walked home 3km in the searing heat. When my parents arrived, I told the story. My father was mad at me for not returning to the depot. 'I'm not going back there again; it's over!' I said. Dad called the manager, whom he knew from the bowling club, and they spoke for a while. As they talked, I was scared of what was coming. After he hung up the phone, nothing happened. The whole affair was dropped and never discussed again. I lay in bed that night confused about the whole episode. I had been cheated, sunburned and dealt with summarily by the manager for my shortages. I finally decided to put it down to experience and fell asleep.

Dad studied at night till I was in my teens and eventually became a company secretary. We then started to see him a bit more during the week. My parents never came to a school function or watched me play tennis. It didn't bother me at the time, but in later years, I thought it was strange. They were always proud of my achievements in a way, but never expressed it. My father always told me I could do better, regardless of the outcome. If we won the tennis competition, he would say, 'Oh, were they cripples?' I think it was the dry Australian approach at the time. I was a war baby, and life was simple but hard. 'Don't expect too much' seemed to be the general advice.

When the subject of religion arose, my father always described himself as a Callithumpian. Mum had been raised a Catholic and taught by nuns.

After the summer break, it was back to school and the same routines. At the end of third year, we sat the Intermediate Certificate and my results put me in the middle of the pack. This was an improvement on my poor start. Dad was constantly making improvements to the house and had added a room at the back of the garage. It became my bedroom. He explained that I could be 'independent', and it was handy to the outside toilet. I thought it was a bit strange, but eventually I liked it.

In fourth year, the subjects were more interesting and the year rolled on. Outside the classroom tennis was still my main focus. Barry Spooner often hit tennis balls with me on his court next door. I quizzed him about his studies. He was doing chemical engineering at University of New South Wales. 'It's very hard, and you spend all your time doing assignments.' He wasn't encouraging, but I pressed him. 'You must like it to continue?' 'I love chemistry, and the lab work is good. It's all about getting a good job, to do the things you like. The hard work will give me options on graduation if I get that far.' I trusted his judgement and felt it might be a good path for me. He was a good mentor and had helped me many times over the years with my questions.

I was coming up for my final school exams, the Leaving Certificate. This determined whether you could go to university and what courses you could study. I knew that a good result would give me options, but I was uncertain what course I should take. I felt I should go to university, as all my friends had that goal. During high school, my results had improved, with technical subjects shining. After the exams, it was a several-month wait to learn the outcome. Early in the new year, D-Day came. The results were posted. Relief flooded my body as I located my name and saw I had done quite well.

I decided to go to the sand hills near the house and contemplate who I was; what happens now. Sitting on the edge of the drop to the beach, I felt I was on a track, but I had no idea where it led. I stared at the small waves breaking and running into the sand. Over and over they approached and disappeared.

I reflected on my situation; good at tennis, nice place to live, some friends and a family who had supported me. But I felt something was missing. In a way I was lonely but how could that be? I had no one to share my inner most thoughts. Barry Spooner had been the closest, but there were limits there. Years later I would reflect on the community in which I grew up. The stoic protestant ethic of hard work brings its own rewards was stamped in my DNA.

I stubbed my foot into the sand, stood and taking off my shirt and shorts I ran down the hill and dove into the water. I swam for a few minutes and lay on the sand to dry. Retrieving my clothes I started for home turning my thoughts to the future. I was very happy.

School tennis team

Three generations

2. Falling into engineering

When I learn that hard work will give you options...

A friend of my father was visiting and discovered I had just passed the Leaving Certificate. He asked me 'Have you decided on a career?' No, I think engineering is likely, but I have no real understanding of what I would like. My neighbour, Barry Spooner is doing Chemical. That might be okay.' He suggested I try out for a NSW Railways traineeship. 'How do I contact them?' I enquired. 'Don't worry I can fix it' He called the following day. 'You have an interview next Tuesday at 10am. Go to Railway House on York Street in the city and ask for Norm Webster. I've suggested civil engineering would be your preference.' 'Civil? Is that what I should be doing?' I stuttered out. 'It will give you a broad base to decide on a direction once you get going.' 'Thanks.' I put the phone down and went to the lounge room to look up civil engineering in the encyclopaedia.

A panel asked me a slew of questions. I answered well but wondered about their relevance. It was a grilling. Afterwards, I was asked to wait in an adjacent room for an hour or so. A couple of other applicants were there too. 'How did it go? What are you going for?' I got the idea that they had applied for several other traineeships. I sat wondering whether I should have looked at the Water Board and other state utility possibilities. Eventually, I was called back in before the panel. I sat and scanned the four faces. The chairman looked up from his papers. Clearing his throat he intoned 'Grahame Campbell?' 'Yes' I replied nervously 'We're prepared to offer you a scholarship,' I stared for a moment trying to take it in. I didn't expect a result so quickly. 'OK.' was all I said. I should have thanked them, but I was in a bit of a daze. It seems I'm going to be a civil engineer!

I spent January reading books on civil engineering, wondering what it was like. My family had no more questions. I had been sorted, and they got on with their lives. I had won a traineeship with the NSW Railways to study civil engineering at University of New South Wales in Kensington. It was a wonderful opportunity, as I only needed to go to university and keep passing my exams and NSW Railways would pay me as a qualified draftsman for the four years I was studying.

UNSW Orientation Week was a revelation. I arrived alone because none of my friends were interested in going. There were hundreds of students milling around in a carnival atmosphere. The campus was largely open grasslands then, with sandy patches. As you looked from Anzac Parade, it gradually rose up a hill to an area with multistorey brick buildings on the right and a new science theatre on the left. I had passed the scene many times as my school bus sped by towards Moore Park. In the bottom corner of the campus the Roundhouse, the main student recreation centre with cafeterias and lounges, had recently been completed. This was where my orientation started, with rows of stalls promoting the university's religious, political and sports groups. After a quick browse, I found a jazz tent and was told of a concert up the hill. I followed the directions and found Mike Nock and his Three Out Trio in the Science Theatre. I had never heard anything like it, although I had heard a lot of jazz recordings. I think it was the immediacy and power of that hard-driving modern jazz that grabbed me. I have never forgotten it – it was life-changing. I decided to be a musician, and I bought a clarinet with my Railway money and some help from my parents as a reward for my scholarship win. However, university classes were starting the following week.

Civil engineering subjects for the first year were physics, chemistry, maths, technical drawing and English. There were no options. The English course was a surprise, and initially I was irritated. Yet as the year progressed I found English was the subject I looked forward to most. It wasn't grammar, as I'd feared, but the history of the language and a reading program. I had always been a good reader and had a good general knowledge. I was now exposed to the world of ideas.

Generally, our class comprised forty 'civil' students. However, several of the classes involved all those undertaking engineering disciplines, 120 of us. It was a bit daunting seeing the sea of faces, probably all as dazed as I was. We started with four girls, but by the end of first term they had disappeared. I had no idea why they'd left – possibly the overwhelming testosterone. I'd sit in the lecture theatre and wonder what everybody was thinking, planning. All I was thinking about was how I could keep passing exams so the NSW Railways cheques continued to flow. Like my fellow students, I had little idea where I'd end up.

Graeme Pont lived around the corner from me in Kyeemagh. We had grown up together, but he had gone to Sydney Tech High and won a scholarship with the Sydney County Council to study electrical engineering. We were sitting at one lecture when he said, 'Do you think you'll pass at the end of the year?' 'Yes.' 'That's an arrogant view' he responded. 'The majority in the room will fail. Do you think you're better than most of them?' I really hadn't thought about it. I'd do my best, and that was that. The others could do what they liked. Graeme did fail second year. I think he failed so as not to be seen as superior to the group. I never did understand his attitude.

It took a while to adjust to university life. There was no pressure exerted on me to work hard, even turn up for lectures, but I realised the cost of failure was high.

Away from uni, my weekends were filled with tennis. However I was warming to jazz after the Mike Nock exposure, and I found a clarinet teacher and acquired music theory books to start my new endeavour. What remained of my spare time was spent on clarinet practice. I bought some Artie Shaw records and new horizons kept appearing. In my early teens, I had listened to pop music, but the jazz in all its forms was fascinating. Harmony, rhythm and melody lines leapt into my brain.

At the end of first year, after our exams, the twelve NSW Railways trainees were summoned to head office for further instructions. We were briefed on general railway engineering issues and then despatched to the trainee workshops in Strathfield for an overview of all the trades utilised by the construction and maintenance divisions. Our instructors were terrified. Engineering students apparently had a history of messing up the place. Discipline was difficult, as they knew that eventually the graduates would be drafted into the senior jobs within NSW Railways' hierarchical structure. The railways were run by engineers! We did not understand this at the time, but sensed we had a power that carried with it a freedom to do things. Learning welding, boiler making and working with lathes was a new world for me, and I respected the supervisors whose job it was to give us a once-over-lightly exposure to trades in a few weeks, where 'true' students, potential tradesmen, would spend years developing those skills.

In January, I learned I'd passed first year with good results. In my year of 120 engineering students, only about forty progressed to second year. We were joined by twenty students who had not progressed to third year. So sixty students, half of the prior year's class size, continued. Our NSW Railways contingent had been reduced to nine, a much higher success rate.

In second year engineering, after the standard subjects we had to choose between a range of subjects in the Arts faculty: I opted for philosophy and psychology. Our philosophy course was basically studying logic, which was pretty dry. The lecturer wasn't very good; he was sorry he had to take engineering students who showed little interest, and we struggled. University was now an obstacle course for most engineering students; it seemed more like a jail term than a learning experience. The thrill of first year, for a lot of us, had been supplanted by the reality that achieving success meant doing a lot of hard work.

By now, I was eligible to try for my driver's licence. Dad, who'd upgraded to an FJ Holden, gave me lessons, and I passed the test. On the following Friday night, I asked if I could take his car and go to the pictures with Graeme Pont. Surprisingly, he agreed. After sitting through my father's detailed driving instructions, we were off. Heading up Bay Street in heavy traffic I felt very adult. We arrived at Princes Highway and stopped at the lights. When the lights changed to green, I put the FJ Holden into gear and accelerated. *WHAMMM!* I looked at the gear stick and then across at Graeme. Blood was running down the side of his head. I then realised that the car had mounted the footpath and was facing a shop. I was too confused to be alarmed. A priest was knocking on my window. I rolled it down. 'Sorry,' he said, 'my brakes failed.' In my confusion, I stared at him and then glanced behind to see a large black car angled across two lanes sitting on its wheel hubs ... no wheels, the wooden spokes had shattered on impact.

I looked back at Graeme. His bleeding had worsened. A crowd was gathering, and I opened the door to get out and staggered a little as my leg was sore. I helped Graeme out, and we sat in the gutter together, using our handkerchiefs to stem the blood. A man standing behind us said, 'An ambulance is on its way. We'll get you to the hospital.' A woman next to him exclaimed, 'Young people today! I don't know why they're allowed on the road. That poor priest must be so sad about his beautiful car.' I found out later that his beautiful car was a 1929 Erskine with running boards, something Eliot Ness would have used in Chicago. The highway was blocked by our accident and the Friday evening traffic was jammed.

An ambulance eventually threaded its way through the gridlock and Graeme was laid on a stretcher. Dad's car's headlights were still on, so I turned them off to save the battery. However, a flat battery would have been the least of the FJ's problems. The whole front of the car was almost torn off. An ambulance officer sat me down on the footpath beside Graeme and told us that we could make phone calls at the hospital. A policeman arrived. He was very nice and explained that the priest would be charged for running a red light, and I was not to worry. My father had been notified and I just needed to rest. I was still trying to remember what had happened. At St George Hospital we were taken to a ward for overnight observation.

Later, Graeme, with a bandage on his head, sat up in his bed and said he was going home. I was asleep, but woke. 'Don't be silly, we'll go in the morning.' He climbed out of bed and donned his bloodstained trousers and headed for the door. I went after him, pleading for him to return to bed. He kept going, and so did I. We hobbled up to Kogarah station and jumped on the train back to Rockdale. It was near midnight, and the other passengers were staring at the blood. We had no tickets; it didn't matter. We limped down Bay Street towards Brighton. My bruised and sore knee made it difficult to keep up with Graeme. Suddenly a police car stopped beside us, and two constables got out. I tried to explain. 'Don't worry, we know who you are. We'll drop you home.' I was relieved, but Graeme starting yelling, 'Are we arrested?' I slumped in the back seat, very tired. I was dropped off first and was greeted by my parents and went to bed. Later, Mum brought breakfast in to my room, and I started to worry that I'd miss tennis. 'Forget about that – this weekend you're going to rest. And don't worry about the car, your father understands.' 'How's Graeme?' 'He's fine; I've just spoken to his father. He's sleeping. The blow on the head must have disturbed him.' Christ, I thought, what if the priest had hit *my* door.

Towards the end of the year, my interest in music had grown and I was practising clarinet more diligently as an antidote to my university studies. NSW Railways didn't bother us during the year, but after the exams, the trainees were assigned to various district offices for exposure to divisional operations. I was posted to Newcastle, under the supervision of John Brew, who eventually became the commissioner. I was becoming more depressed about my future career if I stayed in the Railways. You could pretty much tell which job you would have for the next forty-five years, maybe even ending as commissioner if you kept your nose clean. I spent the summer checking bridge integrity in the district and contractor progress on the Honeysuckle goods yard upgrade. Living in an old hotel in Newcastle provided an interesting nightlife in the bar. Most of the customers were NSW Railways employees, playing darts, drinking and shooting pool to fill the evening. I became acquainted with a couple of the patrons, whom I recognised from the rail yards. After a few beers, they asked me what I did. I explained it was part of my training to become an engineer. One looked thoughtful and replied, 'Stick at it, you're lucky, you'll have options with your life. We're stuck here.'

The family home with the FJ and my sister

3. On the road

Floating along the river with the current.

In summer 1962, at the end of my Railways assignment, I had a month's leave. My co-trainee and good friend, Ian MacDonald, suggested we take a trip to Western Australia. Ian had grown up in Kempsey on the NSW mid-north coast. He was a country boy with a very practical approach to life. We discussed the journey with our mates, who declined to join us, and Ian made a bet with them that we could do the entire trip without once paying for travel or accommodation. We didn't have much money and took only a small tent, sleeping bags, towels and a couple of changes of clothes. We entrained from Central to Broken Hill and then on to Port Pirie in South Australia, making the most of the free travel that was our due as railway employees on NSW trains. As the scenery swept by it changed from farmland to dry, flat plains. We were starting a great adventure. I was to learn a lot about surviving without much money and mateship.

At Port Pirie, we were confronted by an industrial landscape not inviting for our camping plan. We walked some blocks and finally found a church that Ian said would be a good place to sleep, as the walls had buttresses that formed a protected area. Ian was quite religious,' We'll be right here, they won't turf us out!' I was sceptical, but we had few options. This worked fine until the bells sounded at 5am to raise the nuns for their morning observances. As they streamed past us in their gowns, we pulled our heads into our sleeping bags and hoped they wouldn't notice. At 6.30, with activity in the church quickening, Ian thought we should go. We wandered down the road looking for a breakfast place, which took more than an hour. Over breakfast, we decided we needed a better plan for each day's travel. Food, accommodation and travel plans needed to be set for each day.

We hitched a ride on a truck to Port Augusta, further north, where we came upon a camping place. It wasn't a campground as such but a large paddock. We set up the tent in the back, out of the way, for we didn't want to blow our bet by paying at a regular campground. Immediately water was an issue – we needed it for drinking and a shower and washing up the dishes. Ian felt we could survive, but I was sceptical. Finally, we realised that we needed a tomahawk for chopping wood for a fire and barbecue tools to cook. We found a hardware store and bought the stuff. This was not an auspicious beginning as our cash reserves were low and we had hardly started.

Crossing the Nullarbor Plain was our next big challenge. Only one road connected the continent in the south, and we needed to find someone to take us the 2,400km. We walked a couple of kilometres out of town to a large truck stop with many heavy vehicles parked in front. It was very hot and dusty, and we were glad of the air-conditioning in the basic coffee shop. 'Hi,' I greeted a large man in a blue singlet. 'Can we join you?' He looked up quizzically and nodded towards a chair. We sat and asked about hitch-hiking. 'All the boys put their trucks on the train now. It's cheaper, as the road's unsealed and there's a lot of corrugation. After you've done it once, that's it – you put it on the train next time' he said with purpose.

This news sank us. I noticed traffic heading west, away from the train marshalling area, and I hoped we'd find a truck bound for Western Australia across the Nullarbor. We walked a couple of hundred metres along the road to find a good hitch-hiking position and extended our thumbs. Several cars and trucks went by without stopping, then finally a truck stopped. Great! We ran up and he asked where we were going. 'Kalgoorlie.' 'No, I'm off to Whyalla. I don't think cars or trucks go across the plain.' In the next couple of hours, two more trucks stopped, and their drivers gave the same response. In the early afternoon, we trudged back to the coffee shop to eat and get relief from the burning sun. We didn't have shoes or socks, as we'd thought thongs would be lighter. The tops of my feet were red. An hour later we were back on the road, with a similar lack of success. As the sun set with still no good fortune, we returned to our camp to discuss alternatives. If we couldn't find a ride, we'd lost the bet, but that seemed trivial compared to not getting to Perth.

The next day we set up again at the truck stop for several unsuccessful hours. By lunchtime, the sun was killing us, and we resolved to go to town to check the bus and train options at a travel agent. More gloom, 'Your only option is the Indian Pacific train, but it has been booked out for several months,' said the agent. 'You could go to the station and check for cancellations.' The stationmaster explained that an hour before the train's arrival he'd have the passenger loading details. Maybe we'd be lucky. We asked what it would cost and found we didn't have enough money. Could we go cheap, foregoing meals? He explained that it was the law that we had to be fed, as there had been problems years ago when passengers had died. What to do? We were stuck. Ian suggested we return to the hardware store, give back our tomahawk and barbecue tools and get a refund. I thought we would be lucky, as we'd used them. Yet it was our only hope, and we set off. The store owner was sympathetic and examined the goods. 'OK, I'll help you, but just this once.' I smiled; I didn't think we'd be back for a while. We pooled our money and found we had enough for the train fare, just!

Back at the station, we waited in the shade. Eventually, the stationmaster came out. 'I've found a seat for you!' Only one? 'Well, there may be another one tomorrow.' We looked at each other glumly and replied we needed to go together. We could not split up, as we had no communications. 'Well, I'll tell you what. Since you work for the railways, I can check after the train arrives – it stays about half an hour – and if the crew haven't used the emergency berth they keep for maintenance people, you might be in business.'

The train steamed in and we watched the crew prepare it for passenger boarding. The conductors wore white tie and tails. The Indian Pacific was a grand train. We were in shorts, T-shirts and thongs. The stationmaster came running towards us, gesturing success and pointing to the ticket booth. We handed over all our money bar two shillings, and he explained that our berths were at opposite ends of the train. He was very excited for us, and we thanked him for his efforts. We split up and I found my carriage. The conductor looked at me and my pack, and I gave him my ticket and climbed onto the train.

I found a cabin for four, with seven people in it. Struggling to be heard over the music they were playing on a tape machine, I asked if I was in the right cabin. 'You must be in the top berth there. Don't mind us, we're having a party. Did you just get on? We were wondering if that berth was vacant when we left Port Pirie. Find a beer and I'll introduce you around.' 'I don't have any money.' 'Don't worry, you can pay us later. We just set up a tab at the bar.' They were well-lubricated, and I tried to remember all their names. After a couple of beers, the train crept into motion, and I sat and watched Port Augusta slip by as evening descended on the landscape. I chatted with one of the girls, Jenny, who explained they were students from Melbourne Uni on an excursion to Perth for a couple of weeks. I explained our trip, and she asked how we would manage without money. I told her we had lodged money in a Perth bank for emergencies, and that would have to do. 'Come on, let's dance!' she said. 'Dinner will be called soon.'

Dinner was held in several sittings. We had numbers designating our seats in the dining car. Most people dressed in suits and ties, but my group was more casual. I had a shower and changed my underwear. I was a little embarrassed, but once seated my shorts and thongs weren't visible. It was *haute cuisine*, with silver service. I wondered how Ian was doing. It was impossible to find him, as the train was very long and each cabin private if the curtains were drawn. I would have to wait for a stop and hope he got off.

The next day I sat in the club car at the back of the train and watched the scenery. It was mesmerising; there was a constant vista of red earth interrupted by nothing. The sky was cloudless and blue, and the track disappeared into the horizon in a straight line at the top of a curve that made it clear the earth was a sphere. I sat for hours, entranced, as we raced across this massive reddish-brown billiard ball. The rail line is well north of the road, which only clips part of the Nullarbor in the south, and is on the plain for 478km with no deviations in alignment or elevation. The only scheduled stop is at Cook, on the plain. Aborigines sometimes camp on the track to stop the train and sell artefacts to tourists. We saw no wildlife, although camels and roos were sometimes spied, according to Alan, a fellow passenger who I had met in the observation car for the spectacle. He had made the trip three times and filled in gaps in my knowledge. For the entire day, we mostly sat in Zen-like silence. I had taken advantage of my friends' bar tab and kept a note of my beer consumption.

As the sun set, we slid off the plain into scrubby country with low hills. I returned to my cabin to find the group sleeping in odd positions. Some had formed relationships and were spooning in corners. Jenny was awake and offered me the remnants of a drink. I declined, but spooned up to her for comfort. Dinner was called, and I showered again and put on a clean – or cleaner – T-shirt for the occasion. We were treated like kings and I took advantage of it, as we would be leaving the train later that evening.

Stepping off the train at Kalgoorlie around 10pm, I looked for Ian and farewelled my new friends, who were taking the connecting narrow gauge train on to Perth that night. I swore I would send them the money I owed them and they thanked me for my company, and I kissed Jenny and promised to write. Ian appeared and we sat down to swap notes and plan where to stay. On spying a welcoming message from a nearby church on a sign at the station Ian asked the platform attendant where it was. 'Two blocks over there.' He pointed across a field. We strapped on our packs and headed towards the residence next to the chapel. We knocked, and eventually a priest materialised in his pyjamas. 'We saw your welcome sign at the station and wondered if we could doss down in the recreation hall.' (We were assuming he had one.) He told us the church's offer didn't extend to accommodation, then relented. 'Ah well, you can stay in the shed over there. Just for tonight, mind you, and don't bust anything. The door's unlocked.'

We thanked him and went to sleep there in our clothes on our sleeping bags without turning on the light. At about 6am, I woke to see broken windows, broken chairs, rubbish everywhere. It looked like there had been a big party. I woke Ian and we decided to leave quietly, in case we were blamed for the mess. The priest clearly had problems with dossers who didn't announce themselves and trashed the place. We had two shillings between us and a couple of packs of biscuits and peanuts that Ian had found on the train. I regretted not having Ian's foresight. We found the main street and wandered under the awnings looking at the shops. Crossing the street was a problem, as it was about 100m wide and very hot on our thonged feet.

After a couple of hours, we decided to try to leave for Perth as a lack of money was our main problem. We waited for a ride and finally a truck stopped. 'Where are you going?' 'Perth.' 'Well, you better get on the other side of the road, I'm going to Coolgardie.' We'd walked to the edge of town, and now we needed to walk all the way back and out the other side, about 6km. It was coming on dark when we were finally in position, but we had only waited a few minutes before a truck pulled up. 'I'm going to Perth,' said the driver, whose name was Alf. 'So are we.' He was a large, cheerful man with a red check shirt. We jumped up in the semi and got set. 'Glad of the company. Where you from?' We chatted for a few hours, and he finally stopped in Merriden for fuel and food. He asked if we were coming in, but we declined, said we'd eaten earlier, which was a lie. We had one small bag of peanuts left, and two shillings. The semi set off into the night again, and we fell asleep. As dawn lightened the sky, we were pulling into Perth, into a goods unloading area. Alf bid us goodbye, and we walked till we found the markets and bought two bananas with our last coin. We found our way to the CBD and waited for the bank to open. At 10am, we were back in the money and found a cafe to have breakfast, the full fry-up.

Where to now? We walked down to the Swan River and along some boat berths. It was Saturday morning, and people were out and about. We noticed a boat full of people preparing to leave. The captain looked at us and said, 'You'd better be quick, we'll be off in a minute.' With our packs, he'd mistaken us for late arrivals. 'What do you think, Ian?' 'Seems okay.' We jumped aboard, and the boat eased itself off the moorings and started cruising. We found a seat among the throng and looked around. 'Nice estuary. I wonder how far it goes,' I said to Ian. 'Never been here before,' he said, and turned to the person next to him. 'Where are we going?' 'To Rottnest Island for the weekend. Why? Didn't you get a ticket at the booth?' Ian turned to me and said, 'Apparently we're going to an island ... for the weekend.' I looked around. Everybody had sleeping bags and gear; they must be camping too. The passengers were young and in high spirits, so we relaxed and waited for the next surprise.

The boat nosed its way out of the river and into the ocean, picking up speed as we cleared the channel markers. Soon we were approaching Rottnest, and nobody had asked for our tickets. We disembarked and went across to the hotel, which had some maps. The rest of the passengers diffused into the buildings, and we left our packs in the lobby corner with other luggage. We walked a kilometre around to a sheltered bay with our towels and swimmers. It was busy with holiday-makers and families setting up picnics. We swam for a while and dozed in the sun for a few hours before returning to the hotel for lunch and a beer. In the afternoon, we found another beach and repeated our morning. Around 4pm the wind picked up and we started to think about a camp. Nobody else seemed to be setting up and I wondered where they all were.

We ate in the hotel, and I drank some beers while Ian had lemonades. We went back to the beach to find it deserted – strange! We crawled into our bags and quickly fell asleep. I was awoken by a quokka – a small wallaby unique to the island – landing on my leg; Dutch sailors had seen them centuries ago and thought they were giant rats. I pulled up my legs and found several of them around me. I shooed them off and went back to sleep. When I was unconscious, the insects attacked. In the morning, I awoke, but couldn't open one eye. I called out and Ian looked at me. 'Your face is swollen, just on one side.' My other eye was OK, but my mouth hurt. My lip was swollen. As well as having been punctured by insects, I was sunburned. We packed up and joined the people having breakfast at the hotel. A fellow at the table asked, 'What happened to your face?' 'Insect bites. We slept on the beach.' 'Why didn't you stay in the camp like the rest of us? It's only a couple of bob a night, bring your own bedding.' I looked mournfully at Ian with my one good eye. 'We didn't know; we're from Sydney.'

The temperature rose quickly during the morning and a short walk around the headland was uncomfortable. We retreated to the pub to wait for the Perth ferry. It left at about 6pm, so we had a long wait. As we boarded, the wind was picking up, and we found a protected corner at the back. The other passengers were jolly and tanned. They were drinking and starting a party and singing. I had a beer to take my mind off my condition, and we steered out past the point. The boat lurched as we hit the open sea and quickly it was dark, with tossing waves. I felt a cool wash of water envelop me as we dove into a wave. People were laughing. I was soaked through. I sat down again and felt miserable for the rest of the trip. As we walked off the gangplank, the salt on my clothes rubbed against my legs. Ian looked at me and laughed. 'Come on, we need to find a place to sleep.' We caught a bus to Cottesloe Beach and bunked down in the sand hills behind the beach. I slept soundly and awoke to find a sparkling sea. I stripped off and swam lazily for a while. Yesterday had washed away, and we were in heaven. My eye, however, stayed stubbornly closed. We used the surf club showers and, leaving our gear in the sand hills, walked to the shops to find food. At a chemist, I bought antiseptic cream to treat my swollen face. Our adventure was having its ups and downs.

We decided to head south and went to the railway office to find out the alternatives. I mentioned we worked for NSW Railways, and we were given free travel on the Bunbury express –wow, things were going our way. On the train, we found the conductor, who said we could stay in the barracks in Bunbury for free, just sign the book with our home station – another win! As we headed south from Bunbury, the population thinned out. Our journey to the Margaret River was slow, for few cars passed. The area had only recently been settled, and only a few people had set up farms. On the plus side, all cars stopped to help. A lady asked about our trip and suggested interesting features including caves which had recently been opened. We made for the Jewel Cave, just north of Augusta, the south-westernmost point of Australia. The 6km walk to the cave from the highway turn-off was arduous but worthwhile, for the caves were wondrous. The place was deserted except for the guide. He gave us a personalised tour where we found a subterranean lake which has now gone. As we penetrated deeper through the caves, we felt a magical aura surround us in the silence. With only three of us, it was very special. Afterwards, we asked if he was going back to town. 'No, one more tour to do.' I said, 'But there are no people.' 'Well,' he replied, 'we have to wait and see.' Two hours later, no one had showed, and he drove us to Augusta. At last, my eye had come good, and the sunburn had settled down, so I was feeling great. We were very fit from walking, and the outdoor life suited us.

We slept on the cape beach at Augusta, and for two days saw no one. A dead dolphin was the only feature of the windswept escarpment. The flora was quite different to that of the east coast, probably because of the winds blowing across the Indian Ocean. Barbecuing over a fire on the beach was ideal. The wind dropped in the evening, and the throb of the surf was a settling backdrop for a beautiful location. Looking at the vast night sky, Ian asked me, 'Why are you doing engineering? You seem more interested in music.' I thought for a while and said, 'It just evolved. I seem to just float along the river with the current. Parents have expectations, and I didn't have a better idea.' The question stayed with me for quite a while.

It was hard to leave our piece of heaven, but we had to restock our supplies and continue the journey. Albany was our next destination, and we hitched via Manjimup to an old whaling town that had become a grain export point for the state. The tourist agency gave us a map and suggested the rugged coast was impressive. A bus left in an hour. Unfortunately, it was not worth the driver's while to go if he had fewer than four passengers. No one else came, so once more we were on Shanks's pony. A car took us to the turn-off, but it was still 12km to the coast. Once again it was worth the struggle. We found ourselves alone in a wilderness. Spectacular rock cliffs and natural rock bridges laced the high escarpment. As we completed the walk along the cliffs, we came to a car park to find a car there but no one around. We strolled out to the point. There was a girl at the lookout, the driver of the car. In Bermuda shorts and with long curly hair, she was staring out to sea. She swung around as we approached, 'Hi,' she said, smiling. We joined her and chatted about nothing. Eventually, she excused herself and headed back to her car. We followed, caught up and chatted some more. Reaching the car, she noted there was no other. 'Where did you put your car?' 'Oh, we don't have one.' 'You must like walking.' she said gaily. 'No, we prefer to ride.' 'Well, you'd better get in and I'll take you back to town.' Relief and thanks all round. We told her our story, and she explained that she was a nurse in Perth. She was on holiday for a few days and was driving back via Bunbury to visit friends. 'Would you like a lift?' We said no, we had come from there, but thanks anyway. It was a pity; she would have been a good companion.

We'd planned to go north to the Kimberley. Time was against us, particularly against Ian, who was pining for his girlfriend, Elaine, who lived near Shellharbour on the NSW south coast. We returned to Perth and were resigned to taking the train from Kalgoorlie again. The trip home was less eventful, because as Nullarbor crossing veterans, we knew the ropes. A truck took us east to the railhead, and we convinced the stationmaster to let us sleep in unused maintenance staff berths. Boarding in Kalgoorlie brought back memories, with the conductor in white tie and tails. Our own dress had not improved, going by the look he gave me. Our last-minute berth allocations meant that we were again separated. After dinner, I went to the club car to check out the patrons. I met Sarah, a petite brunette from Perth, who was visiting the east coast for the first time. It's amazing how the promise of romance can focus the mind of an 18-year-old. It was love at first sight for me. But nothing occurred on the train, in spite of my overtures. (I called a number she gave me a few days after I arrived back in Sydney to be told by her uncle not to bother his niece.) Ian and I alighted at Port Pirie. It's quite industrial, and we decided to hitch-hike to Adelaide the same day. That proved easy, and we camped in a park near the beach. After a day in the city, we hitched a ride to Melbourne. A few days there caused Ian's desire for his lady to accelerate our departure to Sydney.

Our odyssey was quickly coming to an end. We caught a ride in the afternoon heading north. Ian slept in the back seat. As we approached Queanbeyan, Ian woke and asked if he could get out at the Shellharbour turn-off. I continued to Sydney and Stan dropped me at my house. 'It's not too far out of my way, and you guys have made the trip tolerable.' My parents greeted me warmly, after noting my beard and general state of disrepair. It was nice to be home. Ian and I had had a life-changing experience. We had met warm and helpful people right across the country. I had learned to be observant and respectful but mostly to travel successfully with a mate.

4. Learning curve

You can't make a career out of music.

My studies continued after the break, and I reflected on the prior year. I had done well in the exams but had mixed feelings about the future. Some 40% of my university class failed second year, leaving twenty-four of us to proceed to third year. We were joined by eight third year students of the previous year who hadn't progressed, which made a total of thirty-two in our year. Our streams were totally separate from the other engineering disciplines, so we were all Civil. The NSW Railways trainees were reduced to seven. We still had to take one humanities elective subject, so I continued with psychology, which had been interesting because the lecturer was interesting. He treated the class as he would his patients! He was a clinical psychologist and generally arrived with stories of his last client to illustrate the lesson – a novel experience for engineers. He would quiz us with oddball questions like: 'Who walked to class on the path and didn't tread on a crack?'

Despite our psychology lecturer, I found third-year university a drudge. I had come off a high with the trip around the west and now here I was, sitting in class taking notes. I knew I had to concentrate and be organised, and I was ... but I did it without enthusiasm. Practical subjects such as surveying provided a bit of outdoor relief as we measured the university buildings and squares. I felt I was caught on an endless treadmill, What lay ahead for me was two more years of study and then a five-year bond period.

At nineteen, I was starting to experience a broader world. It came over the news that President Kennedy had been assassinated in Dallas. I wondered why there was so much fuss. It seemed to me that most presidents were at risk in the USA, and many died. I thought the Cuban missile crisis had something to do with it. It was a long way from my world. Music was my refuge. The clarinet was absorbing more of my time because university work was easier than the first two years. I was still playing tennis most of the weekend; my social life was almost non-existent. By the end of the year, only five students had failed, and we went into our final year with a class of thirty-one, the number bolstered by part-time students doing their final year on a full-time basis.

NSW Railways assigned us to various locations for the summer break at the end of the year. I ended up spending a month with a survey group in Bathurst, 200km west of Sydney. It was very hot, around 40°C during the day. We camped in canvas tents next to the track. Reg, an old rail hand with a bad back who walked with a limp and always seemed preoccupied, was camp manager. He kept the camp clean and prepared our meals. It was disconcerting being only metres from the main western line when freight trains sped by during the night. One of the labourers put detonators on the track about a kilometre either side of our work to warn the driver of our presence and us of an approaching train.

We were on the rail tracks all day; I acted as a chain man for the surveyor, which was good training. It's basically the surveyor's assistant. Other men cut pegs and brush. The camaraderie was great, and I generally enjoyed the routine. One morning Reg juiced up the fire for the billy by pouring kerosene on it. It flamed and burned his arm and face. We jumped up and applied first aid before taking him to the hospital. I asked Brian, our leader, how Reg could have done such a stupid thing. 'Grahame, we get these blokes from all walks. He's from the city and was sent out here because he's on disability. We'll have to cook our own dinner tonight or eat in the pub. Now, let's get out on the track.' The incident made me think about how many people live alone or in camps like this, away from their families. I was starting to understand better my privileged position in the world. It was a humbling revelation to me.

For the final month of our university break, our group was sent around the state on bridge repair inspections. This was a very practical exercise, and I learned about the old designs using wood, wrought iron and steel construction. In Grafton, the major crossing of the Clarence River had the deck stripped off one track and we were forced to walk on the beam over the river to inspect weldments of plates being used to strengthen the girders. The beam was at least fifteen metres above the river and about fifteen centimetres wide. Traversing it proved more a test of character for young engineers than a technical exercise.

We were given the weekend off, and I visited my grandfather, who was still at Yamba, at the mouth of the Clarence river. His father and grandfather had worked at Iluka, near Yamba, in the 1800s on the marine works there. Iluka was the site of the first mineral sands mining operations in Australia. (I would eventually become a director of Iluka Minerals, but that comes later…) Hitch-hiking from Grafton, I was surprised to be picked up by an old couple. 'We can only take you to the McLean ferry. We're on our way to Brisbane.' I thanked them, and they asked why I was heading to Yamba. I told them my grandfather lived there and had grown up near Ulmarra, which we were then passing through. 'Ulmarra, you say? We used to live there. What's his name?' 'Ossie Campbell.' 'Oh, Ossie! We went to school with him. What a coincidence! By the way, I'm Alan, and this is Frieda.' Alan talked about the war. He and my grandfather had both enlisted at the same time. When we reached the McLean ferry, Alan and Frieda asked if they could meet Ossie. That suited me, and we reached Yamba mid-afternoon. I knew Pop would be at the bowling club, and we went straight there. What a reunion! They hadn't seen each other for nearly fifty years, and it went on till dusk. After Alan and Frieda resumed their journey, Pop took me home and marvelled at the occurrence. 'You know, Alan was in my company in France. He was wounded and went back to Australia. I haven't seen him since the day he left.'

Pop and I enjoyed being together. It was sunny, and I bodysurfed and spent the few days chatting while he cooked his fry-ups. 'How are your studies going?' 'It's a bit tedious. I'd rather be playing the clarinet.' Pop had played the trombone in the army. 'You can't make a career out of music. Stick to your studies, young man.'

An event in my younger years brought reality rushing into my life. At the end of 1962, while my parents were attending the Commonwealth Games in Perth, our neighbour Barry Law committed suicide. Barry was about my age, and I knew him well from school, though he wasn't a part of our Jacobson Avenue group. His death was horrific. He had a girlfriend in the next block, across Bestic Street. They had argued, and he went home and took a shotgun back to her house. He killed her and her mother. He then put the gun in his mouth and blew half his face off, but survived to stagger next door for help. No one answered the door, and he managed to return to his house and get more ammunition to finish the job. My bedroom was at the back of the garage, about twenty meters from where he fired the last shot. I didn't hear any noise and only discovered what had transpired in the morning when I saw police crawling over the fence.

I was starting to see a world where life was transitory and needed to be valued. Barry Spooner and I sat on the front step and talked about the future. We both were shocked by the shootings. He had graduated and worked at the glass factory. 'Value your education, it will be the bedrock of your life.' I looked at him with mixed feelings. I knew I was privileged, but my music aspirations confused my thinking.

Back at university, I was facing my last year. Once you were in fourth year, it was difficult to fail. I found the study quite easy and opted to do an honours degree, as it included statistics and a practical thesis. I was enjoying engineering better, but it wasn't my main focus. I was approaching 21, and facing a dilemma. My parents were pleased that I was about to graduate, but I was leaning strongly towards a music career.

Professor Shaw, our structures lecturer, tried to instil some philosophy into our studies, and our final exam was oral. He asked questions and marked our responses; there was no hiding. This was very innovative and quickly found out students who learned by rote without understanding the underlying principles. During my whole undergraduate experience, Prof Shaw was the first to try and expand our horizons beyond the science and mathematics to philosophic concepts. I did quite well, as he had opened my eyes to new ideas in engineering – the concept of the real world and our inexact characterisation of it in the design process. The whole of university life had been learning facts and formulae, but the connection with the real world was to some extent ignored. I began to see the world in a different way, and events started to connect my thinking.

My graduation thesis was related to concrete testing. I enjoyed the work in the lab and teamed with a Malaysian student who became a good friend that year. Moh'd told me about his home life, and I became keen to visit. He had grown up in Sarawak, on the island of Borneo. I hadn't been out of Australia, and a foreign project sounded exotic.

We eventually received a high distinction for our thesis. I felt I could succeed at anything I put my mind to. But music remained at the top of my list.

5. My love of music

I learn about minimalism.

I had been studying clarinet with Mal Cunningham in Paddington during my second year of uni. Mal played flute with the Sydney Symphony, and also worked with Johnny Wade, a mainstream show band at the Brighton Hotel. I aspired to be like Mal. To play professionally it was necessary to play the saxophone. Nobody employed a clarinettist; you had to play saxophone as well. I asked Mal if he could teach me sax. He couldn't, and, besides, he was giving up music teaching. He suggested I talk to Al Meader, a clarinettist in Marrickville. I would have to put the saxophone on hold. I was disappointed that Mal couldn't assist, but there was no other option. It was a trek to Marrickville, but I had a car by then, and off I went. Al had four kids and a harassed-looking wife. She was generally out shopping when I had lessons on Saturday morning, so my first job was to get Al out of bed and able to teach. He needed a 'silver bullet' (a Resch's pilsener) from the fridge to kick-start his day, so his lessons were a bit of an eye-opener for a teenager.

Al played at the Musician's Club in Pitt Street. He was a regular at the club and drank relentlessly. Al was nicknamed 'The Bird', not for Charlie Parker but for trying to fly out of the club window on the fourth floor one night. He ended up in hospital with a broken leg. For all his faults, Al was a beautiful clarinettist with a smooth, liquid sound.

Al's penchant for silver bullets kept him in a blur. The club was featuring a big band one Sunday afternoon, and I asked Al to take me, as I wasn't yet eighteen. I arrived at his place at about 1pm – the show started at two. No Al. He hadn't arrived home from the night before. His wife and I waited in the street till a cab pulled up, and Al motioned for me to get in. He was still in his dinner suit. 'Sorry I'm late, got caught up.' The cab quickly took us to the club where I joined the throng of musicians. I looked around for familiar faces but saw none. It was wonderful to hear the band up close, and I was inspired. I asked Al how you got to be in a band like that. 'Reading music is the main thing. Discipline is something I don't have, and I don't like the constraints,' was his response. I looked around the room; it had a vibe I hadn't experienced before, one that I wanted to be a part of.

A few weeks later I arrived for my lesson to find that Al had decamped to the country. No teacher! I had been going to the weekend dances in Hurstville. There were two venues, the Rivoli and the Civic Centre. Each featured an eighteen-piece band in the Count Basie style. It was a great opportunity for the local musicians to play in that format. I loved the music, and also tried to meet girls ... with little success, although I did meet Margaret eventually. She was a country girl from Armidale. I noticed that in the breaks the musicians gathered in a coffee shop on the corner; the venues were quite close. I spied Don Burrows, a well-known clarinettist who played saxophone, sitting at a table with other musicians.

I bowled up to Don. Could I have a quick chat? I told him my story and finally asked if he could take me on as a sax student. He sighed, and my heart sank. He thought for a moment, then turned to a young guy next to him. 'Graeme,' said Don Burrows, 'I want you to meet a friend of mine, Grahame. He wants to learn the alto sax. Do you teach?' Graeme paused, looked at me. 'Sure, I can see you on Saturday afternoons. Is that OK? I live in Randwick.' 'Great, thanks! And Don, I can't thank you enough.' Immediately, all the musicians started to leave to go to work, and I was left there by myself. I began to realise what Don had done. If he hadn't introduced me as his friend, things might have come out differently. I eventually found out that Graeme Lyall didn't teach; he had no students. He took me on as a gesture of goodwill to Don, whom he respected. Graeme was the hottest tenor player in Australia at that time; he was only twenty-one, a year older than me. Graeme would go on to dedicate his life to teaching, principally at Edith Cowan University in Perth. I had bought a Selmer alto with my Railway salary. It was the best sax you can buy.

My first lesson with Graeme Lyall was unusual. We sat and talked. He asked me about my philosophy of music. What did I want out of music? What did I listen to? At the end, after about two hours, he asked me to play an open note, while he walked around me. I did so, then stopped. 'Keep playing!' After five minutes we sat down again. 'How did you feel about that?' 'It was exhausting!' 'What were you thinking?' 'I don't think I *was* thinking.' 'Well, we have a lot of work to do. Reeds, I was taught a non-pressure system by Frank Smith in Melbourne. One and a half is what I use. Focus on the sound you make, keep it steady and play long notes for a couple of hours a day. You can start soft and build up to forte, then go back to soft. That'll make it more interesting.' With that, I left.

After a while, Graeme moved to Forestville. We drank green tea and mused about music for a couple of hours for our weekly lesson. Graeme never seemed to notice the time and the two dollars I gave him seemed irrelevant. I felt I had learned more about music in a couple of months than I had in my entire life. We seemed to get inside it and focus on the core, wipe away the frills. Graeme had the best technique in the country. How did he achieve it? 'Be a minimalist. It starts in your brain and ends up out there. Everything in between is an impediment if you let it be.' I noticed that when Graeme played, he didn't seem like he was playing. He suggested I read Mahler's book, *First Principles*, his view of music theory. I did, and it was then when I really started to understand music. I also began to doubt my ability as a musician. I felt I could never be as good as Graeme. He had a phenomenal memory for music. He could hear a piece then write it down; remember solos from a year ago and play them note for note. These are skills you have to be born with.

Graeme wanted to know if I had ever played in a band. 'No.' 'Well you'd better start, so you can listen to other instruments.' He called his friend Billy Weston, who said I could start with his rehearsal band at the Musician's Club in about a month. I was terrified. I took that month off work and played eight hours a day to get my sight reading and technique up to scratch. On the day, I met Billy in the lobby and confessed that I was a little worried, as this was my first try. 'Don't worry, if Graeme says you can do it, I trust his judgement.' Billy was short and had a thin moustache. He had a nervous nature and spoke in quick, intense bursts. At the club, there were seventeen other musicians, each of them a professional, discussing current gigs and so on. Billy told me where to sit in the second alto spot and called 'Twenty-three'.(it was the number system for the band book) I looked at the guy next to me and watched what he did. One, two three four, *pow, pow, pow, STOP*! I thought, it can't be me – I haven't blown a note. 'Second trumpet, what was that all about? Phew, not me, I'm the second alto.' 'Attack the note.' And so it went, for three hours. I was exhausted. As I walked out, Billy came over. 'You did well. Concentrate on your tongue.' I went home elated.

We played at the club every Wednesday night from seven. Because I had never been in a band or played a real gig, I was nervous when the other players asked me where I worked and sometimes invited me for a jam session. I could read music well, but at that time had no ability to improvise. I wasn't sure how to start, didn't feel I could fit in with the club scene. My guitarist friend Paul McCabe worked with me on improvisation, but it was amateurish. He had a couple of friends who played piano and drums. We'd hang out at the pianist's house. Ross McLean was older and came across as very 'cool'. He didn't seem to have a regular job or play anywhere. He was into 'philosophy', but it didn't seem to fit anything I had experienced. He drank neat scotch and had a 'bohemian' girlfriend. This was all new to me.

Paul called me one day and said he had a gig at Balmain Town Hall: the darts club of a local hotel was having its annual ball. 'What are we going to play? Who's in the band?' I asked Paul. 'Don't worry, Grahame. We'll play what feels right on the night.' I bought some standards books at Nicholson's music store and started practising. With my books, clarinet and sax, I turned up at the hall and met the drummer and bass player. Paul was warming up his guitar with some fast riffs. There was a crowd of about 200. They seemed pretty happy. We started with a couple of Cole Porter songs. Paul tried a solo but got tangled in some chords and the bass player lost his way. The audience didn't seem to notice. We finished the first set and the darts club organiser, whose name was Greg, came up and said they wanted a barn dance next. He then went over and turned the lights down 'to create a mood'. We went backstage and sat in the corner. 'Paul,' I said, 'how do you want to handle the barn dance?' 'These morons don't understand music,' he replied. 'We'll speed it up with some modern stuff.' I protested, 'I think they want to dance, and if it's a barn dance it has to be the right tempo, as it's progressive.'

Suddenly came a loud yell from the hall caretaker across the stage. 'Who turned the lights down?' He strode towards us with a menacing look. 'If you guys do that again I'll turf you all out!' 'It wasn't us, it was the darts club guy!' explained Paul. 'I don't care. Don't do it again.' Just as we were about to start, the organiser bounded up the stage. 'Who turned the lights back on?' 'The caretaker.' 'Well, tell him to get stuffed. It's our party.' 'He seemed pretty pissed off that you didn't ask him.' 'Well, tell him to fuck off if he comes back.'

With a sense of foreboding, we started the barn dance. *If you knew Susie like I know Susie, oh, oh, oh, what a gal.* Out of the corner of my eye I could see the caretaker advancing on us. 'I told you, I told you! Stop the music!' Then, looking at Paul, he said, 'That's it, you can all piss off!' He strode over to the panel and the lights came on. The organiser jumped up and grabbed the caretaker. 'Are you trying to fuck our party?' A menacing group of darts players had gathered at the base of the stage. 'Pop him one, Greg, the arsehole.' The caretaker looked around and backed off 'You can have some of the lights off, I'll do it, but that's all!' He went over and dimmed them a bit. Greg glared at him and barked, 'A couple more!' The caretaker glanced at the crowd, whose number had doubled at the front and were calling out obscenities. The caretaker turned off a couple more lights, then stood there defiantly. 'Oh shit, let's get on with it, you old turd,' Greg said to him. Then he turned to Paul and yelled 'Let's play!'

Paul began a riff for 'Surf City'. 'I'll give them something to get excited about.' We stood amazed. Paul continued his solo, ripping out a fast surf beat. The dancers, expecting a barn dance, gaped at him. We had reached the progressive stage and no one could figure out when to change. A group gathered at the stage. 'What the fuck is that?' they cried. 'Play it properly.' I looked at Paul, who growled, *'I'll give 'em some good stuff, the morons.'* The noise on the dance floor rose. 'Tell him to stop!' 'Get a proper band!' 'Don't they know a barn dance?' A balled-up napkin flew past my head. Finally, Paul stopped playing and yelled at the audience. 'Cop that, you dickheads!'

There was silence. I thought the audience was going to rush the stage. I stepped up to the microphone and started playing. *If you knew Susie, like I know Susie…* The drummer chimed in and the bass player started. The dance floor started to move, and the aggressors were dragged by their partners into the swirl. Paul looked at them and exclaimed, 'You can stick it up your arse!' and promptly packed up his guitar and stalked to the back of the stage. I played song after song till the dancers wilted and sat down for their dessert. 'Where's Paul?' I asked the drummer. 'He's gone home.' 'It's going to be a long night, with just the three of us.'

At ten to twelve the caretaker came on stage, grabbed the microphone and announced, 'You've got five minutes to piss off. I'm turning the lights off at midnight.' He was rewarded with a boozy chorus of obscenities. At midnight, Greg the organiser came on stage holding a bunch of dollar notes. 'Great job,' he slurred. 'Best music we've had. You blokes can come back next year. I hope this is enough'. It was twice what we were expecting; I guess partly because Paul had missed out. As I drove home, I mused about my life as a professional musician. Next day I called around at Paul's place.

He was very maudlin and declared he wasn't playing for people who didn't understand his music. I replied, 'They're paying, and they'll tell you what to play.'

Billy Weston had started a show band with many of the top musicians in town. They played at the State Ballroom on Sunday nights. I went along to learn how a big band should sound. Graeme Lyall, Neville Blanchette, Judy Bailey, Doug Foskett, Warren Daly and many more attracted a good crowd. After several months, Billy asked if I would like to join the band, because the second alto sax player was leaving. I was overcome. I took six weeks off work and practised eight hours a day. The rehearsal band was OK, but this was a big step up, playing in a proper band with the elite. Graeme was very helpful and told me to concentrate on being calm and practising long notes to focus my thinking. Things worked out well enough, although my peers knew I hadn't done the hard yards in the clubs, learning standards and current pop. I couldn't play the songs without music; I couldn't improvise.

I did get a couple of gigs. Reuben F Scarf, the clothing king, had a bar mitzvah for his son in his house in the eastern suburbs. I received a call from my agent asking me to arrive at 7pm and play. A drummer, bass guitar and guitarist also turned up. 'What do you play?' I was asked. I had my books and that was it. I suggested we play some bossa nova while they were inside the house, as a warm-up. We were on the veranda. After an hour, we were asked to be quiet while the bar mitzvah ceremony was held. By ten thirty, the ceremony was over and people started to come out onto the veranda, so we played some standards. 'Can't you play some rock 'n' roll?' one of the guests asked. I replied, 'I know a couple of Buddy Holly songs.'

We played 'Peggy Sue'. The crowd got very excited. We played it again. And again. Eleven o'clock came around and we stopped. 'That's it; we're finished.' 'No!' a fellow called out. 'We'll pay $500 for another hour.' 'OK, what do you want?' ' "Peggy Sue"!' There being no foldback speakers, I couldn't hear myself play, and that was weird. I just screamed my saxophone against the guitar riff. The dancers got wilder. We played 'Peggy Sue' for an hour. The man offered us $700 for *another* hour. I looked at the band. The crowd was chanting, ' "Peggy Sue, Peggy Sue!" ' Off we went. I became more adventurous and played whatever came into my head. As long as the bass and drums kept the thumping rhythm it didn't seem to matter about the rest. Every now and then I'd play the head and then launch into wailing sounds, or what I thought were wailing sounds, as I couldn't hear a note. Finally, at 1am, we quit. I had a big headache. Some of the crowd asked what our band was called and where we played. I realised I couldn't remember my bandmates' names, as we hadn't met before that night. As it turned out, I never saw them again.

I drove home feeling good and bad. I'd made quite a lot of money and was glad that the crowd had liked what we played, but I didn't think this was a career. I have never played 'Peggy Sue' again!

The show band was booked for the Musician's Club, to start at 12.30am Sunday morning. That was when everybody could make it after their regular gigs. At 12.20, Billy was walking quickly back and forth, muttering. I looked at Graeme Lyall. 'What's up?' 'Neville's not here.' At twelve thirty-five, Billy came out from the side, glared at the band and called, 'One, two, three, four!' very quickly. That was the first four bars. The band leapt into action at a pace I had never heard. I think I started playing after the first eight bars. Billy was super nervous because a number of musical stars including the Woody Herman orchestra were in the audience. I spied Don Burrows sitting quite close and thought I might freeze. The night sped along and everybody was happy, including Billy, who gave me a pat on the back. At 4am, I was on a high. As the sun rose, I reflected on the evening. Where to from here?

The show band played at Sydney Uni after a folk concert featuring Doug Ashdown. It was packed, but half the audience left before we went on. I couldn't work out why the students went more for a guitarist/singer than the best band in the land. The Sydney University jazz secretary was Carolyn Best. She invited the band over to the Forest Lodge Hotel across the road when we finished and after a few drinks asked me if I would take her to the Sunday gig. I said yes, but later realised that Margaret, my girlfriend, would be coming, as she came to most of our concerts. I suggested to Margaret that she might want to give this one a miss, but she was insistent. As a way out, I invited Paul McCabe to join us so it would look like a foursome.

Carolyn lived in Paddington and was the last to be picked up. I suggested she get in the back seat of my car with Paul, but she declined, and both girls sat in the front. We arrived at the State Ballroom and I left them to it. At the break, the trio greeted me and Robert Edwardes, a good friend who started out as a NSW Railways trainee but failed first-year uni, arrived from his shift as a male nurse at Callan Park. I rushed to introduce Carolyn and then returned to the bandstand. When the gig was over, I packed up and Billy invited the band to the Piccolo Bar up the Cross. Robert came and sat with Paul in the back while Carolyn and Margaret squeezed alongside me in the front. I took Robert aside when we arrived and pleaded with him to take Carolyn home. But she declined, telling him that she was my date and *I* was taking her home. It was a difficult evening, and I was ill-equipped to manage. After a bit, Carolyn did go out with Robert, and eventually she became Mrs Edwardes.

Billy was finding it hard to sustain the Sunday night gig at the State Ballroom. For me, it was the highlight of the week. The rehearsal band still played at the Musician's Club on Wednesday nights, and I had been promoted to lead alto. I did a couple of club gigs but found that soul-destroying. I was not equipped to ad lib the bits required for some of the acts, and couldn't see myself spending time learning them.

The ballroom gig folded, and my engineering work, which had grown, became more interesting. Two years had elapsed since I finished university and it seemed that Margaret may be my future wife. Still, I was feeling confused, as I'd hoped music would be the centrepiece of my life. I was spending time at the El Rocco, where Graeme Lyall, Judy Bailey and Johnny Sangster, among others, played. The Macquarie Hotel had Ray Price and the Port Jackson Jazz Band, along with Graham Bell and his band. I admired Merv Acheson at the Criterion Hotel, and, of course, Don Burrows, who played at the Sky Lounge on a Sunday night. Bernie McGann was a favourite; he sounded so different; he had his own sound. I had visions of being a part of all that, but no idea how to get a start. It seemed you had to get set in the clubs and work your way through the system. Pay your dues! I wasn't prepared to do that, as I felt I had played with the best and wasn't going to go backwards. Also, in my heart of hearts, I didn't feel that I thought like a musician. I had observed Graeme Lyall closely, and he had absolute focus on harmony, sound and composition. My world was broader and lacked that intensity.

Part II
Learning about projects
1965

6. I join the workforce

We don't all think the same way.

My foray into music as a career had hit a wall, so now my story reverts to the parallel life I had been leading for my 'day' job.

After university, NSW Railways beckoned, and the six remaining trainees were called to head office to discuss their future. Norm Webster had been our mentor from the start. I liked Norm as he exuded warmth and positive energy towards us. He explained the plan for the next several years: 'I'll be your supervisor till you are finally assigned into the divisions and start your formal career.'

My first assignment was to the design office at Wynyard, as a junior designer. I was introduced to Fred Dawson, my section head. Fred was stooped and wore a grey cardigan. He explained to me carefully in a soft voice that I had a lot to learn and that I should pay attention. A drawing board was assigned, and I was issued with pens, pencils and stationery. I was given a minor job, designing cross-beams for a small bridge in Petersham. It took me less than a day. Fred Dawson came to me next day suggesting that four cross-beams rather than three would be safer. I changed it. Next job?

'Don't rush things,' he replied. I asked what the others were doing, and learned it was generally altering what they'd already done, to little effect.

Fred finally gave me a larger design task: the abutment of a large old bridge with many spans across a flood plain near Narrabri, in north-west NSW. I studied the existing structure and other designs that had been used on similar structures over the years. After some time I decided concrete was the best material and set about sketching the standard abutment wall, with wing walls at 45 degrees swept back to deflect flood waters. Most of the concrete was in the front wall and needed a large foundation with a horizontal slab behind to resist the tipping forces. As my ideas developed, I realised that if I brought back the wing walls parallel to the tracks and made a big concrete box each wall would support the others and I could reduce the thickness dramatically to reduce the cost. I grew excited and finalised the box design. My plan was then to build a riprap rock wall of loosely packed rocks outside the wing walls to resist floodwaters and stabilise the box.

I asked Walter, an engineer sitting close by, for his opinion. He studied it for a few hours and said it would work; and added that Fred wouldn't like it as it was new and Fred didn't do *new*. I thanked him and finished the work. I thought I should cost it out to make sure it was cheaper than the alternative, and found that concrete was the major cost and I had halved the volume with my concept. Walter was right, Fred wasn't happy. I protested, 'But the cost is much lower.' He responded, 'That's not the way we do things here. Now do it the standard way.' I went back to my board and stared out the window. What was the point of being an engineer? Fred wouldn't discuss the merits of my work, but I was buoyed by Walter's support. He told me to package it all up and put it in the file room. 'Walter, I want to see it built.'

I went to Norm Webster and asked if I could be given a field job as the design office was not my cup of tea. I had been there eight months. A month later I was assigned to work with Trevor Favell at the Concrete and Soils laboratory at Sydenham.

My new boss, Trevor, was a very energetic but slightly eccentric engineer with the air of a distracted professor. He explained that my role was to supervise the soils laboratory, which performed soil and foundation tests for railway and also local council projects. There was a diamond drilling truck which travelled the state drilling and collecting samples, mainly for new bridge works. It was a totally indigenous crew, led by Tom Callaghan from La Perouse, south-east of Sydney. Tom was rotund with a constant smile. The laboratory was staffed with workers with disabilities. Reg North had been there the longest and had a bad back. Reg reckoned that Trevor was an evangelist; every couple of years he saw a travelling circus and hired the clowns – that's how he put it. I'm not sure if Reg placed himself in that category. The group was a happy one, and I enjoyed the freedom that Trevor afforded me. He was only interested in building the concrete batch plant customer base as it also catered to many non-railway clients to boost the profitability of the operations. Robert Edwardes' father, Harry, called and asked if I could get his son a job. Harry was working for UNESCO in various parts of the world helping universities with consulting assignments. He didn't like the idea of Robert working as a nurse. I was able to take him on as my assistant and driver.

There was an assignment in Bourke, 800km northwest of Sydney, where a firebug had burned down the town hall, the community hall and the railway station and we were to do the soil tests for the designers of the replacement buildings. Robert and I were confronted with the charred wreckage at the railway. Bourke is one of the most remote towns in Australia with serious social problems. The loss of their public buildings cast a pall over a streetscape already pocked with shops boarded up and abandoned. We didn't hang around and caught the same train back east.

On the way back we stopped at Narrabri to meet the district engineer who was coordinating the work. He mentioned they had had flooding and part of the train track on an old bridge had been washed away. I became excited. Was it on the flood plain? 'Yes, we're starting work next month.' Could I see the drawings?' We went through them, and I saw my abutment design. 'This is a bit radical,' said the district engineer, motioning to my work, 'but it was all they had available. It looks interesting.' A wave of pride swept over me. My design was to be a reality.

After eighteen months I was told I would be reassigned as part of my training. I would remain in Sydenham, but at the construction office across the compound. It was a large dusty area to the north of the railway station overlooking an industrial tip that was slowly being filled to expand the available land. A circular dirt road connected the wooden construction buildings with the two-storey brick divisional offices next to the railway tracks. The soils laboratory, my old office, was on the opposite side. All construction for NSW Railways was controlled from this office. It was a big job covered by my new boss, Gordon Vogan, who supervised three recent graduates – a small team for such a large portfolio. Gordon was overweight but always jolly. He sported thin-rimmed glasses on his ruddy face. The new construction projects for the entire state were split between the graduates. I was given the Liverpool-Campbelltown electrification, which included a 90-span flood plain bridge at Minto, five station upgrades and the rebuilding of the Campbelltown rail yard. I had to supervise around 2,000 workers and several contractors. My responsibilities also included the train servicing centre at Eveleigh for the new Southern Aurora train, as well as other works around Redfern.

Engineers were required to do their own surveying for the set-out of the works. Surveyors seemed only to be assigned to the main divisional operations, and this was probably my biggest responsibility. I had a car and a driver who doubled as a chain man. Most of the time I could handle the work, as the general organisation was managed by the sub-foremen. I had to check the quality of the work, agree to overtime and perform other administrative tasks. One day the chief construction engineer came out on the job. This was a rare event. I had to take him through the various sites and explain the current activities. He asked when it would be finished. It had never occurred to me that I could predict a finish date. I told him I had no idea, but we would be as quick as we could. He nodded and said, 'If you need help, give me a call.' I suddenly realised that management of construction was not sophisticated, and I had a lot to learn.

As I went around the jobs over the next few days, I pondered how things could be better organised, how efficiency could be improved. I saw gangs waiting for materials, such as concrete, to be delivered. How long did deliveries take? When did we need to order them? The design office in Wynyard did the design and there was a capital works program, but they seemed to be disconnected from our office, and there was no overall coordination. I began taking notes while on-site and quizzing the sub-foremen about the activities. They were very helpful and glad I was taking an interest.

7. I stop the Southern Aurora

Multitasking with work, family and university.

Engineering was the main game now, and I made enquiries about further study to reorient my thinking to an engineering future. My leaning was towards project management, of which I seemed to have the least understanding. I enrolled in a Master of Engineering Science degree at UNSW in 1967. The university staff advised me it could be tough as I had been out of the academic environment for three years – I might find the discipline too difficult. However, for the first time it was fun to go to university. I was more mature, and my music experience gave me good backup. The big band discipline of being on time, listening and being organised was valuable.

The master's course consisted of a number of postgraduate subjects and a major thesis. The university world had changed with the introduction of computers; we had done all our computing at undergraduate level with slide rules and log tables. Now I was learning computer languages, FORTRAN, COBOL and BASIC, as well as studying PERT diagrams and logic networks with linear programs. I was being exposed to the tools I needed to manage the construction work at the Railways. My course work included coastal engineering and systems analysis. I immediately took to the lectures and did much background reading to put them in context.

Meanwhile, my private life took a twist. Margaret fell pregnant, and we decided to get married. She had been an anchor in my life but with the pressure of work, coming to terms with my music aspirations and the university study I was not focused. The church wedding and the realisation that I was assuming new responsibilities gave me a sense of purpose. Margaret provided the stability and organisation my private life lacked. Our parents were very supportive.

As a father-to-be, I needed to come to terms with buying a house. Margaret and I had no money, and my father explained the options for obtaining finance. My father was very keen for us to get a good start. A visit to the bank manager and filling out a lot of forms was the first step. Finding the deposit was a hurdle, as I had just $300. We found a house in Forestville in Sydney's north for $12,000, and amazingly the pieces fell into place. The bank accepted my deposit and funded the balance. I was the owner of a three-bedroom wooden bungalow in a leafy neighbourhood. It felt strange but nice to be settled so quickly. I revelled in university studies and began to understand construction problems better.

In the railway hierarchy of importance, keeping the trains running on time was sacrosanct. For the electrification program, we had developed a work train to install the overhead structures to support the new electric wires. At the front of the work train, a boring machine dug a hole for the foundation. The holes were dug at about 50m intervals. Next, a steel RSJ (rolled steel joist) was inserted in the hole and supported by a crane until coarse blue metal was poured around the steel. This gave it enough support so the crane could be released. Next, a slurry of cement was injected to finish the foundation and leave a steel pole to which, in a later operation, the cantilever and dropper for the electrical apparatus could be clamped. The plan was to erect twenty of these per day.

I teamed with traffic manager Ron Tidyman to get the work done and keep the trains running. After a couple of months, it was clear that we might never finish. There were twin tracks. For four hours per day, we were supposed to have possession of one track. However, when the crane was swivelled to hold the steel pole it 'fouled' the second track and trains couldn't pass. Ron accepted that we might stop suburban trains for a minute or so, but that was it. The reality was very different. Our train was delayed almost every day by traffic restrictions, so we only had two or three hours in which to work. Sometimes the train was marshalled with the carriages in the wrong order, which meant we could do no work. I tried to reason with Ron. He said he didn't care if we ever finished. I discussed the situ-

Pouring concrete on the railway

Filling the train with concrete

ation with the foreman. Clem was philosophical 'You can't beat traffic. We are at their mercy.' We improved the marshalling problem, but our productivity was still low. Under these conditions, we would be years late and costs would balloon enormously. Ron had no interest in our problems.

One morning, after more delays, we were finally underway. Then Ron came over: 'The Southern Aurora is coming! You need to shut down for half an hour.' No, let me know when it's close, and we'll see. Oh and by the way, it should have come by early in the morning,' I said. He fumed. 'You know you can get the sack for stopping it!' 'It must be very late and a few extra minutes won't hurt,' I said. I thought Ron would burst – his face was red and the idea that I would stop the train was apparently unthinkable. I stood my ground, and he turned on his heel. I told the foreman to ignore Ron and complete the installation. The train came and was delayed about five minutes. Ron stormed off to write his report. 'That's the end of you!' I heard him shout in the distance. Hmmm. Soon after I went back to the office and made some calculations. If we continued, the costs would blow out from $78 million to $288 million, and it would take an extra three years to complete. I typed up my report and went home.

In the morning, there was a summons to appear in the commissioner's office at 10am at Railway House,

Wynyard. I donned my jacket and headed in with my report. Ron was in the anteroom, glaring at me. 'I warned you,' he said. 'Nobody stops the Southern Aurora and gets away with it.' We were summoned into a large, ornate room, and I got my first look at the stern visage of Commissioner McCusker. 'Ron,' he said – they seemed to be on first-name terms – 'what happened?' Ron ran through the whole scenario accurately; I was impressed. The commissioner turned to me. 'What do you have to say, young fellow?'

'$210 million, sir.' I replied, pausing for effect. 'That's what it will cost extra if we don't change our operations.' 'I don't understand,' he said. 'Well, it will take three extra years and the extra money.' 'I still don't understand,' the commissioner said. I showed him a schedule and some of my calculations. 'I've never seen anything like this,' he said, looking at Ron. 'Are you aware of this? It's serious.' Ron suddenly realised that his story was falling apart. The focus had shifted to time and cost. His job was to keep the trains running, not to worry about anything else. 'Sir, I just wanted to get the Aurora past. Grahame refused to let it,' Ron said.

The commissioner turned to me. 'You should have come to me earlier. I'll get someone to review your report, and we'll issue some new directives. And by the way, don't stop the Aurora again – it's bad for publicity. You're both dismissed.' I looked at Ron and we trooped out. He was shattered. I still had my job. I actually felt sorry for him. He was at the end of his career, was on first-name terms with the commissioner and I had won the battle.

A few hours later I received a call from my boss, Gordon Vogan. 'What have you done to the commissioner?' 'Nothing.' Gordon's voice went up a notch 'He just called and wants a detailed report on the electrification. He said the budget is blown. We don't normally involve the commissioner with the details.' 'I told him it was over by $210 million.' 'Why?' 'Because I stopped the Aurora for five minutes.' 'Christ, you didn't, did you?' 'Yes.' Silence… 'This is serious. You could lose your job for that … and mine too!' 'I told him it would be three years late.' 'Grahame, what's got into you? All you have to do is follow the rules, and stopping the Aurora is out of the question.' 'Well, it's *been* stopped and the commissioner wants a more detailed report.' 'What do you mean, *more* detailed?' 'I've already given him a summary report, and he was very interested.' 'You've seen him? You must tell me about these things before they get out of hand. What did you tell him?' 'That it will be over budget $210 million and three years late unless he gets Traffic to be sensible.' 'Keeping the trains on time is his main mission,' said Gordon. 'I don't think I can save you. Be in my office first thing in the morning.'

I explained to Gordon the theories on planning I

had learned at university and how we could reschedule some of the activities to make up ground. Concrete pumping had just been commercialised, and there were a few pumps available for trial. We needed to check that the concrete could be placed without segregation, which is when the cement separates from the aggregate. Gordon listened intently. 'Now, about this meeting with the commissioner...' said Gordon. I replied, 'I told him we can develop a plan to get things back on track if the traffic people assist with the available track time.' Gordon looked glum. 'I've been here 25 years, and I think you're wrong, OK, if I go so be it.'

I now had my chance to try the concrete pumping technology. Several sections of the work did not allow for the erection of our standard foundation. Conventional concrete foundations were needed, due to rock. The inaccessibility posed problems of getting concrete to the locations. Pumps were expensive, but shutting down the railway track and doing weekend work was too. I wanted to see how far we could pump and still produce quality concrete. After our trials with the pumps, I set up a major pour near Glenfield. We had 300 men positioned and three pumps organised. I planned to pour 400 cu m for the day, starting at 6am. I was told I had to use Marley concrete; Marley had the government contract. I called the company and set it up. Next morning on-site we waited. At six forty-five the Marley concrete delivery was late. Des, my supervisor, came over agitated. 'They're on strike. When the men heard of the big order, they walked out.'

Christ, who else supplies concrete? I raced back to the hut, rang Pioneer and asked the manager when they could get the first truck out. 'Seven thirty.' I gave him the spec. 'Can you do 400 cu m?' 'Yes.' 'Go for it!' I told him. I returned to the men. 'They'll be here at seven thirty.' 'Who?' Des asked. 'Pioneer.' 'You can't do that! We don't have a contract.' 'Well, it's done. Get the men ready.'

By ten thirty, we had completed two thirds of the pour. Des approached and said, 'Marley is back at work. Should I call? … went back when they heard Pioneer was doing it' Are we set up for tomorrow to do another 400?' I asked 'Yes.' he responded 'Call Marley and tell them.' Des was back in ten minutes. 'We should have put the order in before ten. It's in the contract, and they're dirty because you went to Pioneer and want to put you in your place.' I went back to the construction shed and rang Pioneer. 'Can you do another 400 tomorrow, six thirty start?' 'No probs.' I thought … in for a penny, in for a pound.

The following day the district engineer, Doug Neil, stopped by to watch the pumping, which was going very well. I was unaware at the time, but this was the first major use of concrete pumping in Australia. The men enjoyed it, as it removed a lot of hard work. 'Grahame, I notice you're using Pioneer? They're not our supplier. Marley have the contract.' 'Did they call you?' I replied. 'Yes, pretty upset, to say the least.' 'Well, suppliers are supposed to supply. They didn't. If they get their act together, we'll use them next time.' 'Grahame, this is a hanging offence in the railways – you've spent $80,000 without authority.' 'Yes, but I've saved more than that with the new system.' I went back to the office to write my 'cover your arse' report and plan the next attack on the schedule. Surprisingly, I didn't hear any more about it for several weeks. Then Gordon Vogan called me into his office and showed me an invoice from Pioneer concrete. 'It's only $1 a metre more than Marley, but don't do it again.' It was a mild rebuke, and I asked if he'd seen the pumping and showed him my new schedule. 'I think we can bring this back to the original plan, but I'll need Traffic to cooperate.' 'Don't worry, the commissioner's watching very closely, and Ron Tidyman is under orders to cooperate.'

To speed up the project, I had a plan to bring on extra crews and work Sundays when rail traffic was light. I discussed it with the sub-foremen, and they liked the idea of earning extra pay because Christmas was coming. We devised new procedures to install foundations in major cuttings. One Sunday, south of Campbelltown, I walked into a major cutting to see men suspended from ropes guiding concrete buckets down the face. I was shocked. It was drizzling rain and very slippery.

The concrete transit trucks were on crude tracks at the top of the cutting. I ran to the subbie, Matt Blessington. 'Stop everything!' He looked at me, nonplussed. 'You said you wanted to accelerate the program.' 'Matt, it's too dangerous. Stop everything now.' The next morning I called all the sub-foremen to a meeting at the field office in Campbelltown. I explained that all innovations for special works would require a work plan and a run-through of the logistics. I emphasised that we would meet the schedule and that I would try to have them paid a bonus for finishing before Christmas.

For the first time in my life, I realised safety had to be number one in any work plan. It was a revelation for me, as I had thought that all workers would realise this and act accordingly, but men look to the leaders to show them the way and rely on their judgement.

My coursework at university was opening my eyes to new possibilities. Coastal engineering showed how primitive was our understanding of the effects of storms on structures and beaches. Storm surges were poorly understood. My work on computer programming and modelling was also starting to bear fruit. I was enrolled in operations research and was starting logic analysis of construction problems. Historically, major developments had evolved sequentially, starting with a concept that was designed and costed before procurement and construction were started. Government was largely responsible for public works and infrastructure. I began to apply logic analysis to my railway work.

Undergraduate courses in English, philosophy and psychology had spiked my interest in big-picture thinking. Working with the NSW Railways management made me realise how confined was their approach to their work. I had read a book by Frank Hardy, *Power without Glory*, and been amazed that the events he described could have occurred in Australia: corruption at the highest levels of government, police and the public service. I started to question everything in my own world.

Back in the construction world, I had to deal with an Italian contractor who had won the contract for a new 90-span bridge and viaduct over the Minto River flood plain. There were two larger spans over the river, and the rest were concrete culverts about 4m long. I met the project manager at the site, and we ran through the construction methodology. Immediately, I realised there was a problem. He wanted to construct a level crossing for access, rather than using the path under the existing bridge span. 'Not enough head room for some of the equipment,' he explained. I countered, 'This was covered in the contract, along with other restrictions to improve safety with train operations.' 'Oh, you're not going to use the contract against me?' he sighed. 'We're here to get this thing built as quickly as possible, and you're already quoting the contract?' I was taken aback. This man was the first main contractor whom I'd had to supervise, and I had no experience of what was normal behaviour and good practice. 'Why didn't you bring it up at the contract negotiations in head office?' I asked. He replied, 'I've only just been hired by the firm. This is the biggest job they've ever done, and I think they may have underbid it to get into the bigger league.' If I let him put in the level crossing, I would have to provide four flagmen to monitor trains. The track was the main connection between Sydney and Melbourne, and carried the Aurora. 'Are you going to pay for the flagmen?' I asked. 'Don't be crazy!' he said. 'Well, that's it. You'll just have to drive down to the main level crossing,' I said.

All the workmen were Italians with good knowledge of concrete, but not on this scale. They started excavation of the main bridge piers with driven sheet pile, next to the old bridge. The track was to be realigned at an acute angle to allow for the new construction, so the old and new work was quite close at this point. I received a call to authorise the first pour of the foundation concrete for the bridge piers. It was about 6m below grade. As I arrived, I noticed eight mobile concrete agitators lined up ready to deliver their loads. Mario, the construction boss, was anxious to get started. I had a look at the steel reinforcement and formwork – it all seemed in order. I then checked the despatch dockets for the concrete to see the right mix had been ordered. All OK. 'How are you going to get the concrete into the base?' I asked Mario. 'Pour it in from the trucks,' he replied. 'No, you can't just pour it in,' I said. 'The concrete will segregate, with aggregate on one side and sand and cement on the other.' 'We'll make sure that doesn't happen,' he replied. 'No,' I said, 'you have to have a tremie [a large metal hopper and pipe] to control the flow. Why don't you use the new concrete pumps?' 'Too expensive.' 'Well, I can't authorise the pour,' I said. 'What! Are you trying to screw us? I'll have to tip all the concrete in the creek.' 'Your problem,' I said, and left him fuming.

Next morning, a note was on my desk: 'Meet me at Minto for meeting with contractor at 9.30am. He's claiming large damages for your actions,' signed 'Gordon'. Hmmm, I thought … I might be in trouble. There was no way I could get there in time, so I resigned myself to a late arrival. As I drove up, five people were standing adjacent to the bridge pier. Gordon greeted me with, 'It looks bad. You can't go around stopping the works like this. I've spoken to the owner and said we'll try to arrange some compensation. You need to work with these people cooperatively.' I looked at him wide-eyed. 'Have you looked at what they propose to do? I did my honour's degree thesis on concrete technology, and I understand the problem we could be causing,' I said. 'Grahame, these people are experts, and I think we should take their word for the quality of the concrete,' he said. 'Gordon, I don't think they have a clue. This job is too big for them,' I said. Gordon looked at me and sighed. 'Grahame, you're going to have to learn how things operate in the real world.' 'OK,' I said, 'let's do a trial. They're pouring concrete for the other pads. Let's use some of it to test my theory.'

We walked back to the others, who were sneering at me. One said: 'Has the boy got the message?' I wondered what he meant. 'OK,' I said, 'bring some concrete over here and pour it into the base,' It took half an hour to get organised. We stood where we could watch the concrete cascade off the rebar as it dropped to the bottom. After a couple of minutes, I signalled for them to stop. It was clear the concrete was segregated. I asked Gordon and Serge, the owner, if they could go down and check how it looked. After a few minutes, they emerged from the hole. 'Amazing, Grahame,' said Gordon. 'I didn't know that could happen.' He turned to Serge. 'You're going to have to get a tremie, as Grahame asked.' Serge turned to the project manager. 'You're fired. Leave immediately.' He then turned to Mario. 'And you can go too.' Serge turned to me. 'I'm sorry to have put you to this trouble. We'll get a tremie in the morning.' With that, he left. I looked at Gordon, and we departed together. 'Keep up the good work,' he said. I smiled inwardly and wondered what had transpired before I had arrived.

The overhead wire structures were going in at a faster rate, and I was pleased to see the enthusiasm of the crews. One Sunday we were tying in the new track at Minto to the main line. I watched the fettlers handling the long strings of rail, which were like spaghetti. They used long steel poles to manoeuvre the rail into position. I was enthralled but wondered if there was a better way. Then I heard a scream. The rail had been turned over and at the far end a worker had been distracted and his bar, stuck in the rail, had swung over and hit him on the side of the head. Several of us rushed to him and held his head up to see what damage had been done. He was unconscious and bleeding profusely. One of the men stanched the bleeding while another called for a ute and got some blankets. I thought quickly. 'Do we have any medical supplies?' 'Only some basic bandages, not much.' Somebody yelled, 'Take him to Campbelltown Hospital!' That seemed a good idea and one of the men drove off quickly with the patient and a helper. About five minutes later a worker came over and said, 'There's no hospital in Campbelltown... it's in Liverpool.' I stared at him. 'Christ!' I took off in my car after them. Just out of Campbelltown I caught up and signalled them over. 'You have to turn around and go to Liverpool.' They sped off again. I had time to reflect. Safety was at the forefront of my mind, but I had failed to plan for this emergency. The next day I called in at the hospital to see how the injured worker was getting on. I had phoned the previous evening and been told he was OK. He smiled and apologised for all the fuss. I told him it was our fault for not being better prepared and wished him a speedy recovery.

As Christmas approached, I started the final clean-up tasks, for there was to be a grand opening at Campbelltown. I asked Gordon how it was being managed. The local council was in charge and working with head office on the arrangements. I found out by chance that nobody who had worked on the construction would be invited, including me. Welcome to local government. My boss was invited, and I felt bad that the people who actually did the work were excluded. I called a meeting of the foremen and told them we would have a celebration in a pub in Liverpool and all the men were welcome, and the party was on the house! From lunchtime on Saturday, a large crowd of around 500 converged and we had a great time. This was my first construction job, and I was so happy for what we had all achieved. I told my boss what I'd done and presented him with the bill. He didn't blink and thanked me for organising the event, commenting, 'I'm sure you had a lot more fun than I did.'

Shortly after Christmas, I received a note saying that I was being posted to Narrabri to work under the divisional engineer in Moree. The fun was over. I needed to make a decision on the direction I wanted to take. I could stay in NSW Railways or go into private construction, as many of my peers were doing. It was strange that the railways provided the best training in Australia for engineers, not to be railway engineers but construction managers.

I reflected on the past couple of years. I had married, had a son, David and a big job in construction at the railways. I lived in Forestville, in the north of the city, and had work and university in the south. Nighttime lectures and a 7am start in Sydenham made for a long day. In the winter, Margaret made me a thermos filled with soup for dinner on my uni nights as I went straight to lectures from work. It had been exhausting but exciting. I don't think I had ever been so happy in my life.

I was lucky to have been exposed to a wide range of experiences and often remembered my structures lecturer Professor Shaw's comments about theory and the real world during my oral exam at the end of my undergraduate years. The increasing role of computers in engineering and management would create a new world I was only just beginning to understand.

The railways had been a fantastic training ground for me. I had been exposed to design, soil mechanics, concrete and construction management. More importantly, I had been challenged to deal with aggressive contractors, technology and indifferent bosses. Overriding all this was the reality of safety and my responsibilities to the workers. Engineering has many more dimensions than I had been taught at university and in a few short years I had been given solid lessons to build my future.

With wife and first son

8. The harsh reality of private enterprise

When the price of something is always too high.

My formal studies were nearly over, but I had a major thesis to write. My engineering friends gathered at a pub in Sydenham, generally on a Friday after work. They were my sounding board, and I was particularly interested in how the big construction firms operated. I learned McDonald Construction in Mascot, the largest construction company in Australia at that time, was hiring. Was that my new direction? A financial bond kept me in NSW Railways for five years, three of which I had served.

I secured an interview with Ed Riddle, McDonald's state manager. Ed was a tall, gaunt man with only a fringe of hair around the base of his skull and over his ears. Ed listened to my story and was complimentary. I then broached the bond issue and wondered if he could help. He said he would think about it and get back to me. About a week later I received an enticing letter of offer from McDonald's. It was the moment of truth. I discussed the McDonald's offer with Norm Webster, my NSW Railways trainee supervisor. I told him that while I had enjoyed my work with the railways, I didn't find exciting the prospect of years in the bush, going through the rail promotion system. 'I'm doing the university work to bring a higher level of competency to develop projects.' Norm noted some of my past breaches and my meeting with the commissioner, but assured me that I was held in high regard and my postgraduate studies were appreciated. Then he smiled and said I needed to follow my heart, and wished me well.

I was reasonably well paid and had a wife and child to support. If I was going in another direction, I needed to consider all aspects. My parents were very conservative and still reeling from my music deviation; they were not much help. My wife Margaret was supportive and encouraged me to follow my instincts. I called Ed and accepted his offer, which included helping me pay off my bond. I had joined free enterprise!

My first day was a shock. I was shown a desk and told to meet the supervisor in an hour. I introduced myself to the others in the open-plan office and found the stationery cupboard to get set. I sat at my desk and thought, 'I've just left a job where I had an office, car, driver and secretary. A couple of thousand people were under my control. Now I have a desk among a dozen others. Hmmm.' I sat with a cup of coffee and met my new boss, Ray Daley, the chief estimator. Ray had slicked back hair and a purposeful manner. He was curt and to the point. He gave me the history of the company, its structure and some of the rules. We spent about two hours exploring my background and his expectations. He then handed me a large file and said to study it. I opened the cover and found an 'Invitation to Bid' from the Wheat Board.

The task was to build twelve wheat silos at several locations through the mid-west of New South Wales. It was a massive task, and I was surprised Ray thought I could pull it together. After a couple of days, Ray led me through the company procedures for bidding work. I asked if we had any alliances with suppliers and local contractors, how the client managed contractors and the terms and conditions that would drive our planning, and myriad questions. Ray gave me a list of names and contact details, and suggested I spend a couple of weeks going to all the locations stretching from Forbes to Tamworth through the central west. I was a little overwhelmed with the responsibility, but set off optimistically.

After a week I had covered only two sites and was bogged down in obtaining prices for materials and sourcing local equipment. I called Ray with a progress report. He was a bit short with me and told me to get help from the purchasing department. He said I should not get into too much detail, but talk to local contractors and see if they were bidding to any of the other contractors. He suggested they might have already done a lot of work, as this was a big contract. I arranged to meet the local rep of one of the big concrete suppliers at the pub that night. He was a goldmine of information. His company had hoped to supply all sites, and put a plan together. He was also in contact with earthmoving firms and crane hire operators. I realised a lot of my work had already been done – I just needed to tap into it. My main task was to develop a strategy to build these silos with minimum overhead, utilising an integrated local team. I thanked him and set about methodically building a plan. In two weeks I had covered all the sites and formed some good relationships with a group of suppliers.

I presented my first cut to Ray a week later. He quizzed me on every aspect of my plan and cost build-up. Then he declared the bid 20% too high and told me to go back to all the suppliers and force their prices down. I said these were good people, and I couldn't treat them so badly. Ray looked at me hard for a few seconds. 'Do you want to be in the construction business or not? They expect you to do this and will think you're soft if you don't.' With that, he left me to my thoughts. I was on the phone the next day, battling suppliers. Most reacted positively, but a few told me to get stuffed and hung up. I saw Ray in the corridor later in the day and gave him an update. 'Fine,' he said, 'this is round one of ten rounds. Keep finding ways to shave their prices till they bleed. They have to think you're the winning contractor and want to be on the winning team. This is a big deal for them, and you can tell them it's a long-term relationship.' 'Is it?' I asked. 'Who knows?' he replied. 'The world is a funny place.'

After two weeks of honing, I was ready to put my final plan and costing together. Ray had one of the senior construction managers vet it, and I made a series of corrections. During a final meeting with Ray, he asked if I would be prepared to manage the construction if we won the bid. I hadn't thought about it; I had expected one of the senior managers to be appointed. He explained that he would give me some experienced foremen and site managers. I was chuffed to be asked and accepted.

The next step was to present the bid to state manager Ed Riddle. Ray and I spent two hours going through the plan and our approach. He wanted to know how financially solid the local contractors were. I said I assumed they were all right as I had spent time with them on-site. He was dismissive. 'Get a credit check on all of them.' This was new to me, and Ray offered to show me how to do it. Next step was to get approval from the board subcommittee for bids. They would add the profit margin and risk premium. 'What's the risk premium?' I asked. Ray explained: 'The board assesses each project for its location, union and client risk. If there's a history of problems, they add money as a contingency.' The following week Ray told me the bid was approved with a 7% profit margin and a 20% risk premium. I asked what he thought, as I thought the risk premium was high, we'd put in a lot of work, and it would be a waste to lose the contract because of that. Ray shrugged. 'It's out of my hands. We'll know in a few weeks. They generally call to have clarification meetings. You can't tell what the other contractors are thinking.'

I sat at my desk wondering what happens next. I didn't have to wait long. Ray gave me the documents for an upgrade to a CSR plasterboard factory in western Sydney. I devised the plan and costing. He then submitted it to the client. 'Ray, don't we have to give it to the board tender committee?' 'No, it's under their limit.' 'Well, we need to add a profit margin.' 'No, we bid it bare and make it up with the extras.' 'How do you know there'll be extras?' I asked. 'Grahame, these guys are so disorganised they just issue a package and then immediately start changing the scope. The extras end up being worth more than the original bid.' 'How do they justify that to their bosses?' 'They just change the production values to show they're improving productivity.' I was learning. Ray was right – at the end of the first week, the supervisor at CSR called me in. 'Here's the new plan. Can I have a revised estimate?' I showed Ray back at the office. 'What do you think it's worth?' I said. 'I thought around $100,000.' 'Tell them

$200,000,' he said. 'He'll haggle you down to $150,000, which you will grudgingly accept. That's how it works.' This went on for several months.

I kept wondering how the silo bid was going. Ray indicated he wasn't hopeful, as they hadn't called for clarification meetings. I went through the bid again, to be ready for a call. I couldn't find the steel roof figures. I checked and rechecked – no mention. I had left it out. Those figures represented around 20% of the total cost. What should I do? We must be in the running with that omission. I slept on it for a few days and finally called Ray to let him know and receive advice on what to do. But before I got to it, Ray said, 'Bad luck about the silos – they gave it to a small specialist operator, a Dutchman, and he apparently does nothing else. Did say we had a good price, but upstairs put on that 20% loading, which probably knocked us out.' I listened quietly. 'Nobody mentioned the Dutchman when I was out there.' Ray continued 'Apparently he has his own teams, and they move from job to job. It's a blow to the locals we were hooked up with. You live and learn.' My mind raced. Construction was not just pouring concrete and throwing up steel. It was teams, connections and a good understanding of the local scene. I'd been on the sites for only a few weeks. The winning contractor had been honing his skills for years and understood how to work in these remote conditions. If I'd been the winning bidder, we'd be starting from scratch. The outcome would be a lottery. I had a lot to learn. Ray said, 'So what did you want to talk about?' I hesitated… 'Why do we put on those large loadings?' 'I'll tell you over a beer one day.'

That day came one Friday a few weeks later. The team was having a beer at the local. Eventually, it was just Ray and me. 'You asked about the loading, Grahame. McDonald's was the biggest a few years ago. We built the Kurnell refinery for Caltex – the first time an Australian company was given a major industrial project. It went very well and was a credit to Sir Warren McDonald, the company founder, who went on to serve on the Reserve Bank board and several others. We actually part-owned the Francis Creek iron ore mine in the NT and took positions in other mining operations. We then bid on the beef roads in western Queensland, and it turned out to be a disaster with huge cost overruns. The soil conditions proved to be difficult to manage. Then a big silo job came up, also in Queensland, to make up for the losses, but that cratered due to poor management. It nearly brought the company to insolvency. Senior management was sacked, and we became very risk-averse. *That*'s why we put the loadings on with the big jobs.' I took all this in and said, 'If we keep doing that, we'll certainly go out of business.' 'Grahame, it's a matter of confidence and good people. You're a breath of fresh air, but it will be years before they'll believe they can back you. We have a long road to hoe to get back to our former glory.' I went home with mixed feelings.

The next day I was bidding on a 27-km water pipeline at Coonabarabran. I was to put together a construction plan and an estimate to deliver the project, a government job to service the Siding Springs telescope, on a nearby mountain in the Warrumbungles. I quickly read the file and realised that I knew nothing about pipeline construction. I called a friend at the Water Board and arranged to have a chat. Meanwhile, Ray contacted me to say a site inspection was to be held the following week, in which we'd be taken through the job with the consulting engineers. I joined eight other contractors in a hotel back bar to be briefed on the pipeline issues. Our host was an amiable engineer from MWP, a large engineering consultancy. Back in Sydney, I pondered how to win the contract and make some money. We submitted a bid and waited.

The CSR job was finishing up, and we had heard little from the pipeline people. I was beginning to wonder if I had made the right career choice. The pay was good, and I enjoyed working with Ray, but I wanted to get my teeth into a real project. I had learned a lot about construction methodologies and costing, but a year had passed and I still didn't have a project. My discussions with MWP on the water pipeline had opened my eyes to the role of the consulting engineer in the development process.

Consulting engineers seemed to have a bigger influence in how projects were structured, and the work I'd done for my master's degree might have more application in that field. I was beginning to understand the roles of the various participants in project development. The owners employed engineers to design the works and, in turn, contracted suppliers of equipment and materials in different combinations for constructors to build the project. Finance arrangements sometimes influenced the legal documents which brought everything together.

I started exploring the world of consulting engineering. I called several of the major companies to see if there were opportunities. Peter Miller, the CEO at Miller, Milston & Ferris, interviewed me. I was very impressed; this company had a cool office in Sydney's The Rocks and was involved with prestigious building projects in the city. Peter liked my ideas on operational research and planning, but a month passed and I heard nothing.

CMPS, a consulting engineering company in Chatswood, was looking for a project controls engineer, which was a new area evolving with the development of computers. Chatswood was a good location, as I was living in not-too-far-away Forestville. Kevin Torpey, a brash young manager, interviewed me. His speech was peppered with expletives. Computer skills were his main focus, and he was keen to use a new IBM product for project management. After an hour of grilling, he offered me a job … if I was able to pass the scrutiny of the partner, Eric Mansfield.

A secretary led me into a wood-panelled office where sat a gentleman in a pin-striped suit and striped shirt. Eric Mansfield was courteous and offered me tea. Then he began. 'Well, where have you come from?' 'McDonald Constructions, sir.' 'No, what school?' 'Oh, Sydney High.' 'Hmmm, good rowers and quite good at football. Well done. What did you play?' 'Tennis, sir.' 'Excellent! That's my game. I hope you'll be happy here.' I was surprised that he didn't quiz me on my technical skills. I returned to Kevin's office, and he gave me the papers to join the company. 'By the way,' he said, 'the job's in Melbourne.' This was a surprise, but I was happy.

I had to give notice at McDonald's and called Ed Riddle for an appointment. I explained my reasons for leaving and my new job's possibilities. Ed said, 'You're signing on as a project controls engineer? It's very hard to make progress in a company from that position; you tend to get marginalised.' I wasn't sure what his point was. Ed continued, 'You had a great future here as a project manager, but, unfortunately, we have no projects.'

I went home and told Margaret. She was much relieved as she was only a couple of months away from having our second child. It had seemed likely we'd be in

Coonabarabran for the birth, and now it was Melbourne. Things were moving quickly for me on a new track. I only knew it felt right.

McDonalds had been so different to the railways. It had been tough to shave costs and challenge the subcontractors. I had trusted what people told me, but the reality of commercial life meant hardening my thinking and constantly pushing prices down. The alternative was failure. Cost estimating the construction task involved innovation and a good understanding of the processes. Dealing with the client effectively meant understanding his processes to get a successful outcome. All of this was another foundation in building my career.

9. Southern discomfort

I am hit in the face with a dead fish.

We flew to Melbourne for our new adventure. I reported to the CMPS partners' office on the top floor of Clunies Ross House in Parkville. I was ushered into a well-appointed corner office, to be confronted by a short man who introduced himself as 'Nairn'. He stared at me coldly. 'You're the new man from Sydney?' The emphasis was on 'Sydney', as if it was a dirty word. 'Yes.' 'Why are you here?' 'They said you need a project controls engineer.' '*We* don't need one, *they* think we do. I was against it. Never had one before and Melbourne engineers can control their own projects.' Nairn said forcefully. I paused for a moment and said, 'I'm to introduce a new IBM management program that's driven by computers.' His eyes narrowed 'Well, we don't need American technology here. British technology is what we use.' With that, he started reading his mail, ignoring me. I was getting a message: Sydney folk are not welcome.

Nairn's secretary showed me to my desk, and I introduced myself to some of the people around me. I then called Kevin Torpey at the Sydney office and told him about my exchange with Nairn. 'Yes, he's an arsehole. Only likes people from Melbourne and Adelaide. You'll find the project manager's a prick too.' 'Great,' I said, 'what have you got me into?' 'Look, don't worry about that. Get the controls set up, liaise with the main contractors and find out where the project sits, cost- and schedule-wise.' I took some comfort from Kevin's words, but Nairn had shaken me up. I felt isolated. I was still idealistic about my profession. I hadn't realised that personalities would play such a strong role in the engineering process.

Electrolytic Zinc and Goldfields had joined forces to deliver a total change to the west coast mining operations in Tasmania. Copper, lead and zinc were currently being exported via an APT railway from Queenstown to Strahan, and then shipped through Macquarie Harbour. The bar in the harbour was quite shallow and difficult. The system was old and expensive to maintain. The turnaround involved shutting the copper smelter and exporting metal concentrates north via the Emu Bay railway to the port of Burnie. This required new rail-handling facilities at Melba Flat, Rosebery and Burnie with a rail upgrade, principally at the Pieman River, involving a new high-level bridge. Additionally, the iron pyrites (fool's gold) would be transported and processed at a new sulphuric acid plant at Ulverstone, near Burnie. There were many elements that needed to be coordinated. Some of the sites were remote, and the west coast suffered high rainfall.

I started to map out a program and found the other staff members enthralled by what I was doing. They had never seen the planning tools I was utilising, but were willing to give me the necessary data I needed. I visited the IBM offices and outlined my requirements. They were generally unhelpful, as they were largely salesmen who weren't familiar with this product. The experts were in the United States. I liaised closely with Kevin Torpey in Sydney, and we found more helpful and knowledgeable IBM people there. Kevin arranged a meeting in Burnie in Tasmania – 'in the pub by the jetty at 5' – the following week to check the port and acid plant sites. He would be driving from Hobart, as he had meetings with the Electrolytic Zinc people. We had other projects in Risdon near Hobart.

I flew into Wynyard, a few kilometres west of Burnie, and took the shuttle bus to town. Armed with some plans from the office and wandering around the port I tried to visualise our facilities; I began to understand the scope of our project.

At 1pm I headed for the pub and waited for Kevin, who burst into the bar at five thirty, cursing about several things that were annoying him. 'Bloody hell! Simple things seem to trip up Nairn. He has no concept of a project. He's only interested in the status issues, organising lunch and brown-nosing the Goldfield executives. You OK?' 'Yes.' I replied open-mouthed. Kevin dug into his bag looking for memos. He paused, looked up and asked, 'How's Nairn treating you?'

'Fine, he doesn't talk to me.'

'Good, he's an arrogant prick. You need to get with the contractors and come down here for a week a month to keep up with the local gossip. Reading reports is no good – they only want to tell you the good stuff.' He wrote some more notes and I got some beers. We went through all the issues with the rail upgrade, as it seemed the most vulnerable to government interference and delays. More beers and discussion saw the sun disappear and Kevin exclaim, 'I'm hungry! By the way, where are we staying tonight?' I looked at him blankly, and said, 'Your girl made the booking. I've never been here before. How many hotels are there?' 'Buggered if I know. We'll just have to ask around.' We drove off in his car as the pub where we were drinking had no reservation and was full. By now it was eight thirty and every hotel or guest house we found was closed.

'Christ, I have to eat. There was a fried chicken place on the main road next to a service station.' Kevin exclaimed. We went there and tore a fried chicken apart with our bare hands. The chicken was delicious, and we felt better.

It was getting cold, and the warming glow of the Boag's beer was wearing off. I asked the attendant at the service station about hotels. 'There's one on the hill you might have missed, up by the carpentry workshop.'

We drove up, but it looked closed. Kevin said, 'Don't worry, we'll go around the back.' We did so and entered through the kitchen and found the manager. 'You're a bit late! Come into the office.' It was the right place. We put our bags in a shared room, and Kevin started for the bar. 'They have early closing, but we'll be right.' We entered the bar to lots of noise and almost a full house.

'It's my shout. Find a seat.' There were none, but a large timber worker created a space at the bar. 'What are you doing here?' he asked. I explained a bit, and he nodded. 'Great to see the place booming. Good luck!'

Kevin returned with a couple of pints. 'Who was that?' 'No idea, but he was onside.' 'You've got to be careful, there are people against the project.' I left Kevin at ten thirty. He was involved in a vigorous conversation about Irish politics. I was tired and a bit drunk and fell into bed. I walked into breakfast at six thirty next morning to find Kevin halfway through his eggs. 'I didn't want to wake you, and I need to get back to Melbourne. I'll leave you the car if you drop me off at the airport.' He looked chipper, and I felt hungover.

The project was coming together, and the family had settled into a maisonette in South Yarra. Margaret was due in a few days and David, our son, was running riot. We had an unexpected visit from my best mate from Sydney, Robert Edwardes. He was passing through Melbourne at the start of his trip. He and his wife Carolyn were off to Europe on a world trip for a year. They were both school teachers but had taken leave for the trip. He quizzed me on the project while I kept an eye on my wife in case we had to dash to the hospital. He asked, 'Are you spending much time in Tassie?' 'About a week a month. I'm still trying to find out how the company operates. The Melbourne people don't get on with Sydney HO. It's hard when you're new and you don't feel welcome. My boss in Sydney is supportive, and I think things will work out.' I wished I could emulate Robert and do the Aussie thing and *do* Europe, but I had a growing family and work was my priority.

My efforts to introduce structure into the project were frustrated by Nairn and his project manager, Jim Smythe, who came out of the same mould as his boss. I persevered and wrote the monthly report based on my financial and schedule reports. I criticised the acid plant designer and builder for supplying optimistic schedules and not recognising supply chain constraints. I was called into a meeting Nairn was having with the contractor. 'Grahame thinks you don't know what you're doing. How many have you built?' snarled Nairn. 'Sixty-two,' was the contractor's reply. Nairn looked at me, 'How many have *you* built, Grahame?' It was an ambush. I ignored his question and asked how long they had been using their project control tools. 'This is the first time.' Touche! 'Right. The option you used to predict the end date assumed all activities would occur with no delays, and no risk assessment was applied?' Yes, that's right.' 'Well, where are all of the bin liners?' (This was a new high-tech plastic material to protect the steel.) He checked his printout and announced, 'They're in the store in Burnie. They arrived three days ago.'

I said 'I've received a report from a mate on-site that the bin liners had suffered an accident during offloading and were actually in the harbour. 'We have no report of that.' 'Well, you might want to make a phone call.' I looked at Nairn. He walked out of the meeting.

The contractor and I spent several hours going through the detail and agreed there was a likelihood of a delay, but judicious overtime could haul that in. They left, cordially suggesting we might have a drink later in town. I agreed, although I needed to check Margaret's condition as she was nearly due. I found that by gaining the contractor's confidence and sharing information you could break down the barriers set up by the contract.

Next morning Nairn confronted me. 'You don't want to compromise yourself with contractors. We could end up in court, and they could use certain information against you.' I replied, 'If we document all discussions and agreements we should be safe, and the contractor will trust you more.' 'You can never trust contractors. They're just after money and don't have the professional ethics that we have. Be careful'. I went to my desk and pondered this. This elitist attitude was strange to me. I hadn't detected any higher level of intellectual insight to support his position. The contractors employed many fine engineers; in fact, I had recently been employed by one myself. Nairn had never bothered to find this out. I vowed to go with my gut feel and work closely with them.

I needed to find a topic for my master's thesis. After much deliberation, I decided to look at the relationships between design and construction activities. All efforts in scheduling had focused on the logic of the construction task and the resource levelling benefits that this planning tool could bring. I would focus on the complete project task, from conception to completion. My first hurdle was convincing the university and finding a thesis supervisor who would take it on. During my visits to Sydney to brief Kevin and his boss Kevin Napier, I talked to the civil engineering school where I met with a cool reception. They weren't really into the management of engineering, just the engineering itself; they were unaware there were problems there to solve and wondered if my project had any merit. Finally, they suggested I talk to Michael Folie, who had just joined the faculty from the economics school. Michael listened to my ideas and suggested I develop them along the lines of resultant economic benefit, that is, the faster project delivery lowers the cost as production can be sold earlier.

I returned to Melbourne and started gathering data. I needed to spend time with the designers to understand their processes and how the interdisciplinary design needs were handled. I was met with quizzical looks. 'Why do you need to know? It's very complicated; we just work together.'

I started to spend time with the lead designers, asking how they confronted their job. They obviously knew what they were doing, but they'd never had to visualise the process in a forward-planning way. I started to piece together elements of a process and fed it back to the leads. Though sceptical, they played the game. After a while, there was some good banter, with an overtone that my task was a waste of time. 'Design is an art and can't be systematised,' seemed to be their anthem. They felt I was commoditising their profession and that that could diminish their value. As the project developed, I collected data and tried to reconstruct events into logical sequences. I also tried to monitor the crises when packages of drawings and documents needed to be issued for contract bids. I noted that deadlines were achieved by having holds on areas when design was incomplete, either for lack of vendor data or because of client changes. Contractors were asked to price work that was not defined. This led to difficult evaluation processes and unit price quotes. As the many parts of the project started to converge, the planning and costing work that was my main task became more difficult. I was starting to feel inadequate.

The chief estimator was Bob Williams, from Sydney. He was experienced and helped me understand how the particular processes worked. Unfortunately, he too had a bad relationship with Nairn, whom he considered a complete idiot. 'If Nairn could manage the client better and stop snivelling up to them we could reduce the changes. How can you design something when it keeps changing? You have to fix the process flow diagrams and then the plot plan. Otherwise you keep chasing your tail and costs escalate and the schedule is blown.'

Instantly I started to see why I was making no progress. There was no leadership. Nairn never consulted the schedules and trending was a totally foreign concept to him. He started each day as a new challenge, with no reflection on where our plan stood. I felt my best efforts would come from continually talking to the leads and trying to piece together a story.

Meanwhile, Margaret was due. All babies seem to be born in the early hours of the morning, and so it was with my second son, Miles. Margaret and I arrived at the hospital at 11.30pm. Miles was born at 2am. We were very happy.

Back at work, the project lurched into the mid-stages. Nairn came under pressure from the client and became agitated. We were not meeting the target dates due to the numerous changes. He started attacking all the lead engineers, with no real purpose other than to suggest it was entirely their fault. I found his negative attitude to me began to change as he realised my work could help the team get on top of things. They started asking questions about planning, and I tried to organise coordination meetings to share information. I realised that some of them were doing the biggest job of their careers, and we were all as inexperienced as each other.

I was regularly visiting Tasmania and with the persistent rainfall, the work progress in Rosebery was slow. We had hired a local earthworks contractor named Bill Singline to clear the rail-handling site. Bill was a personality in Tasmania. He had a logging business, a supermarket and a fledgling mining company, Tasminex, trying to export iron ore from a mine south of Burnie. His earthworks operators had come to a grinding halt on the site. Bill was totally bogged down, with a pile of cut material that was unsuitable for fill as it was spoiled with water penetration. He had submitted a claim for extra costs that exceeded his total contract value. My job was to find a way to get the site back on track. My background in soil mechanics gave me a good understanding of the problem. The spoiled material could not compact due to high clay content. We needed to locate a source of sand and loam to create the fill.

I met Singline's foreman and ran him through my ideas. Had he considered mine waste? 'Grahame, I just manage the plant. You have to give me a lead on what material will work. Bill will just walk away if you don't give us some money. We're in your hands.' This was a surprise. I thought Bill was a successful businessman. Said his foreman, 'He's all front, runs things by the seat of his pants.'

Next day I visited the mine. The mine manager Ed Jones was very helpful and suggested a few possibilities. He was aware that the project was important for him and went out of his way to have some material tested for its suitability as fill. Over the next few days, Bill's man and I agreed on a rough compensation plan for the new fill material. We had a solution.

Back in Melbourne, *I* was bogged down. I reviewed my thesis data. I had been collecting statistics on drawing numbers, material take-offs and costs. The design functions and their interrelationships were still muddy. I didn't have any benchmarks and the design leads just seemed to respond to crises. I started a new round of questions along the lines of what would they have done better now they could see the recent history. Anticipating the external needs was not easy. The mechanical guys relied on vendor data for the conveyors, bins, chutes and crushers. There didn't seem to be a good system of anticipating the inputs and then refining the design when final data was received. The purchasing group was isolated from the processes because the designers didn't see the value of their input. Contract documentation was not managed well, adding to the confusion.

How could all this be improved? The main problem was that the engineers were focused on their design competency and took no responsibility for the project needs. This gap was the responsibility of the project engineers. However, their role was diminished by Nairn and his project manager Smythe, who bypassed them. I reported all this to my bosses in Sydney. Finally, Nairn was instructed by Sydney to hire a new project manager, Norm Elphinstone. I felt elated but worried as to how the transition would play out.

Nairn treated Norm as he treated me, but Norm was more senior and seemed to handle Nairn well. This improved the office performance, and Norm encouraged me to spend more time with the project engineers, to improve their planning skills. He also gave me more insight into the design interfaces and the potential for different contracting strategies. I started to see ways to package work to improve the overall schedule. I felt I was making real progress.

With Norm on board and some new project engineers hired, the project started to have some structure. I found the new team fun to work with. Nairn was now nice to me. 'I was reading your monthly report,' he said. 'I like the trending section; it gives us a good idea of status. The client likes it too. Join us for a drink this evening.' After nine months on the outer, finally I was in the 'in group'!

I had learned so much in Melbourne, but little of it related to engineering, or my idea of what an engineer is trained to do. After leaving NSW Railways, I had been exposed to the realities of commercial life. It was a shock, but helped me understand the nature of construction. The railways had no cost constraints, and there I had been able to experiment without fear of failure. My experience in Melbourne had revealed a different environment. The different cultures represented by government, contractors and consulting engineering came together with very rough edges. Each had a different view, but all played their role in the development world. Lack of understanding among the groups gave me many hours of reflection and a great source of inspiration for my master's thesis.

10. Master's thesis

My university thesis takes a new direction.

During my final month, Nairn made me offers to stay. He said I would be promoted to project engineer and given a section of the project. I replied that I was returning to Sydney after my year's commitment and, exactly to the day, I returned. The Tasmanian project was coming to a close on a solid basis under Norm Elphinstone, so I left satisfied, if not a bit bruised.

I needed to start my thesis documentation. I spoke to Michael Folie, my supervisor at the university. He was warming to my idea of managing the integration of design and construction activities for a project, but wanted an outline of what I planned to write. As I sifted through the data, I realised I had gone off on a tangent. I was trying to measure design development in the wrong way.

Meanwhile, I was assigned to a new project to be built at Westernport, a steelworks for BHP in Victoria. It was a grassroots project which took steel billets and converted them to galvanised iron. It was a major project and a chance to test my theories for design measurement. I found the lead engineers much more professional and capable than those I had worked with in

Melbourne. As I set up the systems and planning tools, it occurred to me that my work in Melbourne was flawed. I had collected data that was useless in this environment. I realised that the drafting process was a better place to measure progress than engineers assessing their position. I realised that if I hadn't experienced the chaos generated in Melbourne by Nairn, I wouldn't have been so clear about the structure I needed to create for the current project.

Margaret, David, Miles and I moved back into our house in Forestville and I settled again into Sydney life. Miles and David were growing up and were a handful for Margaret, but she was coping well. I was oblivious to the stresses she was experiencing. My life was focused on engineering, and I assumed the family managed itself.

Construction had started on-site, but there was little progress. I was asked to report on what was going on. After landing in Melbourne, I drove out to Tyabb, a small village on the Mornington peninsular. At the large excavated site next day, I saw that there was no work going on... WS Atkins, an English management firm, had been appointed to manage the site, and they had installed a lean, craggy Englishman, John Harris, as the site manager. He had come from a project in India and was very formal at our first meeting. I remarked on the lack of activity at the site and the large number of drawings we'd issued for construction. Harris curtly dismissed my comment: 'They are not checked and won't be issued until I'm happy.' I paused to take this in and explained that they *had* been checked, in Chatswood, and were perfectly all right. He gave me a pained look and very slowly, as if speaking to a child, said, 'I will check them.'

I talked to some of the site inspectors, who were idle at their desks. 'Harris comes in early and locks his office door, stays there all day and we sit here waiting. The site contractor men have gone on strike because some have been laid off.' I went to the contractor's office. The contractor's site manager looked at me and, referring to Harris, exclaimed, 'Where do you get them, these clowns from the Raj?' I asked him to be patient, and we went through which drawings he needed most urgently. Back at Harris's office, I called Sydney. I needed Kevin's advice. He said, 'Just issue the urgent drawings to get work started and we'll deal with the client representative in Kembla.' I arranged for the Chatswood office to send me the drawings in the overnight bag. In the morning, I collected the drawings and issued them to the contractor. By lunch, work had commenced and equipment was mobilised. Late in the afternoon, Harris emerged from his office and looked across the site. 'What are they doing?' he said accusingly, looking at me. 'Getting on with it,' I replied. 'On whose authority?' 'Port Kembla?' I suggested.

'Like hell! I'm running this site!' With that, he returned to his office. My job was done, and I collected my things. As I was leaving, he came bounding out. 'You'll regret this!' he cried. 'The drawings are possibly faulty.' I walked out and headed for Sydney. The BHP people in Port Kembla were apprised of Harris's performance and decided to replace him. There were several angry meetings, as Harris felt he had been ambushed. Having come from a highly structured colonial environment, he was blind to modern management. He finally left the site, never to return.

I was feeling good about the thesis work; the data was matching my expectations and the draughtsmen were filling out their timesheets with the hours spent on individual drawings. At the end of the week, each section head would estimate the percentage complete for each drawing. It was clear the draughtsmen were better organised than the engineers, and we could get accurate read-outs of progress without much hassle. My error in Melbourne was to concentrate on engineering progress, which seemed impossible to measure. I noticed that many engineers didn't see much beyond their area of interest. They were very tightly focused. It was the project engineer's job to link the pieces, but it could have been made easier if the designers took a step back now and again to look around and get a feel for where they fitted.

As the project developed, I detected poor engineering progress in some areas and quizzed the relevant engineer to find the cause, which was usually client interference or poor management. I was able then to identify potential future problems. Initially, the leads were resistant, believing I was interfering with their work and causing delays. However, after we had some coordination meetings they read the reports and responded positively. The interplay between the engineering groups is strongly influenced by the personalities of the leaders. My role was coming to an end. It had been very satisfying, as I had finally unlocked the key to integrated planning of projects and I was keen to apply my knowledge to new work.

My thesis 'The Integration of Design Functions into Major Projects' needed to be completed. This was the tedious stage. With the flood of new data, I was able to progress quickly, and my supervisor started to give me encouragement. It was hard putting the documentation together when I had a day job. After a big effort, the thesis was submitted, and I was pleased to be awarded a high distinction for my efforts. This was a new area, and I felt I had broken new ground. The university decided the topic had value and tried to encourage me to continue the work to earn a PhD. I decided not to pursue that path. My supervisor Michael Folie would go on to senior positions in Shell Oil and years later he congratulated me on the relevance of my work to his Shell experiences. I knew how important my ideas were for acceleration of projects, but I wanted to learn more from practical experience before developing my theories.

The return to university had allowed me to jump ahead of my peers with my computer skills. I felt I could set up projects effectively because I now had a good understanding of the design process. What could be the next step?

11. Indonesia: Into the deep end

They speak Bahasa Indonesia.

CMPS had established a projects group under Kevin Napier with a full range of skills and systems. In many ways, it resembled a contractor's office, and I felt at home. Kevin was easy to work with, and I settled in well. I was asked to go to Indonesia to set up control systems on a remote mining site in Sulawesi. It was my first trip out of Australia and the start of a life of travel, but I was not to know that then. The site was a nickel mine in the planning stage, with a test pit completed and a construction camp established in Malili, near the coast. International Nickel (INCO) from Canada was the owner. They had formed a development team based in Sydney, which included Kevin Torpey, my former boss. Professor Alex Jenkins, a friend of Eric Mansfield, was the exploration manager, and it had been he who encouraged Kevin, who had just left CMPS, to join INCO. Alex was a key player for the exploration team and combined his role with his Sydney University teaching duties. In turn, Kevin Torpey had asked for me to be involved.

Kevin outlined my task in Indonesia. The project was in transition from an exploration to a development site. Taylor Woodrow (TW) was the general contractor and had commenced preliminary infrastructure works, roads, airport and marine structures. TW was a large English contractor that had been very successful in Africa, particularly Ghana. For all that, Kevin revealed TW had spent $40 million over two years and could not account for much of it. Thirty million dollars had been tagged as transportation and logistics. The other ten million dollars was segregated under three other headings. 'Grahame, I want you to set up systems and a plan to manage the works. TW seem incapable.' There was no suggestion of dishonesty, exploration teams don't think about management but when the operations move to capital investment there needs to be good systems to report on expenditure. TW had not done this.

I arrived at Sydney airport for my first ever international flight. The airline was Garuda, the Indonesian national carrier. I felt very important as I was shown my seat in First Class. We arrived in Jakarta Kemayoran Airport at four on a steamy afternoon. I descended the steps, wondering which way to go. At the bottom, a man darted forward, grabbed my bag and asked for my checked bag docket. 'I'm Hiro, your driver, follow me.' We then peeled off from the crowd and headed for a side door. 'Wait here,' he instructed. I watched him purchase two cartons of cigarettes and return. 'Follow me.' he said urgently. As we edged around the side of the building he gave half a carton to an immigration officer. The officer quickly stamped my passport and we went to the baggage claim. 'Wait here.' He found my bag and headed for the exit to the customs hall, where he dispensed the rest of the cigarettes. Quickly we were out in the clammy heat, full of noises and smells that were new to me. The distinctive smell of clove cigarettes has stayed with me my whole life. 'Wait here.' He disappeared into the crowd. People seemed to be in a constant state of activity.

Ten minutes later a Kia van appeared with Hiro inside waving furiously. We headed into a multi-laned road, and I wondered which side of the road they drove. Cars and vans jostled with mobile shops, *becak*s and cattle. We came to a large level crossing and fifteen lanes of traffic lined up on each side as a train passed, its roof loaded with passengers. As the gates rose, the traffic surged forward into a fractious mess. This gridlock continued for half an hour. No word was spoken during our trip. We passed a rubbish-filled canal with rickety huts perched on the edge. Poverty seemed to be everywhere. My head swivelled from side to side as I tried to take it all in. I had no idea how the locals survived.

People filled every space – I'd never seen so many. They seemed to be living on the street. Finally, we approached a large square with a statue of two people dancing in the middle. We pushed forward with horn-blaring and arm-waving. The entrance to the Hotel Indonesia was blocked by people sitting on the footpath. Hotel employees were trying to move them. I watched as their belongings were stacked to the side to clear a path. Eventually, we arrived at the door, and my bags were unloaded. I was booked to fly to Makassar next morning at the crack of dawn. 'I'll pick you up at 4.30am … here.' Hiro stared at me to see if I understood. I nodded. With that, he jumped back in the van and disappeared into the throng. I looked at my watch: 6pm. What to do? First I would check in and leave my bags in what proved to be a dingy room. I found the Ramayana bar on the ground floor and waited in the doorway for my eyes to adjust to the gloom. Groups of men, several in military uniforms were in discussion at low tables and around a central bar. I found a lounge in the corner, and a waiter brought me a drink. The smell of cloves in the cigarette smoke and the soft percussive sound of gamelan music completed my sensory overload. As I sat watching the girls in their long, elegant dresses serve the business groups I thought I don't know one person in this country of 120 million.

    The 3am wake-up call jolted me to life. I hadn't slept well. The noise of the air-conditioner had kept me tossing. I packed and waited at the entrance for the driver. Even at that hour, it was hot and humid, and the street seemed just as busy as the previous afternoon. The Kia swung in and Hiro leapt out, grabbed my bags, and we were off. The traffic had eased a bit from yesterday, but I still wasn't sure on which side of the road they drove. We arrived at Kemayoran Airport again. It was chaotic; full. Hiro found our airline desk and leapt the counter. He checked my bag himself and worked with local airline Merpati staff to get me a boarding pass. 'This will get you to Makassar; you will have a stop in Surabaya. Look for the Bristow guys there, for the helicopter. Good luck.' With that, he turned and headed off.

I found the gate and waited. The passengers were mostly Indonesian – businessmen, I surmised. Once on board, I settled in. The plane was full. It was an old Viscount; the propellers seemed to touch the ground as we taxied before climbing into a new dawn. I looked down on vast patchwork paddy fields. Through the light mist below us, I could make out dozens of small islands dotting the turquoise sea.

In Makassar, I found the Bristow pilots and discovered there were two flights leaving together. The other passengers were families returning from leave. The airport was cavernous, and unlike the last one, there were few people. Soldiers lounged about, looking very young to be carrying automatic rifles. Eric, one of the pilots, introduced himself. 'I haven't seen you before. First time?' 'Yes, in Indonesia and in a helicopter.' 'Well, I hope we live up to your expectations. We leave at about ten.' He went off looking for more passengers.

Our flight path took us north over paddy fields, and we followed the west coast till we arrived at the village of Pare-Pare, where we peeled to the east across yet more paddy fields till they morphed into thick jungle. Through the mike and headphones, Eric explained that the flight took about two hours and the Jet Ranger was close to its limit with fuel. The weather was important. If the chopper needed to skirt storms, this would take extra time and fuel. Two storms was our limit. The flight plan was to maximise time over the water, for that was the only place we could safely land if we ran out of fuel. There were no weather forecasts, so it was seat-of-the-pants.

There seemed to be no habitation around the Malili River, but I discovered later there was a small village near the mouth. We followed the river up to some low hills, and now I could see the camp. It looked like a napalmed clearing with huts spread around. As we landed, I felt a great sense of isolation.

I was met by the camp manager and left the bags in my *donga* (hut) on the edge of the camp. The camp, set on the side of a hill, was primitive: the pathways were made of duckboards. There were around thirty accommodation units and several larger sheds which, basically, were the smaller units placed together to form offices, mess and a recreation area. There wasn't a blade of grass or a shrub in the area, which was fenced with a high cyclone steel structure, topped with barbed wire. It looked like a prison. The presence of soldiers with AK-47's didn't detract from this image. Outside the fence, jungle loomed in thick profusion. Down the road, a second camp was established for Indonesian staff. Beyond that, it wound down towards the mouth of the river to the small fishing village that I had not seen when flying in.

I located the office huts and met Travers Duncan, the country manager. Travers was rangy and bearded. He was very welcoming and outlined the issues. He hadn't been there long but had decided that TW was the wrong general contractor for the site and was in the process of firing them. Problem was, there was currently no alternative, and he had a big program to contend with, building roads, an airport and wharf facilities. The road to Sorowako – the mine site up the mountain – was poor, and impassable in wet weather. The high rainfall was a huge impediment to progress. Travers asked me to start setting up project controls, to instil structure into the operations. He gave me a rundown of the on-site staff and their skill levels. It was a bit deflating. It looked like I'd be doing it mostly myself.

I set about studying the geography and available reports, but it was important to meet the crew. At 5pm we gathered in a small room at the end of the mess. After dinner, I pumped the Australians for information. The airstrip had been built, but had slipped down the hill at one end due to poor drainage. The rainfall was high and the soil had a high clay content. Getting the airport into service was a high priority as it would reduce the need for expensive helicopters. They were expecting a new site manager in a couple of days, from Adelaide. Relations with TW were poor as it was in the process of being dismissed, partly because of the airstrip failure but mainly because of poor management.

The mine site was at Sorowako in the centre of the island, about 40km from Malili. Sulawesi had no road connections between Makassar and Manado in the north. Manado is largely Christian, due to the Filipino influence, with the south part of Sulawesi Island Muslim. The long wooden ships of Bugis traders plied the coast and were the main connecting influence. The central part of the island was largely unexplored, and tribes of small people, known as Toradjas, inhabited the jungle.

I organised to drive to Sorowako with Frank, one of the Australian engineers. He had been on-site for about a year. We were accompanied by a driver, a couple of mechanics and a soldier. I asked why the soldier. Frank said we had no option. The authorities were insisting we needed protection from communist insurgents, even though he hadn't heard of problems. We set off to the north-east and found the land flat and partly open, with minimal farming. Historically, the area had been explored by Dutch and then Japanese geologists, looking for minerals. The name Sulawesi means 'iron island'. There had been some production in the south around Pare-Pare, but because of its remoteness the discoveries around Sorowako had been passed over and the Second World War with the independence movement had stopped further work.

After driving about 10km we ran out of petrol. I was amazed. We'd set out on a difficult journey to have this happen! Frank was embarrassed, but I'd learned another lesson. Ask questions, even if people think you are being unnecessarily inquisitive. One of the mechanics knew of a group of roadside huts a kilometre further on. There might be fuel there. He trudged off and an hour later returned with a can of petrol. We drove on and purchased enough fuel to get us to Sorowako. As we filled up the locals sat on their haunches and watched us carefully; there was little banter. As we drove into the hills, the dirt road became rougher. We twisted into higher hills, and the jungle hung over the road. The going was slow. Then we found the road had collapsed into the ravine. We couldn't pass. There was a chainsaw on board and Frank and I cut down trees and fashioned some planks that would support the vehicle's weight as we drove over them. The mechanics helped, but the soldier lounged in the Land Rover. Our makeshift thoroughfare had to span 3m, and have a solid foundation on each side. After two hours' work, we were ready. The driver inched the vehicle forward and we held our breath. The downside of the road disappeared steeply into the jungle. The crossing was successful.

After a six hour journey, we arrived at the lake just after 4pm and met the camp boss who took us to huts by the lake and announced, 'The Sorowako Hilton!' We cleaned up and found the bar. There were a dozen men sitting around a couple of tables who introduced themselves and enquired about our trip. In turn, they told us that most of their supplies came by helicopter, but major equipment was flown in to the local airport from Makassar. The road link was important. 'Where was the slip?' they wanted to know. 'Did you see any activity along the road?' Frank responded to their questions while I watched the sun set over the lake and absorbed the evening breeze, which was such a relief after the hot, humid atmosphere of Malili. I spent the following day boning up on the plans for the mine site and the outcomes of the recent test pit. Activity was low as the mine planning was being done in far-off Sydney. Basically, no one knew what was happening next. I managed to get a chopper back to Malili to consider how to put control systems around a project that had stalled.

I was surprised to find that the new site manager was Gordon Vogan, my old boss at Sydenham. He was upbeat about his appointment. I hesitated to ask him why he had left the NSW Railways, and wondered how he would fit in with this crew. Most had come from West Africa and seemed to be escaping domestic nightmares and the law. A few kept to themselves, just doing their job and waiting for their leave.

I seemed to be Gordon's only friend. The TW managers were ignoring him, and he was making notes of their transgressions to present to Travers. I suggested that he confront the boss of TW, Kevin Turnbull, and have it out. He was silent.

On Sundays, the expats had a day off. Some visited the nearby village, while others took the work boat downriver to the Gulf of Bone. A small island in the gulf was the destination. On the island, I had the feeling that no one had ever been there in the history of the world. We anchored off a cove and swam and snorkelled for hours. I have never seen so many conch shells and so much marine life. Unfortunately, on my first outing to the island I was severely sunburned on my back. In this environment, it was a serious problem, as I eventually found out.

I still needed to understand the scope of the operations, so I visited the remote camps around the island. The camps had a geologist and about ten helpers. Half a dozen exploration teams were in the southern and eastern arms. Kolonadale was the most distant. One of the doctors, Ray Jenkins, was on the chopper flight.

He explained that Malili was rife with tropical diseases, mainly carried by mosquitoes. A strain of cholera had started in the local village and swept the world. The vaccines had to be changed because of it. Ray led a team of doctors who were documenting the local population. Elephantiasis was the most visible problem, but many others existed, and controlling mosquitoes was key. When I scratched my back from the sunburn – it felt like a thousand pinpricks – Ray examined me and gave me a tablet to reduce the itching. 'If you tear the skin, it could become infected, and you'll have some real problems.' We arrived at the fly camp where the conditions were primitive. The geologist shrugged it off. 'I've been doing this for decades, and this is not the worst.' We discussed his operations and enquired if we could get him more help or equipment. He squinted with his head on an angle. 'No, I'm good, but thanks for asking.'

As we prepared to return, I noticed a scratch near my ankle had flared up and a red line was climbing my leg. The doctor immediately dressed it and remarked how quickly these problems progressed.

It was becoming clear to me that I couldn't do the job I had been asked to do. I had no one to talk to who was interested in systems and structures. Travers was busy planning the mining operations and, I came to understand later, organising TW was not a priority because the British company was to be terminated. The site communications consisted of a Morse code operator who took your message and translated it into Bahasa before sending it via Makassar and Surabaya to Jakarta, where it was translated back to English and telexed to Sydney. This seemed to take days. I sent several reports over the first couple of weeks and received no response. God knows what message had actually been transmitted by the Morse code man.

I began to worry that CMPS had forgotten about me. Maybe a big new contract had come in and everybody had been reassigned. Next Travers told me he needed to go to Makassar, where communications were better, and that he would be away a few days... Weeks passed, and Travers had not returned. Everybody on-site was in limbo.

By the time Travers had been gone a month, the camp workers had descended into moribund and sullen behaviour. Basically, there was nothing to do except wait for him to return and give new directions for the project activities. Rumours abounded that he had gone to Canada and the project was to be suspended. My reports had gone unanswered. One day Gordon came to my *donga* after work. He sat on the bed and burst into tears. I waited for him to compose himself. Finally, he said, 'He hit me. Turnbull, the TW thug.' I looked at him speechless. I felt like saying 'Why didn't you hit him back?' but held my tongue. 'You have to get back some respect. Confront him.' 'I can't. I'm finished here.'

He went to his *donga*. I went to the mess. Four TW people were there, drinking. I got a beer and joined them. 'Why did you hit Gordon?' I was looking at Kevin. He paused, knitted his brow and said, 'Hit him? No, I slapped him on the back and bought him a beer.' I let it pass. Later, after Kevin had gone, I asked one of the others what had happened. He explained that Kevin had slapped Gordon on the back, like you would greeting someone, but it was a bit hard and Gordon had stumbled and fallen into the back of a chair. His pride was hurt more than anything. Kevin should have apologised. Instead, he laughed and went to the bar to buy Gordon a beer. By the time he returned, Gordon had left. I absorbed all this and finally said, 'He's a prick, he should go and apologise.'

I realised that standing up for yourself is important in these little, closed societies. You can't hide.

It gave me cause to reflect on who I was and did I need this type of experience. I had achieved little. Next morning I was on the chopper to Makassar. I had had no contact with the family and looked forward to spending time with them. It had been the longest time without any message.

Back in Chatswood, I confronted Ken McGlynn, the office manager. Kevin Napier, my new boss, was in Queensland, organising a mining project. Ken knew little of my role and tried to explain that we needed to be flexible and make an effort to fit in. I tried to explain my situation and the lack of support I was receiving in Indonesia. He had no idea what I had experienced and seemed disinterested. My family had not received any news of my situation and had been worried. I took a couple of weeks leave to clear my thoughts.

On return, I asked my boss, Kevin Napier, for another assignment. Kevin was sympathetic, and we discussed the various projects in the office. I wrote some clean-up reports for Indonesia and waited. A week later Kevin came to my office with an unusual request. 'Grahame, you are the only person in the group with computer modelling experience. We have won a contract in joint venture with an American company from Oklahoma, Williams Bros (WB), to build a pipeline to carry natural gas from Bass Strait in Victoria to Sydney along the east coast. They were looking for someone with computer experience to work with the Tulsa engineers, to run computer models for the transmission design studies. Is it something you would like to consider?'

After the misery of Indonesia, this was wonderful. I was keen to work with the Americans, and I accepted on the spot. I had been out of the design role for about five years but had continued to try to understand the design processes, because my project structuring duties demanded it. In fact, I had been exposed to all the disciplines and the interactions required to deliver a complete design. Gas transmission technology would be an exciting new area.

I had spent about six years learning about the structure of projects. How do they start, who are the players and how they are managed. The railways had almost no management systems. They proceeded at their own pace and sometimes responded to prodding if the politics demanded. I was pleased to experiment with new skills from my studies, but I was in uncharted waters. The move to the commercial world snapped me into a new reality. Cost and time needed close attention. Working with suppliers and subcontractors and second guessing their abilities was paramount. Understanding construction methodologies and using new techniques was the difference between success and failure. I felt I had a good grasp until I went to Melbourne and walked into the world of consulting engineering. It was a world in which I would eventually complete my full-time career but at the outset I was nonplussed. I had acquired new skills in computing and system analysis and been told the old ways were proven and best. I was confronted with an elitist attitude I had never struck before. Next I was thrown into a project that had died before it started. I was asked to set up control systems for a contractor who was about to be dismissed. It's a bit like wading into a swamp that has soft mud underfoot. It looks OK on the surface, but you aren't going to get very far walking.

I was fortunate to be presented with a new direction and luck was smiling at me. My next assignment took me into the positive world of new ideas and an industry that was about to change the world radically for the next decade.

Part III
The oil and gas industry
1972

12. Moomba to Sydney Pipeline

Oil becomes the hottest business in the world.

A new organisation needed to be created for the project. An office a couple of blocks to the north of the CMPS Head Office was established in Help Street, Chatswood, to house the pipeline team. Several Williams people had arrived from Tulsa, Oklahoma to take the key positions, eventually over 300 staff would be assembled to design and manage the project. Southern drawls resounded at our meetings, and cowboy boots rattled down the corridors. The wild west had come to town! Williams Brothers had a suite of software that allowed the system designer to size pipelines and, over time, add compressors to the line as the gas sales volumes increased. The pipeline was designed for 20–30 year growth. Marketing projections were important, but the daily variations were equally important, as peak morning and evening loads needed to be catered for. The design of long-distance transmission pipeline systems was a specialised skill in which Williams Brothers had led the world.

Ed Robinson was an expert in this area, and I was assigned to be his assistant. He was urbane and worldly, quite unlike his fellow Tulsans. Ed had worked on many pipelines across the world and was willing to share his knowledge. He had never been to Australia, and we became great mates. He had a dry sense of humour and was critical of 'corporate bullshit'. He told me he was embarrassed by his colleagues' cowboy image.

My first task was to locate computer facilities to run the large models that would be the backbone of our design development. Nearby, in St Leonards, we found some Univac 1108s that fitted the bill. Protocols were set up to run the programs, and we were surprised at the sophistication of the arrangements. Once Ed felt I had sufficient training, he would return to the USA to supervise his team. I needed a communication method with Tulsa and Ed suggested a new product that was developing in the US. A telephone dial-up system had just been established around the world called GE Mark 3 timesharing. It was an early version of the internet. Large Univac 1108 computers in Cleveland, Ohio were connected by the telephone system to dial-up points around the world. Most of these points were in the United States, but some were in Europe, Africa, the Far East and Australia, in Sydney, Melbourne and Perth. You could register and set up files on the computer. These could be data or software output. Telex was the main data communication method at that time for messages. I figured that we could set up protocols to switch messages at one tenth of the existing cost of telex and share software output with Tulsa. I became the link person for the design development and enjoyed the fast pace. I was having the best time of my life. Working in the jungles of Indonesia was a dim memory. However all was not roses.

There was a bigger problem working with AGL, our client. We quickly discovered that they had an internal problem. AGL's head of engineering and technology, Roy Maher, believed that he could do all the studies and engineering for the project with *his* team, and objected to an external group, that is, us, being appointed. AGL general manager Sir William Pettingell had hired John Butters, an outsider, to head the project. John, in turn, had gone outside to retain an engineering manager (WB-CMPS) to deliver the project. We were initially unaware of this.

A compromise was reached whereby WB-CMPS would check AGL's design and, if there was agreement on a particular design stage, then the next stage of the work would be commenced. JV Ray, our project manager, agreed to this reluctantly. He was from Mississippi and very deferential to John Butters. John was a tall, rotund man with an unusual interpersonal style. He made you feel that anything he told you was confidential. I got on with him very well.

I was asked to relocate to the Haymarket to work in AGL's office as liaison between the teams. Leo Kenyon was the design chief for our team from the US. I needed to keep him informed on progress. AGL saw us as the enemy. It was poisonous. My main contact was with Dr Paul Grimwood, an Australian engineer who had trained in the USA. Paul was new to AGL and had a PhD from Cornell University. He reported to Gary O'Meally, an operations research specialist who led the Haymarket project team under Maher's direction. Gary was confident his team could deliver the design. I felt like a shag on a rock, waiting for information to send to Chatswood. The AGL team was technically competent but had no idea of project development. I tried to instil a sense of schedule discipline and received no support. 'It'll be ready when it's ready,' was the general attitude. Each week I'd return to Chatswood empty-handed.

I kept in touch with Ed Robinson, who had returned to the USA, and practised running the models that were now installed in St Leonards. We did dry runs to prove the integrity. There were several stages in the design process, and I became familiar with the theory behind each stage. I was becoming an expert in gas transmission. Several months had elapsed since we'd started and JV Ray was concerned that the key design parameters had not been set. AGL was no closer to an agreed design concept. I suggested to Butters that we perform the first major run and compare it with the AGL team output. In essence, I was suggesting a race. Butters convened a meeting with Sir William Pettingell and O'Meally to confirm the arrangements. Time was of the essence, and both teams would present their results to Sir William in four weeks.

I returned to Chatswood to assist our engineers. Leo Kenyon was briefed and he mobilised his engineers. In three weeks we needed to come up with a comprehensive optimisation of the total delivery system over its thirty-year life. The race was on. After two weeks we had a good conceptual outline. I ran the computer models using Kenyon's input data. It was workshopped with the team and the final refinements completed. I went back to the Haymarket to check AGL's progress – no response. Operations research specialist Gary O'Meally assured me he was on track, so we waited a week. I rechecked. This time, Gary denied there was a race, and said he was working on other problems. I was stunned. I spoke with Paul Grimwood on the side as we had become good friends. He obliquely suggested the AGL team was disorganised. I called Butters and said we were ready to present. A meeting was arranged with Pettingell. O'Meally went to Adelaide for an operations research meeting, and so didn't attend. Pettingell complimented us on our work, and we were assigned the lead role for the design. AGL could review and comment, but WB-CMPS would carry the main responsibility. I was over the moon.

Another major development hit the project. Sir Henry Bolte, the Victorian premier, was keen to protect local industry from Sydney competition. He had secured cheap gas from Esso in Bass Strait and legislated that Esso could not sell gas at the wellhead cheaper than the delivered price in Melbourne. This guaranteed a cost advantage to the Victorians. AGL was incensed and opened negotiations with the Cooper Basin producers in South Australia. If they would sell their gas for 16 cents per MMBtu (million British thermal units), then they had a deal. The Victorian gas price was 32 cents, and we figured that we could deliver it for 16 cents from Moomba, which would match that price. Santos and their partners agreed. This was a massive change for the project. Our route location team switched to Moomba and we plotted a new route, the main obstacle to which was the Blue Mountains, west of Sydney. We would need to cross two state boundaries.

I was enjoying the challenge of refining the pipeline design. We had a unique situation, in which the gas was sourced from a remote field and there were no reductions in volumes due to sales until it hit the coast at Sydney. In other parts of the world, a series of sale points would reduce the carried volumes. Also, due to the largely domestic sales as opposed to power and industrial sales, the daily fluctuations were high. We had an opportunity to design the last section of the pipeline as a storage vessel. This was achieved by running a series of tests using a transient flow model, unique to Williams Brothers. We ran hundreds of options and gained an intimate understanding of the pipeline system. Lateral pipelines to Wollongong and Newcastle were included. The transmission system interfaced with AGL's primary and secondary mains. Close cooperation was required to optimise the overall system and Paul Grimwood at AGL worked closely with me.

Our field team was building up, and I met some crusty cowboys (or good ol' boys, as they were known) who would select the route and formulate a construction plan. I volunteered to set up the schedules on my computer facilities. Jake Cheeves was from Okmulgee, south of Tulsa on the B line. He was a lover of country music. I remember him playing a tape of 'Okie from Muskogee' by Merle Haggard. *A place where even squares can have a ball.* Jake's stories opened a whole new world to me, and we became firm friends. He was equally impressed by Australia, and his forays to Broken Hill and further north brought new tales. The Americans loved Australia. I spent many hours after normal work hours quizzing them about the oil and gas industry. They enjoyed a drink in the boardroom as it was forbidden in their Tulsa offices. Oklahoma was a 'dry' state.

I was given the opportunity to deepen my design skills and attend a course given by a gas processing expert on gas production techniques. John Campbell was a world authority and had written the key book on the subject. During the week-long course, I managed to chat to him about my work. He surprised me by noting that the conditions in Australia were quite different from America. I realised that without that world view, engineering solutions can be suboptimal if you use conventional methodologies. John's design approach was just a large number of 'go-bys'. These are handy design methods. They work if you are careful to stay within the operating parameters. It requires a lot of experience to not make mistakes.

These lessons stayed with me for a long time. I had noticed that American engineers were trained differently. In Australia, we had the standard disciplines – civil, mechanical, etc – but the Americans had pipeline engineers who combined various aspects of these areas and relied more on the 'go-bys' I had been exposed to, without understanding the fundamentals of the engineering problem. I'm sure this applied in other industries.

The Blue Mountains were proving a formidable obstacle. As the early explorers discovered, crossing them was difficult due to the vertical cliff faces in the valleys. The only two known crossing points were at Katoomba and Mount Victoria. Finding a suitable pipeline route adjacent to the road seemed impossible, but after several months a third crossing was discovered to the north. We liaised with the NSW government and the various utilities to plot a path that was acceptable. Large tracts of land had been set aside for possible future airfields, forests and other land uses. Finding out which could be traversed took a lot of discussion, as the government had no experience with gas pipelines. The relevant authority was the mines department.

Environmental groups started to mount opposition in the media, citing the dangers of high-pressure explosive gas. Sydney was supplied by a coal gasification plant that was a pollution-prone business at Mortlake, on the banks of the Parramatta River. The Total Environment Centre led by conservationist Milo Dunphy had the loudest voice. 'If you hear of any proposed development, we will fight to stop it!' was Dunphy's cry. Aboriginal elders were concerned with sacred sites. Our land right of way (ROW) group were busy gathering data and liaising with landowners and other interested parties to explain the construction process. The pipe would be buried at a depth that would not interfere with farming and the land would be returned to its former state, complete with topsoil.

As the time neared for us to apply to the government for a licence to build and operate the pipeline, other gas developments were occurring. Discoveries were made at Palm Valley, in the centre of Australia. Bechtel, an American engineering company, had done studies that suggested the gas could be exported to the

USA via a pipeline to the Gulf of Carpentaria, where it would be converted to liquefied natural gas (LNG) then shipped through the Torres Strait. John Butters asked us to study an alternative plan, enlarging our system and placing the LNG plant at Jervis Bay, south of Sydney. The Commonwealth had developed a site for a nuclear power plant which had been abandoned. The plan became urgent when our chief surveyor commented that LNG tankers could not pass through the Strait – it was too shallow and dangerous. He had been stationed in the area during the Second World War. We resized the pipeline and carried out preliminary studies which showed gas could be delivered to the USA for $1 per MMBtu, a very attractive price. Everything looked good, as the AGL gas transmission cost would be halved.

However the gas producers drilled a second well, and it was a dry hole. All work ceased on that option. The exercise had showed that we could source pipe from Japan at a much lower cost than BHP in Australia. The Japanese also had better quality steel, due to their controlled rolling techniques. John Butters was very excited. He had spent time at the Battelle Institute in the USA and wanted to use their approach to metal failure. Historically, transmission pipelines had failed due to crack propagation brought on by welding imperfections. By improving the notch ductility of the steel and testing the finished pipeline to its specified yield strength, higher operating pressures could be achieved, which in turn improved the flow efficiency. This would bring down the cost of construction and hence the transmission cost.

All this was cutting edge stuff and had not been used anywhere in the world, although some projects were contemplating the theory. Butters wanted us to lead the world, so we pressed on. I became his main point of contact, which the Americans were happy to cede. I received calls at all hours to run our models, as John dreamed up new ideas. It was a thrill for me, and I didn't mind the late-night calls. My involvement in the design development had covered a lot of territory, and it became clear that the processes I had been exposed to in the past were very narrow for the current context. The clear lesson was to keep your mind open.

Australia was at a crossroads, with a federal election looming. It seemed we were in for a change of government. 'It's Time' was the catch-cry, and so it turned out. Labor leader Gough Whitlam was elected prime minister and soon he installed his cabinet of ministers. As well as a change of government, there was ideological change. Labor was opposed to the free-wheeling resource industry and wanted greater control. Rex 'The Strangler' Connor became minister for energy and resources, and announced a total review of energy policy.

In spite of this, AGL submitted the licence application for the pipeline development. The state government immediately called for an environmental inquiry, the first ever. Protocols needed to be established, a commissioner appointed and staff hired. We were treading new ground.

The new commissioner was Eric Coffey, a retired manager from Caltex, who was said to know the oil industry. Coffey may have understood oil, but he knew nothing about gas. A panel was appointed to assist him: environmentalist Harry Butler, John Rankin, an engineer; and a retired judge. What should have been a straightforward inquiry turned into a circus. A large number of people registered to give evidence. The rail union proposed a rail option for transporting LNG; environmentalists predicted the Blue Mountains would be obliterated; Aboriginal advisors claimed sacred sites were at risk. Evidence was taken for about a month. Butters complained that it was clear most of the submissions were incompetent and did not relate to what was actually proposed. The commissioner ignored him and ploughed on. After two months, the advisory panel had had enough and quit. I was called to the stand to explain why 'Interest During Construction' was an allowable capital item. This was the interest that accrues on loans prior to the project coming into operation. This and other capital items were debated for two days. Coffey was out of control.

Meanwhile, AGL was hitting some headwinds with the new federal government, which wanted a role in the project. In fact, it wanted to take over the whole enterprise. The Sydney gas supply project was on hold. Strangler Connor's grand plan was to nationalise the whole Australian natural gas industry. The project ground to a halt.

My new world was collapsing. I wondered about the future, but new doors opened quickly as the oil and gas industry shifted gears. We were asked to study a new LNG project on the North West Shelf, using gas from the Rankin discovery offshore. The plan was to pipe the gas to shore near the Dampier Archipelago in the northern part of Western Australia. Seven potential sites were identified for an LNG plant. I volunteered to join the team as the coastal engineer. It had been one of my postgraduate courses, and I was keen to test my skills. I could also help with the planning of the work. Burmah Oil was the client, and the work was to be done in Perth.

I joined six other engineers and an economist. Our leader Forbes Wilson came out from Tulsa as the LNG expert. Forbes was a dyed in the wool Texan, and we became firm friends. The economist, Ernie Treloar, had a key job determining the waiting times for LNG tankers, as some of the sites meant sharing the shipping channel with iron ore tankers loading at Dampier. LPG tankers would also be in the mix. A complex linear programming model needed to be built, using queuing theory. I helped Ernie with some of the computer programming. The whole team worked well together, and we stayed in the same hotel in Perth, The Esplanade. Forbes was intrigued by Ernie's background: Ernie had put himself through uni with the proceeds of his juggling skills. His wife was his assistant. Forbes could hardly believe this and challenged Ernie after work to show him a trick. Ernie obliged and balanced a glass of beer on three straws on his chin. We were all impressed.

I visited the Dampier area and used a chopper to survey each of the six sites with our Perth civil engineer. I had never been in such a remote and desolate area. Several critical parameters would drive the selection, including sea conditions, the distance from wharf to LNG facility, and the ship channel steaming time. I needed to model the design storm – basically a cyclone approaching the coast from the west – and predict the wave heights at each potential location. The area had just suffered a major storm and a drilling rig, 'Big John', had lost several of its anchors and was in danger of being lost. We were staying in the only motel in Karratha with the drillers, who had been there a week, waiting to return to the rig. It was January, and very hot. We hired a boat and checked the marine environment around the archipelago. The sea water was like a warm bath and gave no relief from the heat when we dove in.

Once the site layout for each option was set, we could estimate construction and system operating costs. The Japanese would be buying the gas. Forbes taught me a lot about the LNG business. When you have a good teacher, the concept is easy. It's just a big refrigerator. You have to clean the gas by removal of the LPG and the water. Then it's all about the efficiency of the refrigeration process. Air Products currently had the preferred design, but an earlier 'cascade' process by Phillips Petroleum was still being considered. The site plot plan needed to minimise the cryogenic pipelines, as they were the most expensive variable part of the capital spend. After six weeks we submitted the report. The Burrup Peninsula was our choice.

During a final party at the hotel, I had time to reflect. This had been my most rewarding work to date, working with professionals in a tight team. Forbes was very complimentary about my work, and we agreed to keep in touch. The oil and gas industry seemed the most dynamic in the world, and I wanted to be a part of it.

Shortly afterwards I was asked to go to Adelaide to help a WB-CMPS team do some economic models for a proposed liquids petroleum pipeline from Moomba to the gulf area in the south. The final location was dependent on a suitable port and a site for a petrochemicals plant. The SA government was keen to establish a new industry on the back of the production in Moomba.

Up till that point, ethane and LPG were being stored in produced gas reservoirs for future extraction. WB-CMPS had proposed a multi-products piping system where several products could be transported in the same pipeline in separate 'slugs'. The concept had been developed by the Williams Companies in Tulsa. The Tulsa team were oil rather than gas experts and new to Australia. Each night I would pump them for stories from the oil fields. Texas and Oklahoma were romantic places for me from my childhood cowboy movies and books, and their tales only enhanced my images. I was now exposed to a new part of the oil business and being with the experts gave me a chance to quiz them on all aspects of oil production. I vowed to go to Tulsa one day, to really be exposed to the business.

In 1973, the first oil shock hit the world, due to accelerating demand and oil prices rose from $2 to $12 a barrel. Oil was the hottest business on earth. The price rise had triggered massive global inflation. My exposure to these problems underlined the power of the computer, which was only just being adopted by the industry. Most of my peers were still using slide rules. A huge revolution was coming. I completed my work and returned to Sydney with a new set of friends from Oklahoma.

Back in Sydney, the Moomba pipeline was still stalled. The government in Canberra was still determined to take a leading role in the development of natural gas. They initiated a Pipeline Authority, with an unknown agenda and no staff. An engineer from Adelaide, Jim Donald, was appointed chief. He had a background in material handling and conveyors. He, in turn, appointed Tom Baker, a former colleague of his, as his deputy. Minister Connor was driving a very public agenda to provide natural gas to all corners of the continent at a low price, to stimulate development, and he pressured AGL to abandon its pipeline and cede it to the Commonwealth. Of course, Sir William Pettingell would have none of it, and ordered that pipe be purchased.

We had a dilemma. In the early days of our studies, a 28-inch diameter line was the right size under standard economics. The Australian pipe mills had been developed to make pipe up to 30-inch. There was a tariff barrier to protect the local mills. We expected to place orders with Tubemakers. When the LNG option from Palm Valley was studied, the pipe sizes went up to 40-inch. This prompted prices being sought from overseas. The Japanese stunned us with quotes that were about half the Australian price per ton of steel. Steelmains, an Australian company, had a small mill that could make the larger size, but there were no others, so Butters started extrapolating this data and asked me to run a series of studies looking at larger sizes using foreign pipe. It was clear that we could justify a 34-inch line, as the construction of compressors could be delayed for many years until the sales gas projections rose. The overall cost of the project fell, and there was spare capacity for future projects.

When we went out to tender for the larger pipe, BHP, Tubemakers and Steelmains were furious. They lobbied Canberra to stop AGL getting by-law entry (whereby if you filled the local capacity you could get duty-free pipe from overseas) but their complaints fell on deaf ears: the new government was not pandering to the 'big end' of town. However, AGL were keen to be good corporate citizens and fill up the Australian mills. Butters and I constructed variations to our model. If we filled the Steelmains mill for the time allowed to manufacture the pipe and increased the size of the Wollongong and Newcastle pipelines to 20-inch from 12-inch, what would be the impact on the overall cost? I ran the changes and computed the increased cost. This was then balanced against the political downside. Tubemakers' smaller mill could only produce pipe up to 18-inch, so it was ruled out. The pipe would have to be produced in the larger mill reserved for the main line. A deal was done, and we ordered the pipe with the bulk (about 80%) being purchased from Japan under by-law entry. All the hydraulics and engineering refinement of the design had been ditched for political expediency.

Rex Connor then dropped the hammer on AGL by blocking their ability to source foreign funding. Australian banks were primitive when it came to project funding. Bill Pettingell was basically at a dead end and forced to negotiate with the Pipeline Authority. Socialism had struck!

Meanwhile, the beleaguered commissioner Coffey was trying to finalise his environmental report. He had little help, as Canberra did not feel beholden to a state report. The Coffey Report was finally released. If we had been hoping for an outcome on thirty points, we were disappointed on all counts. He totally screwed us and his recommendations would have added tens of millions to the cost. Canberra thanked him for his work and ignored it.

Rex Connor had another plan. The pipeline would be diverted south with an extra 105km to come through the town of Young and approach Sydney through the Southern Tablelands. Let it plough through the land of the gentleman farmers and avoid the Blue Mountains, was Rex's reasoning. The main objective was to make a closer connection with the Victorian gas fields and facilitate his vision of a national grid.

Negotiations to finalise the pipeline nationalisation intensified. They couldn't agree on an end point. AGL wanted to retain the markets to the regional centres and requested an end point south of Wilton, near Berry. Whitlam's treasurer, Frank Crean, was working on his first federal budget. I received a call from Crean's office.

'How much is the pipeline going to cost this financial year?' 'Which pipeline? They haven't agreed where it ends.' 'Your best guess will do.' I gave him a number. I asked JV whether I had done the right thing. 'Grahame, this whole thing has gone crazy,' he said, in his best southern accent. Some time later, there it was: $184 million for the pipeline in the federal budget, the exact number I had given. The *Pipelines Act*, which would establish the Pipelines Authority, had not been passed into law, but that didn't stop Connor. He despatched the head of the Minerals and Energy Department, Sir Lenox Hewitt, to our office to inspect progress. An entourage of federal public servants descended and strode through our office. Sir Lenox was surprised to find our contract negotiations for construction were in full swing, with the pipe already ordered and about to be shipped. However, the pipe had yet to be paid for. Hewitt waived the details aside. Connor found the money.

The Pipeline Authority (TPA) was active on a broader front. It announced a national grid study to further the 'ministers vision'. Bechtel was awarded the western section, and we were given the eastern part. The catch was that we had to work with SMEC and TPA people, to teach them how it was done. SMEC, the government engineering spin-off from the Snowy Mountains Project, specialists in hydro projects, had an agreement with TPA to build their own engineering group to compete with us. The Tulsa boys were very unhappy about it, and did not want to train a competitor. Ken Bilson was appointed the project manager. He had come from SMEC and had a high opinion of his expertise. Bilson proved difficult to work with. He had no experience with gas transmission systems, but this didn't faze him. I learned second-hand that Bechtel basically opted out and gave little help. 'If SMEC knows it all, good luck to them.'

We visited Albury to assess the possibility of gas sales. Wodonga was Albury's sister town across the river in Victoria. We decided to explore the potential there. Within 48 hours the Victorian premier, Sir Henry Bolte, announced new legislation to supply Wodonga with gas from the Bass Strait fields. Sir Henry made it clear that he had no truck with the Canberra mob. The political temperature was heating up.

I ran the necessary models and integrated the western work as there was no reason to split the project. We finally produced a report for TPA's Tom Baker after much interference from SMEC. The grid was announced, but no time frame was formed. Building the Moomba line was the prime objective. Sir William Pettingell quit in disgust and the board appointed a 'nightwatchman', John Robinson, as AGL's new GM. Pettingel had a vision to create an energy 'highway', which over time would evolve into a national grid as markets matured. He recognised the total lack of understanding of the ideologically-driven socialist government. Connor's 'dream' would be a disaster if it was built.

JV Ray was totally frustrated. He wanted to build pipeline. The politics were the main event, and he had no idea how to play the game. With Jim Donald in the picture, we potentially had two clients, and a diplomat was required to keep TPA happy. Andy Meyer was a long-time Shell Oil executive from Boston. He was appointed general manager of the joint venture and JV Ray was eased out. A CMPS appointee, David Evans, was slotted into the project manager role. A new team was assembled on all sides to carry the project forward. Andy was a very effective foil for Jim Donald. They had many lunches at the Chatswood Club, with much wine and port consumed.

During this turbulent period I had learned that engineering was not just about physics, chemistry and calculations. There were many forces bearing down on the problem; some of them, it must be said, were imagined, but all were considered and dealt with. We had used sophisticated computer modelling, which had finally been swamped by tariff rules and political pipe dreams. The journey taught me that without our fast-response engineering skills, we could have landed in a very different place. Only by studying the problem on many scales could new ideas be evaluated.

John Robinson proved an able and tough new boss,

although he was at odds with John Butters' style. John was a visionary and did not focus on the detail. His first job was to secure an agreement with TPA for the pipeline termination point and agree a tariff for the main line. The basis for the tariff was to be my economic model. I thought TPA would develop its own model, but Jim Donald was impressed with my work on the national grid and agreed to our independence. The load profiles over the thirty-year life of the project were agreed and the cost estimates were fixed. There were clauses for reconciliation of these estimates with actual costs after the completion of construction, and other operational tests. Delivery pressures were determined for the operation of the primary mains into AGL's distribution system.

The oversizing of the line to capture the benefits of by-law entry of the pipe presented an opportunity to Donald. He couldn't see the point of owning a trunk pipeline where the entire capacity was dedicated to AGL for decades. The episode of the Palm Valley gas convinced him other users of the pipeline would emerge, in line with Rex Connor's proposed national grid. Donald decided to reserve half the capacity of the line for future customers. Robinson thought he had won the lottery. In essence, the gas would be delivered for half price, with no risk. He quickly drew up an agreement and sent it to Donald. Donald convened a meeting with his advisors and I was asked to attend. I pleaded that I had a conflict of interest. Donald said I was just running the models and played a technical role. He had the bit between his teeth and wanted to build a future for TPA.

About a week later I was in the Haymarket with Robinson, who was in the habit of having a drink with his colleagues Maurie Williams and two other managers after 5pm. John left the room briefly to take a call. He returned, filled his glass and proposed a toast. 'It's signed.' It was the happiest day of his life. AGL had the deal of a lifetime, a cheap gas supply for thirty years. To be in that room at that time gave me a warm glow. This was another high point in my career and I felt pleased to be part of the team.

CMPS seemed very remote to me, even though the head office was only a few hundred yards away. I rarely went there and the partners rarely visited our office, which was fully self-contained. Several hundred staff worked in the various groups that had been set up for the pipeline project. Survey, ROW, engineering, procurement and contracts people were engaged, together with a growing field inspection staff. Tension was building, as the project was basically stalled with the development of TPA and the environmental delays. There wasn't much work to do and people were spinning their wheels. AGL was loath to demobilise the team, but costs were building and delay creates friction in any team.

I was invited by Ted Peacock to the RSYS for a special dinner. I had only met him briefly a couple of times. He was the chief executive of CMPS. Forbes Wilson and Wilson Gilliatt, the senior vice-president from Tulsa for Williams Bros, were there, along with some of the partners. I felt very honoured and wondered why I was in this company. During the dinner, Ted stood and called for quiet. 'I wish to announce that the board has decided to offer Grahame an associateship (a junior partnership) with the company. Congratulations!' I was overwhelmed and speechless; it came out of the blue and I had little understanding of what it meant. I discovered I could buy shares in CMPS under a share purchase scheme. I had little money and my only asset was a heavily-mortgaged house. I was now entitled to a company car and a salary increase. Wow!

I went home to tell Margaret. Explaining it all to her. It gave me pause to think about who I was. The truth was that I was so absorbed in my work that I had no perspective of the bigger corporate picture. I was learning so much in my day-to-day activities that I had no time for anything else. I enjoyed playing squash twice a week with my mates at work and we tended to work 10–12 hours a day, which included a couple of hours drinking in the office and debating the project issues. It was all-encompassing and left no time for socialising with my peers in the rest of CMPS.

Forbes Wilson was my best friend in the office. He

had a long history in the oil and gas business and I often pumped him for information about the oil industry, but he was returning to Tulsa. I spoke to Andy Meyer about going to Tulsa, but he said I was too valuable to the current project.

Once I had completed the project controls set-up and trained staff to run it, I contacted the Tulsa boys and discovered I could work in the United States on a company exchange basis. I knew if I was exposed to the US scene I could get deeper into the developing oil boom. I pressed Andy a couple of months later about going to work in the US. He said I would have to get a release from AGL. That didn't seem too hard. John Butters was my best hope. He was enthusiastic, but worried that no one else could run the computer models here, but when Leo Kenyon, our US engineering manager, declared he could do it with his team, I was set.

Forbes Wilson made all the arrangements stateside for me to work in his team.

Margaret, David and Miles were keen, but had no real idea of the consequences of relocating to America. We put the house in the hands of a letting agent. On my last day at the office Meyer saw me in the corridor. I told him goodbye and he hit me with a bombshell. AGL hadn't given formal release, he said, and I couldn't go to the United States till he had a letter. I was stunned. Our plane was leaving that evening.

I went to my office and sat staring at the wall. I had a huge empty feeling in my stomach. I resolved just to go. All the goodwill I had built up over several years had drained away. After an hour I left the building and went home. We organised a taxi to the airport later in the day, and flew out.

13. Tulsa Oil

Where cowboy boots meet the donkey oil pump.

The secretary had given us a stopover in Los Angeles. I glanced out the window as we circled Los Angeles airport wondering about the future. Had I burned my bridges back home? Would the family fit into the Tulsa community? We planned to visit Disneyland on our first day in LA, but we woke around 11am. I called the concierge and asked what time Disneyland closed. 'They don't open on Mondays … it's winter, buddy. But you could try Knott's Berry Farm and the Japanese Village.' I said I didn't think the boys would go for that. 'No, they have rides,' said the concierge. 'You'll love it.' We headed off apprehensively, but were thrilled to find Knott's Berry Farm hit the spot. The boys forgot about Disneyland and rode the big dipper and the log flume with wild abandon.

Back in the hotel that evening I enquired about jazz clubs, assuming that this being LA there'd be one on every corner. 'No, can't help,' shrugged the doorman. I persisted. 'Isn't there a place called Shelly's Manne-Hole somewhere?' This must have jogged his memory. 'Yeah, down on Wilshire.' Later, when the family was settled, I jumped in a cab and found Stan Getz and Chick

Corea were featured at the Manne-Hole. The cab driver, a fellow jazz lover, was so impressed he parked the taxi and came in with me. Stan and Chick had already started. There was only half a dozen people in the audience. I was in heaven – Stan Getz is one of my favourite players. At the break, my cabbie mate had to go back to work. They were playing tracks from their new album *Captain Marvel*. At the end, around midnight, Stan was waiting for his ride. I said hello and explained my background. We chatted for twenty minutes and Stan started to sweat and shake a little. His well-documented heroin habit was kicking in. 'Don't worry,' he said, 'he'll be here in a minute.' Shortly he saw his lift, said goodbye and I was left standing agog.

I hailed a cab, but we were stopped a hundred metres from the Beverly Hilton. 'Best I can do, buddy. It's the Oscars.' I had no idea the Oscar Ball was being held at my hotel. I pressed through the crowd and showed the policeman my room key. 'You'll have to wait a while.' I circled around the crowd, trying to find a gap. I met another policeman, who suggested I try a bar at the side. More pushing got me to a door leading down some stairs. A guard looked at the key and let me past. I pushed to the bar and got a beer and a stool. 'It's a zoo,' said my neighbour. I turned and said hi. He was a guitarist with the Herb Alpert band. 'You playing tonight?' 'No.' 'I've just come from a Stan Getz/Chick Corea gig down the road.' 'Cool, that beats our stuff. Burt Bacharach and the guys were entertaining the movie crowd. Where you from?' 'Australia, heading for Tulsa.' '*That's different.*' 'I'm looking for good jazz in LA. What do you know?' 'Donte's in the valley and the Lighthouse down on Hermosa Beach are about it.'

Another guy joined us. 'Meet Herbie, our boss. Herb, this guy's Aussie, heading for Tulsa.' Herb Alpert the great trumpeter sized me up. 'Do you play?' 'Not in your league,' I assured him. We had some drinks and they quizzed me on the Australian scene. Australia seemed to be flavour of the month. At about 3am I headed for my room. Things had settled down by now, and I had no trouble. I lay in bed and couldn't sleep. My first day in the USA had been amazing. I glanced over at Margaret and the boys asleep and hoped they would enjoy the adventure.

As we disembarked at Tulsa, JV Ray was standing at the gate. I was so pleased but surprised. We waited at the baggage claim. JV eyed the luggage, we had more than twenty pieces. 'Good job I've got the pick-up with the extended cab.' After loading everything we were driven to a motel, the Quality Inn at 51st and Harvard. It was like a jail, with the rooms off a long balcony facing the freeway embankment. 'I'll pick you up in the morning round 7, OK?' I was mystified. I was going to work with Forbes Wilson, why was JV being so nice?

In the morning JV was at reception, all chirpy, right

on time. 'How're you settling in?' 'Fine,' I said, as we joined the morning traffic going downtown. 'I'm really glad you're on the team.' 'What team?' I responded, surprised. He explained that he was project manager for a 3,200km twin pipeline system from Edmonton, Canada, to Detroit. I said I thought I was working for Forbes, but he cut in and said Forbes had had to go to London on other business and that I was to help the Dome Petroleum people. 'Dome?' 'Ya, the Canadian oil people building the pipeline.' I said I'd wanted to learn about the US oil business. 'Don't worry, we'll get to that. We need your help on this project.' 'I thought *you guys* were the world champions at project management.' 'We lied, you Australians have better systems.'

I met the new team and was shown my office. Sitting at my desk I scanned the furniture and equipment. It was spartan. For a moment I wondered how I could fit in. Dome Petroleum was a high-flying bunch of cowboys from Calgary. I was in the middle of one of the world's biggest oil booms and the world was in an inflationary spin. I was told a Kiwi named Elizabeth Harrison was having a barbecue at her house on Sunday and I was to bring the family. Elizabeth was married to Steve Harrison. Steve was to become very important in my life but that was later. Steve was currently in Trinidad trying to develop an LNG plant and hadn't made it back in time for the barbecue. He and Elizabeth had two boys, Chris and Michael, who quickly adopted my sons. At one stage of proceedings, I asked where the boys were. 'Don't worry,' said the petite Elizabeth, 'they're rattlesnake hunting up on the hill. Chris will look after them.' My heart leapt 'Don't tell Marg,' I said, 'she'll freak.'

I became reacquainted with Ed Robinson, my original mentor. He showed me the ropes around the office. I was the centre of attention, for few people had met an Australian and all wanted to chat. The Tulsans had returned from Australia with glowing reports about the locals. They saw Australia as America was thirty or forty years before, about which they had fond memories. It was very flattering.

My job was to set up all the project management systems for JV and his team. I was keen to take advantage of the timesharing system I had used in Sydney, because in the States there were thousands of access points, which made communications cheap and convenient. The project was developing quickly and I wanted to try some ideas I had for procurement logistics. Field offices had been set up at strategic points along the pipeline route for the management teams who would oversee the construction. I planned to install computer terminals in these offices and connect them to the network. I needed to write software to drive my new theories which would log all the materials delivered to each site. My plan was to match despatch information from the suppliers with delivery information from the sites. I could then verify the material quantities and stockpiles at each location. JV didn't see the importance of this. I explained that by digitising the data and comparing the files, accuracy would be improved and we could electronically move files around. He rolled his eyes, smiled and patted me on the back. 'Australians!' He was of the old school and new ideas were resisted, but he indulged me.

To start the ball rolling I took the first computer terminal to West Fargo, North Dakota. I needed to install the unit and train the staff on the procedures. Once in the field office, I located the terminal that I had despatched and set about organising the communications and training the staff. They were not cooperative as the set-up involved a lot more work for them, and I had to prevail on JV to talk to them several times. When we had created some working files I tested the software and discovered some bugs, which we ironed out. Finally the system was up and running and I showed the inspectors the output. They were amazed as what we had produced challenged much of the existing data. Suddenly they saw the value in our creations.

Back in Tulsa, I monitored their work over the next month. They were pleased when they were able to report errors in the despatch data to the pipe mill supervisors. Suddenly the quality of reporting had soared.

We were then able to successfully replicate the terminals in several other field offices. I discovered later that this was the first time computer terminals had been installed in field construction offices in the United States. The real value came with the networking capability of the GE Mark 3 timesharing system; an early version of the internet.

The family had moved into a duplex in south-east Tulsa at 5546 E. 61st Place. Tulsa had no road maps. All the streets were arranged and named to fit a grid so our address revealed the location. We were on a little rise overlooking the city. The rest of Tulsa was very flat. It was the end of winter and very bleak. Our first impression of Tulsa was that it was different, but not *that* different; Australia with an American accent, so to speak. However, in time we discovered that there *were* many differences. One morning, a few weeks after we arrived, I turned the TV on to find a major siege occurring in LA, not too far from the hotel in which we had stayed. The Symbionese Liberation Army was holed up in a house fighting the police and the military. Tanks were in place and missiles were being fired into the house. Patty Hearst had been kidnapped. Welcome to America!

Religion was a constant topic. 'Which congregation have you joined? We love St Johns on 61st street.' The evangelists were everywhere. Oral Roberts University was a mile away with its open hands and prayer tower. On Sunday mornings I surfed the dozens of radio stations listening to the religious broadcasts. The singing and hand clapping was background to soaring sermons predicting death and disaster if the world didn't turn away from sin. This was hot stuff for a Callithumpian.

Tulsa suffered the extremes of weather: very hot, cold, windy and violent storms, the worst of which were the tornados. When we were looking for accommodation, we asked about tornados. 'Plenty around, but they never hit Tulsa. Must be all the evangelists who live here,' suggested one local wag.

Sure enough, on June 8, eight weeks after we arrived, *two* tornados hit the city just before dusk. I'd been out shopping with the family and noticed the yellow sky, lack of wind and heavy atmosphere. When we reached home, I turned on the radio to hear a storm warning. A tornado was passing Keystone Lake, to the west across the Arkansas River. It had picked up the marina with boats attached and deposited the lot in the car park. I was impressed. 'Marg, there's a storm coming," I said. 'Where are the kids?' 'In the yard' was the reply. We followed the radio reports. The tornado crossed the river and headed east along 61st, still several kilometres to the west but coming closer to us. We counted off the major streets till they mentioned Harvard.

I raced out to the front porch. I could see the tornado, and the wind had picked up. I called Marg and the kids. The tornado was bouncing on the tops of buildings and then swirling. It was like an arm of leaden, threatening clouds reaching out. It darted side to side. Its dull roar grew louder as it approached. It looked like it would pass just to the south of us. The family retreated to the lounge room. Loud banging ensued as the intensity of the tornado escalated. Then, ten minutes later, it was gone. Without any particular motive other than to see the damage I got in the car, drove to 61st and headed west, but could only go a short distance towards Yale before debris stopped me. I was the only one on the road. The shopping centre on the corner had disappeared, save for a section of wall. I gazed in amazement, then hurried to our house to tell Marg that the shopping centre was gone. Just then came an electrical storm; hundreds of lightning bolts filled the sky. It was getting dark, but we still had power. Rain started and the TV told us many parts of Tulsa were being flooded.

Next morning the extent of the damage was revealed. We had a call from the Harrisons, who lived east of us. Elizabeth Harrison was highly excited. 'How did you go, did you get in the bathtub?' 'No, we watched it from the front porch.' 'Bloody Australians! Don't you know people were killed? It bounced over our house. The houses either side of us are gone.' Wow.

The Harrisons were preparing to go to Sydney to work with the joint venture. Steve was to replace Andy Meyer as managing director. Later in the afternoon we were able to visit Elizabeth and see the devastation. How lucky we had been!

I had satisfied all of JV's needs on the project and started looking around for the new project that I had left Australia for, but JV said I couldn't leave until I hired my replacement. I set about that task with relish. Mitch Schwartz was hired, and he in turn appointed six people – schedulers and cost and planning engineers. I was off the hook.

My first job as a project engineer with Williams Bros was studying a pipeline link from Africa to Spain to carry natural gas. The leader, John Brown, was an inspiration with his insightful approach to engineering. My contribution was minuscule. I sat at the feet of masters and was all ears. Nobody had built a pipeline as deep as this one would be. In parts it was over a kilometre deep. It started in Algeria and hit the coast of Spain just east of Malaga. Knowledge of fishing and other marine activities had to be married with the latest technical methods of marine pipe laying. This was against a background of political manoeuvring and corporate push. The French were very protective of their technology but at the senior levels realised they needed American help. This was resented lower down and efforts were made

Tulsa house (the duplex in the middle)

Tulsa tornado damage

to frustrate to design development. (I went to Paris to observe the final discussions for the report, but that was much later on, during my world trip in 1977.)

Once in the mainstream of the engineering office I could ask a lot of questions. I seemed to have access to all the current projects. The big one just starting was a massive gas gathering exercise in Saudi Arabia, the Ghawar field. I was assigned to a group designing the gas/oil separators; there were hundreds of them for basically the largest gas field in the world. I learned the fundamentals and set about earning my keep. The John Campbell course in Sydney was my platform, and with the help of the seniors I was able to keep up with my peers. Again, I was struck by the design approach they used. I was constantly trying to improve my work, whereas they settled on a result, checked if it worked and moved on. I felt the need to optimise the designs and hopefully reduce the cost. I also felt if we could standardise some elements we could reduce the number of valves and heat exchangers, and so reduce the cost. I hit a brick wall. 'We don't have time and the client won't reward us for the effort,' was the response to my suggestion. I was unconvinced.

I was lucky to have access to the top designers and spent hours after work picking their brains about these matters. They seemed to enjoy the banter and opened my eyes to the broader industry issues that were totally foreign to me at that stage. Like all industries, companies fight to protect their patch and fight government interference with the pricing and regulations. This can distort the design outcomes. American engineers tend to replicate what has worked in the past and often don't take account of changed circumstances, particularly in foreign countries where transport and environmental conditions are different to those in the USA. Labour costs can change your design outcomes. The design philosophy I had learned in Australia was different. My peers in Tulsa used 'go-by' books along the lines of the John Campbell gas-processing book and rarely were able to go back to first principles to understand the problem. I gained many friends at work as I wrestled through the design development.

Tulsa was not immune to the oil crisis. All the larger businesses in town were car-pooling to lower oil consumption. I was impressed with the American spirit to overcome the OPEC cartel, which was crippling world economies. I was hooked up with three other engineers from my area. It worked well and was a chance to meet some more of my colleagues. We became friends and I learned their routines. Some musicians in the office invited me to play clarinet with them and a regular gig in Broken Arrow, a small town east of Tulsa, ensued. I was in heaven.

Don Brown ran the section I was assigned to. He

had decided I needed a challenge. He was organising for me to join the team studying a gas supply to Fairbanks Alaska from the North Slope. We did the preliminary work and waited for ARCO, the oil company, to make an investment decision. Don wanted me to be the location manager. Another project emerged: designing a production system at Port Harcourt in Nigeria. This was in the delta region and an important increment to the national oil production growth. However, decision making was slow. I was in demand, but the projects relied on client investment decisions and Williams Bros being selected for the role.

In the short time I had been in Tulsa, the office had grown from 500 people to 2,000. I watched the new people settle into unfamiliar roles and take on all the study work that was in progress. Jake Cheeves, my buddy from Sydney, was unhappy. 'We haven't any real projects and these people have no experience. They're just out of college or some business school on the east coast.' The operating companies were happy to spend the money on these studies as it was all rolled into their rate base for the natural gas pricing. Williams Bros was making a lot of money and they kept hiring.

My family was revelling in the cultural exposure. Margaret had been protective of the kids in a new environment but had made good friends to give support. The Perry family from Canada became life long friends as we shared our experiences in this boom environment. Years later I arranged for Bob Perry to come to Australia and help me with the big projects that emerged.

14. Trial by fire in Iraq

The Kurds want their own homeland.

Out of the blue I was asked if I'd like to work on a gas collection project in northern Iraq. Williams Bros was leading a team to study 'putting out the flares' of the northern Iraq gas fields. My Saudi work had given me an insight into the gas separation techniques required for this project. I was appointed project manager – my first role in this senior position. I was unaware that they had struggled to find an American to do the job. It was against company policy to have a non-employee as project manager, even if I came from a joint venture in Australia. The job had been won as a three-way joint venture: Procon in Des Plaines, near Chicago, was the process expert and Keplinger from Denver the reservoir consultant. This was a major promotion for me and one I recognised would elevate my position in the group. I told my family that I would need to travel to Iraq with my new assignment. They got out the maps and we found Baghdad and Kirkuk. They asked if it would be dangerous and I explained that the government would look after me as it was an important project for the country. We all went out for dinner but it was clear they had little idea of the promotion I had achieved.

As the leader I reviewed the brief and laid out a plan to gather the data and prepare a preliminary approach based on our bid documents. The project was major. Iraq was producing in excess of 1 million barrels per day (bpd) of oil from three oil fields, and had been since 1927. The associated gas was being burned at the rate of 1 billion cubic feet per day (cfd). This gas contained more than 100,000 bpd of LPG. I set our initial targets and convened a meeting in Chicago with the three parties, as Procon was responsible for the main gas-conditioning plant and I wanted access to its top designers. Once the plan was agreed we booked flights to Baghdad to meet with the ministry of petroleum, to acquire the data to develop the overall project definition. The ministry had two objectives: first, to utilise the gas for power plants in the Baghdad area; and second, to eliminate the use of kerosene for domestic heating by using the LPG.

Salim Jarrah represented Procon and Robert Blake was the Keplinger geologist. We met a few weeks later and flew from Chicago to London to join an Middle East Airline flight to Beirut. In Beirut we were stalled when the connecting flight to Baghdad did not have our reservation. The girl on the desk said there was no record of our booking. I showed her our tickets and the confirmation. She was unmoved. The next available flight was in three days. She commented that this flight was delayed by four hours, even if we were on it. Salim was excited. 'I can show you Beirut, the Paris of the east.'

I was unimpressed, it was important we got on the flight for we had no visas for Iraq, only a telex guaranteeing entry via a representative of the ministry who would meet us. I told Salim we should wait to find alternatives. Shortly afterwards I thought I heard the flight being called over the fuzzy PA. I went to the desk to enquire. But the girl said no, it was four hours away. I asked her to check. With irritation all over her face, she made a call. Then she replied, 'Yes, it's going.' 'Can we get on?' I excitedly asked. 'Of course,' she had sent everybody away.

We secured our boarding passes for our scheduled flight and Salim rushed off to buy presents for our hosts. As we approached security I saw two lines 50m long. Salim was dividing up the liquor and cigarettes when I noticed an American behind us who was very agitated and waving to one of the guards. 'My flight is leaving. Can I come forward?' The guard was unmoved, but somehow the American interpreted that as a yes and ran forward only to be confronted by a soldier who raised his semi-automatic. The American stopped, turned and ran straight back into the line. Meanwhile my queue was progressing quicker than my colleagues'. Eventually I was through, and waited for the others. Two soldiers came to me and told me to move on. I was about to explain I was waiting for my colleagues but they pointed to the bus terminal with their weapons. Reluctantly I made my way down the stairs. A bus was just leaving and I clambered on with the 'contraband' that Salim had loaded onto me.

As we disembarked in Baghdad after midnight I finally saw Salim and Robert ahead of me. Salim was in high spirits. He took my 'contraband' and we entered the terminal, where we were met by the officials. They explained that our mission was high-profile and that Iraq television would be waiting outside to film our arrival. Salim was the only Arabic speaker among us and he took the lead. After some filming and interviews we were shown to separate cars to take us to the Alibassy Palace, a recently opened hotel. I was alone in the back of a limo, wondering where the others had gone. The driver said I was lucky to be going to the Alibassy Palace. I had been told in the States that the only decent hotel in Baghdad was the Baghdad Hotel. 'Can't we go to the Baghdad Hotel?' 'No, this is better.' I slumped in the seat. The time was 2am. The car pulled up in front of an impressive building, but had to walk across a plank to get in. The lobby was huge, but the check-in was an improvised table. I went to the room to find it only partly finished. No ceiling, and holes in the wall where light fittings and switches might go. I was too tired to care.

In the morning I was woken by strident wailing outside the room. Christ! What was that? It was the call to prayers. It went on for a quarter of an hour as I lay in bed recounting the previous day. It was a bright day outside and I was hungry. I couldn't remember having dinner. I showered and went down to find the cafe. There was one, but all they were offering was toast and coffee. I was idly looking out the window, when a baboon bounded along the parapet. The toast came. I realised it was Friday. No work today. The driver had said he would pick me up at 9am Saturday. I was slowly starting to focus on the job in hand. What was that baboon all about? I didn't think they had baboons here. Maybe it was an illusion!

The telephones at the hotel were useless and I had no way to communicate with my colleagues. I found out later that Robert was staying at the Baghdad and Salim was with relatives. I wandered into the lobby and realised that while the hotel was operating, it was months from being in any way complete. My thoughts were interrupted by a large Englishman with ruddy cheeks. 'Sir, excuse me,' he said, 'are you well?' I nodded and he continued, 'I've organised a taxi to Babylon and wondered if you would join me? Eric's my name. Might I enquire yours?' 'Babylon? … Sorry, I'm Grahame' 'Yes, Grahame it's not too far and might be fun. What do you say?' 'Fine.' 'Right, I'll see you outside in ten.'

I went to the room and put on walking shoes and met Eric by the taxi. 'Hop in, thanks for being a good sport' he intoned. We headed out across the Tigris river and turned south. Soon we stopped at a roadblock. Soldiers were inspecting papers. I didn't have my passport. The airport officials had taken it to install the visa. 'Don't worry old boy,' said Eric, 'mine will do.' We passed successfully and travelled another 15km where we encountered another road block. 'What's going on?' I asked. 'It's the war, old chap. They're checking for arms coming from the south, from Yemen.' 'There's a war?' 'It's the Kurds. They're fighting in the north. There are about 150,000 troops engaged, I've been told.' 'Oh...' I thought for a while. Nobody had mentioned the war. In my research I had only come up with the Israel-Palestine conflicts. The Yom Kippur War had happened the year before, but no mention had been made of the conflict Eric was talking about in the north, where our project was located.

As we sped south my companion was telling me about his trade, selling aerosols, but I was thinking about the project. Another road block appeared and reality set in. No one knew where I was, I didn't have any papers and I was with a character I'd only just met, who sold sprays to the Arabs. Eric was explaining our mission to a soldier, pointing to me, saying that I was his assistant and travelled on his passport. I thought, 'One of these guys isn't going to buy it and all shit will break loose.'

We stopped at a roadside building and the driver got out to talk to a local. With all the gesturing, it became clear he didn't know our destination. Eric became agitated and, turning to me, said, 'By Jove, the chap's lost. Do you have any idea?' 'I have no idea. I thought you were the expert.' 'The chap said he knew the way, and I believed him.' 'Maybe he's on the track now.' The driver returned and we U-turned and took a side road a little way on. 'He seems confident now,' I said encouragingly. 'I hope so. I've wanted to see the hanging gardens since I was a boy.' I thought to myself, 'I think they fell down thousands of years ago.' We saw some buildings in the distance and Eric exclaimed, 'There's the Ishtar Gate! We're here.' We parked near a large building and went in. It was a museum and held some impressive artefacts. We found an English-speaking guide and Eric indicated that we wanted to see the gardens. The guide looked mystified and said the site was a large excavation. There were no gardens.

We walked down towards the river and passed the Lion of Babylon. Eric perked up and his rosy cheeks shone. He was very overweight and struggled with the terrain. We were led into several chambers where there were people and animals carved out of stone. The guide explained the complex water and air-conditioning systems the Babylonians had developed in ancient times. The models in the museum had shown this, but what had been there originally had to be imagined from what remained. We must have walked several kilometres when the guide declared the tour was over and some money was required. I realised I had no Iraqi money, but Eric was happy to pay him. 'My treat.' We headed for the car and spent time looking for the driver. I was surprised there was no control over the diggings. Being Friday, families were cooking and playing in the archaeological ruins; children were sliding down the slopes and throwing balls.

We left and found the main road again, but stopped a few kilometres on. We were out of petrol. It took half an hour to find a source and ensure that it wasn't diesel. The trip back was uneventful. If the gun-running was from the south, surely they would search more diligently on our return. It didn't seem so, and we arrived back after dark, much to my relief. I invited Eric to join me in the bar and found they served alcohol. I had done a pretty stupid thing that day. A spur of the moment indulgence, without any regard for the country I was in. I resolved to be more responsible. I didn't see Eric again after that.

The black limo returned the next morning and took me to the oil ministry. I was pleased to see Salim and Robert. We were ushered into the minister's office and I introduced the team. He welcomed us with tea in what resembled liqueur glasses. The other bureaucrats in the room introduced themselves and we exchanged pleasantries for half an hour. The minister wished us well and emphasised the importance of the project to the country.

The senior bureaucrats took us to a conference room where I outlined our concept for the work. We had sent a long telex requesting various documents and maps. Had any been obtained? No, they were still being compiled and we would have them shortly. We needed to go to Kirkuk to see the facilities. 'Yes, that will be arranged,' said the department head, whose name was Abdul. 'There are formalities to complete. Is there anything else?' 'No. But why am I staying in a different hotel to Robert? 'We thought as the leader you would prefer a higher standard of accommodation.' 'No,' I said, 'I would be very happy in the Baghdad Hotel.' 'Then we will arrange your transfer and your passports will be ready in a week,' continued Abdul. 'In the interim we have prepared these documents for your stay.' He handed over a little card covered in Arabic. 'If that's all, I'll leave you now. Ali here will attend to your needs.' Abdul left us.

I stressed to Ali that we couldn't start until we had some data. What was going on? He shrugged. 'It's up to the various managers. Wait a week.' 'A week? We were only planning on being here ten days, including a trip to Kirkuk.' 'The fighting slows things down. There is a curfew and travel is difficult. I'll call by in the morning with any news.' With that he left. At least, Salim was happy. 'It will give me a chance to see my relatives. See you later.'

At 1pm Robert and I walked down the road looking for a restaurant for lunch. We found a place that sold pasta, which Robert declared they couldn't mess up. The restaurant was dingy and the tablecloths were torn. A waiter took our order and we drank coffee. 'Grahame, you realise there are few westerners here,' said Robert. 'The government evicted most of them in 1968. They've been trying to run things locally, but there aren't many educated people around. Anyone with a degree does postgraduate studies and eventually leaves to work in the west. Saddam has cracked down on that recently, but there's a big gap. We're the first outsiders back under a new policy to get the oil fields working more efficiently. The Kurdish War has highlighted the problem, as the Kurds believe the oil is theirs. The Iranians are helping them to destabilise the Iraqi regime. It's a proxy Iran-Iraq war and we'll be in the middle of it.'

I realised I knew nothing about the Middle East. All the press focused on Israel and ignored the other conflicts. My job was to deliver a plan for harnessing the gas, but without a feeling for the politics of it I would be hamstrung. I thought Iraq was Arabic, but already the Kurds were playing a part and Ali, our main contact, was Turkish, as Robert pointed out. I looked at Robert and asked, 'How do you feel about this contract?' 'From my point of view, it's easy. Keplinger worked in Iraq in the '60s. We have a lot of the reservoir data in the office in Denver. It's a bit out of date, but we employ Iraqis in the office who were here a couple of years ago. The Kirkuk fields are so prolific that secondary recovery was unnecessary. They just drilled a few extra wells. I heard that they were looking at a water flood operation, but didn't have the technology. Some Russians were helping and I'm not sure how far they went. My only task is to verify the production figures and check the reservoir pressures. I can probably guess them now.'

We went back to the Baghdad Hotel, which was nearby, and I found my bags were in my new room. The hotel was old and had a big crack in the lobby floor. A bar and a casino were off to the right at the entrance. There was a very French feel to the place. Unlike at the Alibassy Palace, there were ceilings and light fittings. Salim had disappeared, but Robert was in the bar at 5pm, nursing a scotch. We had a few drinks and dinner, and Robert left me in the bar to go to bed. I was the only westerner there. In time I visited the casino where they were playing roulette, but the main crowd surrounded a couple of *chemin de fer* (baccarat) tables. The language spoken by players and croupier was French and it was a lively scene. I watched for a while before jet lag set in.

In the morning Ali came by to accompany us to the ministry. When Robert didn't come to the lobby where we had arranged to meet I called his room on the phone at the hotel desk, but there was no answer. Ali and I left without him. At the ministry, keen to read up on Baghdad, I asked the clerk if any publications or books were available to peruse in the library at the ministry. He informed me that there was no library there but there was a city library. 'Can I go?' 'What do you want to see?' 'Maybe some books in English that could give me some background on Iraq.' The clerk disappeared for a few minutes and returned to say, 'If you give me the titles, I will have someone fetch them for you.' Exasperated, I explained I just wanted to browse the shelves. 'I promise I won't pinch anything.' 'That is not permitted,' said the clerk. A visit to the library being out of the question, I asked Ali if I could have a car to look around town. 'I'll arrange it,' he said.' I waited an hour in the conference room for Ali to return. 'Follow me.' We went to the street and Ali and I got into the back of the limo. The driver and another Arab were in the front. 'Where do you want to go?' 'Do they have a mosque?' 'Of course. One of the most famous is across the river in Kadhimayn.' He gave the driver directions and we sped off. 'Who's our friend in the front?' I asked Ali. 'That's our security liaison man.'

We arrived at a golden dome that glistened in the sun. 'Wow, can we stop so I can take a photo?' 'No photos. You can buy a postcard.' We slowed, but didn't stop. This wasn't a sightseeing tour apparently. Our trip took us to the main business centre which was dusty and uninspiring. Other parts of the city were equally drab and finally we cruised along the side of the Tigris. It was muddy, spotted with rubbish flowing slowly south. I was starting to get a sense of the size of the suburbs and the architecture. It was hard to see buildings, as they were behind high walls and there were few high rises. Eventually they dropped me at the hotel and I looked around for Robert, with no luck. I walked the streets in the area around Abu Nawaz Street, near the river, and came across a bookshop. Most of the English books were printed in Poland. I found a Frank Hardy book, *Dead Man Running*, and bought it. There were no books on Iraq.

I returned to the hotel and sat in the bar, reading. I was alone with the barman, a surly, non-talkative person of an ethnicity I couldn't determine; he didn't look Arabic. Robert eventually arrived and apologised for his absence. 'I haven't been well,' he explained.' 'You've been hard to contact,' I said. 'Sorry.' He ordered a double scotch, which seemed to perk him up. I updated him on the lack of data. He speculated that the managers in the department were fighting to protect their sections and it would take an order from the boss to release what we required. We had several more drinks and I started to relax. After dinner I heard a commotion in the casino. I looked in to find a customer being ejected by a large Arab in traditional costume. Robert said that patrons bet large sums and it could get a bit testy. After a couple of more drinks we retired.

In the morning I was worried that Robert, once more, had not appeared, and nor had Salim who had also been a no-show yesterday. Ali picked me up and, without my colleagues, we went to the ministry. I was handed a couple of pages of production data. After glancing at it I said it was useless. There were no dates or locations. Ali shrugged and said more was coming. I requested an audience with the department head, but was told he had left town and was away for a week. 'Can I see the minister?' The clerk looked nervous and said he didn't know. I went into Ali's office and said things were intolerable. There was no way I could do the job, and I wanted to register my displeasure with the minister. We had sent our request a month in advance and if the ministry wanted a report from us, then we couldn't help them under these conditions. Ali looked worried. 'Grahame, we only received your request a week ago, just before you arrived. There are a lot of forces in the ministry and your pressure may produce an unanticipated reaction.' I wasn't sure what he meant, but I felt he was the only person I could trust. I thought quickly how we can use our time... 'We may as well go to Kirkuk,' I said. 'How quickly can that be arranged?' 'I'll get back to you tomorrow.' Upset, I went back to the hotel to work out if there was anything useful I could do. Days were passing, with no result. I felt stranded. I couldn't call Tulsa, as I was told a call had to be booked and there was a six-week delay. I had no data to start the concept design. I also had an issue with my colleagues. Salim was in Kuwait, I was told, visiting relatives. He was becoming a liability. Robert seemed sick all the time.

The next day Ali came to the hotel and told me we were set to go to Kirkuk in two days. I asked him if there was any progress on the documents and he shook his head. What to do? I called Robert in his room but when there was no answer, I left a note in his box at reception. Ali said he would contact Salim – I wasn't sure how, but he seemed confident of being able to do so. I thought I'd walk around town to see what was happening. It was cool as I took the path along the river. At one point I glanced behind and noticed a man following me. It put me off a bit, so I headed towards the ministry. I went up to Ali's office and told him. He was unfazed. 'You will never be alone, so don't worry. The ministry doesn't want you getting into trouble.' I left wondering if this was good or bad, and decided it wasn't bad.

I had a free day and after again unsuccessfully trying to contact Robert I was getting worried. I hadn't seen him for several days. In the morning, Salim appeared at breakfast unexpectedly and our car arrived for the journey to Kirkuk. No Robert. I went to his room and knocked. No answer. I knocked again and thought I heard a noise. I waited, then knocked again. Suddenly the door opened and he stood there in his pyjamas, with several days' beard growth on his face. 'We're going to Kirkuk.' He blinked and started to speak. I realised he was drunk. 'Get dressed!'. 'okay, give me ten minutes,' he slurred. I went back to the lobby and apologised for the delay. Ali explained we needed to go right now as there was a strictly-enforced curfew at Kirkuk. Robert finally appeared with a small bag and we drove off. He immediately passed out. I was in the back of the car with him and Ali. A secret service man, Khalid, sat next to the driver. He reminded me of Omar Sharif. Khalid dressed well and draped a stylish gabardine coat over his shoulders. Salim and the other officials travelled in a second car. We were crossing the Tigris in heavy traffic when a truck nudged the back of our car. The driver got out and abused the truckie, who in turn yelled at our driver. Khalid got out and approached the truckie, who stood his ground. Khalid then pulled out a pistol and pointed it at the man who turned and fled, leaving his truck in the middle of the bridge. Khalid got back in the car and we drove on. I sat there nonplussed, what next!

We sped north into the desert to beat the 4pm curfew. At one point the desert to the west was covered in military aircraft; there seemed to be hundreds of them. We passed in silence. Our conversation was inhibited by the secret service man in the front seat. We stopped for a brief lunch at a roadside cafe. It was dusty and the food dubious. The war began to emerge in front of us. On the road were armoured vehicles, a machine gun on top with a vigilant gunner crouched over it. The buildings we passed were guarded. We crossed the river at Tikrit and headed north-west. The country became undulating and grassy. Shepherds tended herds of sheep and goats. The contrasts were stark; war then rural normalcy.

Finally we reached the oil camp on the fringe of the town and showed our papers at a large guardhouse. The area reminded me of rural Australia. There were many eucalypt trees and the roads were well maintained, with bungalows lining the edge. We turned into a sprawling building which housed the apartments for visitors and a mess with recreation facilities. It was a big surprise. After finding our rooms, we met in the club bar for a drink. It was like the British had never left. On the ringing of a bell, servants brought dates and cold drinks. Our Arab hosts seemed quite at home. I asked when we could see the production facilities and visit the GOSPs (gas–oil separation plants). 'Plenty of time for that,' Ali responded. 'Relax and enjoy'. I heard a dull *thrump* and then another. 'It's the field guns, don't worry,' explained Ali. After dinner I walked around the camp, wondering what it had been like ten years earlier, when Iraq Petroleum was in charge. The Iraq government nationalised the company at short notice. I discovered over dinner that the British expats were given only a few days' notice to leave. Some of them had been there for decades. More distant gunfire brought me back to reality.

At 7am the next day we all met in the mess. Ali had organised a tour of the crude stabilisation facility and for the first time I could view some drawings of the plant layout. The manager was keen to show us his improvements, and Salim and I pored over the detail. After a couple of hours we had a good understanding of the operations and had managed to obtain several drawings. I felt we had made the first progress since we arrived several weeks before. Robert had gone off with the reservoir engineers and we didn't see him till dinner. He seemed to have recovered.

The following day Salim and I, with Ali, boarded an armoured car and joined a convoy that filed up into the hills. There was not much vegetation and the road was steep in parts. We rounded a corner to see a well site with a GOSP totally covered in sandbags, machine guns poking through small gaps. As we walked up the rough path, Ali dug me in the ribs with his elbow and, grinning, asked, 'Are you worried?' I had been fine till then. I asked, 'Should I be?' He laughed and we passed through a makeshift steel door to an open area. The headman greeted us. Ali was an old friend and of course a fellow Turk. 'What do you want to know?' said the headman. In his office we reviewed his production data, most of it in Arabic. Salim translated. The whole oil field consisted of three separate areas: Bai Hassan, Jambur and Kirkuk. Wells were grouped and separators took the gas to a flare site. Some gas had been gathered under an older design, to be piped to a Baghdad power station. This was refined in the central process facility we had visited the day before. We noted the production values and toured the facility. An enjoyable lunch of barbecued goat and flat bread ensued. The same convoy visited two more sites along a dusty road and then headed back to the camp – curfew was approaching.

Over dinner I met more of the managers, who gave us a rundown of the operations and their plans for development. They acknowledged that the war was a brake on their plans and that the nightly destruction of parts of the works made planning impossible. 'How will the conflict be resolved?' I asked. They shrugged. 'Saddam will fix it.' The next day we worked in the conference room consolidating our data. The weather was fine for our stay, but cold at night.

I reviewed our findings with the team. Robert felt he had all the information he needed to complete his section. He had the benefit of the files that he had obtained earlier in his Denver office. Salim was a different case. He required well-defined feedstock specs to scope the design task. We had not reached that point and we needed to talk to the department in Baghdad to firm up a strategy. After dinner, Robert invited me for a drink in the lounge. He had a map and a bottle of scotch. 'I think Iran will invade Iraq. This war is just an excuse, I heard there are two Iranian divisions in the mountains helping the Kurds. It's just a matter of time.' 'What do you suggest we do?' 'Well, we go through Mosul. That's our escape route to Turkey.' 'How do we know when to make a run for it?' 'My friends in the reservoir group are Turks and they're in contact with some Kurdish sympathisers. They'll tell us.' Robert's scotch bottle was half empty. It was coming together … Robert was an alcoholic. 'Look, Robert,' I said, 'I'm an Australian and I don't fancy a race across the desert to Turkey. If they come, I'll be here and take my chances. The Iranians are allies of the US, so why are you worried?' 'I don't trust them,' was his reply.' We then talked about the oil business. Robert was a fountain of information on reservoir development and techniques for secondary production with water flood and gas injection. He finished the bottle and excused himself.

It was time to return to Baghdad and see what progress the ministry had made. I travelled with Salim and Ali, while Robert stayed to work with the geologists.

We were dropped at the hotel in the afternoon and Salim asked me to eat with him and his uncle in Al Mansour, an upmarket suburb. We took a taxi and arrived at seven. Salim's Egyptian cousin, Tawfik Saleh, was a film director who had been honoured at the Cannes

Film Festival. He had been hired by the government to establish a film industry in Iraq. He offered me a drink and said he had never met an Australian. Salim kept bringing the conversation back to politics, and particularly Palestine. I knew Salim was a Palestinian, so I was confused as to how the family was structured. Tawfik was interested in Australia and quizzed me on the arts. We got on very well, to Salim's annoyance.

During dinner Salim asked what themes Tawfik would pursue to promote Arab positions in the world. Tawfik waved him away, saying he might do nothing. The government had misled him. They had invited him to set up a film industry now he was being told to help develop the television industry, and he wanted nothing to do with it. He hated TV, he declared, and would sit his contract out in the villa if they didn't give him a film to work on. Salim pressed his case on the promotion of the Arab cause. Eventually Tawfik told Salim he had made the film 'The Dupes' in Syria and had no more interest in that theme; he was interested in the art of film and creating engaging personal stories. Salim exploded. 'What a waste! Palestine is in flames and you talk about personal stories. Come on, Grahame, we're leaving.' I looked at both of them, pleasantly drunk. Tawfik said I could stay if I liked and I remained seated. Salim stormed out and Tawfik poured another drink. 'Salim is a child, really. He would like to kill all Zionists. What are your favourite Australian films?' We chatted for a couple of hours, till Tawfik called his driver and sent me on my way. 'Come again, I'm not doing much.'

At breakfast Salim asked how I felt. 'Fine,' I replied. He then chided me about my behaviour. 'Tawfik is a counter-revolutionary and not a friend of Palestine.' I did not enter that conversation. Instead, we discussed the project. Salim let his frustration bubble up. 'The government is useless. There is no point in waiting around in this boring town.' I asked him to calm down. I said we had a contract and an obligation to see it through. Salim ate his breakfast and left. I returned to the ministry.

Ali had no good news– several key people were away – but he had arranged a meeting at the power station to discuss the low gas delivery problem. The Kirkuk gas supply was designed to deliver 100 mmcfd (millions of cubic feet per day) of gas, but only 10 mmcfd was arriving. We drove to the plant in the afternoon and met the manager. He looked harried and dishevelled, but was knowledgeable. He took me through the turbine house and finally settled down in his office with a cup of tea. I asked if the gas supply was reliable, and he said it wasn't. Pipeline failures across the Tigris at Beiji had interrupted supply several times. Also, only 10 mmcfd was being delivered. I asked about pressure profiles and he said pressure was fine; in fact, there was *too much* pressure. I told Ali that we needed to go back to Kirkuk to track the gas through the system, to analyse for any weaknesses. I felt I might as well do something useful. Salim had disappeared again, and was rumoured to be in Kuwait.

Two days later we were on our way; same driver but a different bodyguard, Soran, a Kurd. I was surprised: I thought they were on the other side. This time we went into the city and the others did some shopping. I stayed in the car on the pretext I was tired. I wanted to take some photos of the streets. Unfortunately, they were full of soldiers and every time I tried to take a shot a soldier was looking at me. I was too nervous and finally gave up. We drove to the camp and I caught up with Robert. Another pleasant evening and another bottle of scotch for him. I ribbed him about the invasion. He told me I'd be sorry.

At the gas plant in the morning Ali and I and sat down with the chief operator. I was armed with more information now, and asked him to take me through the system. He had two customers, the Darra power station in Baghdad and the pump stations along the oil line to Syria. 'You send gas to Syria?' I asked him. 'Yes, there are gas turbines driving the pipeline pumps. We use an old oil line, converted for gas use.' 'How efficient is it?' 'Don't know,' he said, 'when they did the conversion they used 12-inch block valves on the 16-inch line, so you can't run an inspection device through it. We just keep as much pressure as possible.' 'You don't seem to produce much gas for Baghdad.' 'Well, we're constrained by the gas plant. We could process 200 mmcfd more if we could de-bottleneck parts of the plant. We have enough feed gas. The problem is in the stripper.' I went on, 'So you could deliver more gas to Baghdad if that was fixed?' 'Yes. We generally only can send them 10 mmcfd.' 'The pipeline isn't a problem?' I asked. 'Not if the Baiji crossing is whole. We've replaced it several times, but with smaller diameter pipes. It gets washed out periodically.' 'So,' I pressed him, 'if you put 20 mmcfd down the line, they'd get it?' 'Yes, of course.' Problem solved! I felt I'd achieved something. I asked Ali if we could go to the river at Baiji to see the pipe crossing. 'OK, but we need armour. I'll arrange it.'

Back at the camp I asked Soran if he would take me to the town. He was a big cheerful Kurd and proud to show off Kurdish culture. We drove to the base of a huge ancient castle. As we circled the walls I noticed small caves at the base, in which artisans were making Roman swords. Soran explained that the best steel was created by the techniques they used. I pointed out that the Roman army might not be still in the market for these. He laughed. 'They are collectors' items.' Further around, the market unfolded into a sea of colourful stalls ringed by robed Arabs and Kurds haggling over the goods. I stood there, thinking that a film-maker could shoot any biblical movie here and not have to change a thing.

Soran seemed to know all the merchants with their large sacks of fruits, nuts and grains. He took a handful of dates and nuts, mixed them, and handed me some, saying, 'Try this.' It was new to my taste. We did this several times with different combinations, all good. I worried that the merchants would baulk, as we didn't pay for anything. Soran laughed. 'They are my friends.' I asked if there were any jewellery shops. 'Of course. I have a favourite.' He introduced me and I perused the stock. Some of it looked a thousand years old. I chose a gold brooch and some earrings for Margaret. Soran insisted he clean them up and make them look like new. I protested. 'No, no! I want them to look old.' Soran would have none of it and the jeweller took out his blowtorch. When he had finished, the earrings looked like something from Woolworths. Soran checked them and smiled, saying, 'Your lady will love them.' I felt sick, and not from the dates and nuts. The blowtorch had burned all the romance from my gift. What I did value was the magical scene in the market as the sun set – at least I had that. It was hard to believe that I was in the middle of a war zone. Kurds, Arabs and others were at peace here, as lanterns were lit and dots of colour twinkled under the brooding castle.

We returned to Baghdad and I insisted on seeing the head of the ministry to report progress, or the lack of it. I was granted an audience the next day. He was very polite and we had tea. It seemed the custom to spend ten minutes discussing nothing in particular before the purpose of a meeting was broached. I said we still had not received the bulk of the data requested, after a month of waiting. However, we *had* solved the mystery of the Darra Power Station gas supply. The minister called his senior heads and asked why the data had not arrived. They shuffled their feet and offered various unconvincing explanations. Clearly there was another agenda here of which I was unaware. They left bowing and walking backwards. The head of ministry turned to me and assured me I would get what I needed. He suggested I visit Mosul with my team, to see the progress they had made in promoting LPG in the country. I left a note for Salim in the hope he might return for the trip. It was three days before it could be arranged.

On our travel morning, Salim appeared and joined us, as if nothing was amiss. It was quite a long drive and we had curfew deadlines. Khalid was our guide, as he was supposed to know the area. Salim was very excited. 'This is where we train the Palestinian terrorists,' he announced. As we approached the town, a guardhouse and gate blocked the way. I was sitting in the back between two Arabs when the soldier checked the driver's papers. He used his gun to wave us through, but thrust it in the window as the driver started to go forward. 'Khalass!' The driver stopped, and the guard pointed to me and talked to the driver. Khalid pulled out his pistol and told the driver to move on, as the guard had earlier indicated. It was a stand-off. I volunteered to give him my papers, but Khalid said to drive on. We waited a few seconds… I gave my papers to the driver. Khalid holstered his pistol with a curse and we passed.

We went to a small, quaint hotel in the old part of town. After dinner we walked around the narrow streets while our car tried to follow us. It was near freezing, but very exotic for me. After an hour, Khalid looked around for the car, which was nowhere to be seen. Salim berated him; he was supposed to be our guide. Apparently Khalid had never been to Mosul. We decided to walk in one direction to find a main road, hoping to see a taxi. That worked, but Khalid was embarrassed.

The next day we visited an LPG filling station. It looked fine at first glance but the smell of gas was strong and cylinders passing the water dunk checkpoint were obviously leaking. It was scary. The inspector seemed oblivious to this and disinterested when I pointed it out. We then went to the distribution centre, where we met the manager in his office. Our visit seemed of minor interest, as people constantly burst into the room waving papers to be signed. I glanced out the window into the yard below. Hundreds of people were fighting to load carts with cylinders, and yelling at officials who were in their way. It was all very colourful, but chaotic. After half an hour he started to focus on our questions. 'We have a very popular product. I have to ensure the right people are happy.' It was clear that bribery won the day.

Back at the hotel in the evening we joined the crowd in the bar and I drank some *arak* to get in the mood. A local drew my attention to a TV in the corner, black and white and fuzzy. 'Australian city gone in big storm!' I tried to make out the images, but with the Arab commentary it was impossible. He became more excited and pointed to the screen. 'Whole city gone, blown away!' I thanked him and went back to our group. I had no understanding and thought he was mistaken. When the crowd thinned I sat and, and oblivious to the tragedy that was unfolding back home, watched the TV again. The blurry, flickering news footage of the destruction of Darwin by Cyclone Tracy had been replaced by, I think, a sitcom. It was hilarious. One of the ministry guys came to me and suggested I not laugh, as it might be thought that I was laughing at Arab culture. That was too much for me. I went to bed, even though it was Christmas. I wondered what my family was doing. I hadn't heard from them in over a month.

The next morning we returned to Baghdad. You'd never have known it was just after Christmas. I called in on Ali and he was upbeat. He showed me a report that had been prepared by Bechtel in the late '60s for Iraq Petroleum. The company had been commissioned to do a feasibility report on a similar scheme to that which was currently proposed. A part of its scheme had been implemented. Ali emphasised that the report was confidential and that no one should know I had it. I asked why? He intimated that there was rivalry in the department and many there wanted our work to fail. I asked if I would get the balance of the information. He felt that it would eventually come.

I studied the report at the hotel. It was a big leap forward, as it had a different perspective on the development plan, with more emphasis on the Jambur field. It was hard for me to know how to proceed because the Kurds were destroying elements of the fields and the fields' recovery was not certain. I was keen to share my thoughts with Salim, but he had gone again. I had the feeling he was politically active, but I had no feel for the local scene.

I received a note from Tawfik asking me to join him for dinner, and saying he would pick me up. We went across to the Tigris, where restaurants had been set up on the river bank. Tables and chairs were arranged on the grass and the cooking was done on the ground next to your table. The idea was to select a fish, a *masgouf*, from a bathtub and the chef would kill it and gut it. As he took it from the tub a wrestling match ensued as, he told us, the fish was big and strong, having been caught that very day from the river right where we were sitting. Tawfik laughed at that and confided to me that the 'wriggling' fish served by the vendors was often dead, and the cook had a way of pretending to fight it so it appeared to be hale and hearty. Wooden stakes were driven into the clay next to the table. The fish, which had been seasoned, was hung with the inside facing a wood fire. The chef would periodically fan the flames towards the fish, with a cigarette drooping from his mouth under his bushy moustache. It was delicious and I thanked him for the hospitality. As I glanced around the other tables a low hum of conversation infused the swinging lanterns and cooking fires. It was hard to believe a war was being waged in the north. Tawfik and I drank *arak* and whiskey and talked about culture. He told me he had made a film about the Palestinians in Syria which he felt was his best. Salim should be satisfied with that. Tawfik was at an impasse with the government, but felt they would eventually come around and let him make films and not television programs. He was interested in music and wanted to learn about Australia. We talked and drank for hours. This was the highlight of my trip to Iraq. I was privileged to talk to such an urbane man.

Back at the hotel I tried to integrate the Bechtel ideas with our brief. My colleagues had disappeared and I discovered that Robert had left the country. The ministry told me he had retrieved his passport and said he needed medical treatment. After the *masgouf* experience I walked the streets looking for good restaurants. In the evenings the men promenaded along the street next to the river in their gowns, often hand in hand. It was a male tradition and few women appeared. Vendors offered snacks from trolleys and it was a peaceful scene as the sun set. I found a good place to eat a few blocks away, shadowed by my escort. The restaurant was upstairs and overlooked the river. I'd grown used to dining alone, but when I saw an Iraqi couple waiting for a table, I enquired if they spoke English. They did, and I asked them to join me. They hesitated, then agreed, but only for a drink. He was a professor of petroleum geology at Baghdad University.

What happened next struck me as strange. When I told them my mission, they became very nervous and said they had to leave. I tried to persuade them to stay but they were insistent. I invited them for a drink in the back bar of the Baghdad Hotel. They said they had never been there, so I gave them directions. They said they'd come for one drink. I ate quickly then it was back to the hotel to see if they would come. I waited an hour in the bar by myself, not at all surprised that they hadn't showed. Then they appeared looking furtive. I took their order and relayed it to the barman. They looked around the bar and finally sat in a corner. I asked them, 'What's the problem?' The professor replied, 'You are being followed by the secret police and we will be noted if we meet you.' I mentioned I was aware of that and apologised if I had put them in danger. The drinks came and we talked for fifteen minutes. They were interested in my project and had seen our arrival on TV. I said I'd not met any Iraqis outside the government, and asked if life was OK. They gave no answer, but invited me to their home on New Year's Eve. I gave the man my details at the hotel and they left shortly afterwards. I sat and pondered. I had no idea what was going on in this country. There was an unknown war in progress in the north, the people I'd just met seemed frightened, yet walking in the markets seemed normal and safe.

This was my first project management role. My team had deserted me and Robert was sick, I didn't know how badly. I wondered if I was a bad leader. I was pining for my family whom I had left in a foreign country for the festive season. I had many reasons to feel sorry for myself. But I had responsibilities.

Over the next couple of days I worked in my room at the hotel on strategies for the design. My routine with the barman continued till New Year's when the hotel seemed empty. My university friends did not send a note, so I was alone. With nothing much else to do, I sat at the bar rather than at a table to talk to the barman. I ordered my usual Heineken and when he brought it I asked where he came from. 'Baghdad.' 'Did your family originate from here?' 'Yes,' was his response. He then went into the area behind the bar and emerged at the side door to clean tables that looked already clean. My strategy of befriending the barman wasn't working. I wondered what Iraqis did on New Year's Eve. I left the hotel and walked down the short road leading to Abu Nawaz Street to see a crowd looking very untidy, obviously drunk. I watched a while then decided to go back to the hotel. I looked around the public areas, the casino was closed and the barman was busying himself arranging bottles. Down heartedly I went to bed and read my Frank Hardy. Towards midnight I heard yelling and some fireworks or maybe gunfire... I looked out the window and could see nothing. Happy 1975.

Back at the ministry, Ali said a large package of drawings would be available the next day. In the adjacent room I chatted with Soran the bodyguard about the Kurds. How did he reconcile his position? He laughed. 'I am friends with everyone, even generals. I asked him if he would take me to the Golden Mosque. 'No problem, we can go this evening.'

Soran picked me up at the hotel and we drove for a while through the streets. The driver let us off in a crowded area and I followed Soran across a square. There it was, the Golden Mosque, its huge dome lit in the night sky. We approached the main gate and saw a milling crowd. What was happening? Soran looked at me. 'Shall we go in?' I said. 'Is it allowed for an infidel?' 'Yes, why not?' He went over to the guards, who wore red fezzes, and gestured to me to join him. We entered a large area surrounding the mosque. I was transfixed – there must have been a thousand worshippers sitting cross-legged on the pavement, mostly facing the mosque. I had only walked a few paces into the area, but felt acutely aware that I was being watched by an increasing number of people. Soran was still talking to the guard. I looked around again and decided to leave. I had read of Muslims attacking people who didn't respect their religion. Soran came over and said we could go into the mosque proper. I said, 'No, I'm not going to step over all these people.' My gut was telling me to get out of there. Soran was moving forward, but I turned and departed. Thinking I might be followed, I tried to blend into the crowd. I looked back and people were watching me, so I kept walking as fast as I could without drawing any more attention to myself. Eventually I found a taxi and managed to tell the driver to take me to the Baghdad Hotel. An hour and a half after I got there, Soran arrived. I'd been expecting him, so I'd stayed in the bar. He was unhappy about what I'd done, as he was responsible for my safety. 'Why?' he asked. I told him I respected my gut feeling that I was in danger, and had felt most uncomfortable. He sighed and left.

At long last, Ali brought me a box full of documents. 'I have given you two copies, one to keep and one for the secret police. They know you have the information and will want to check for security issues. Just give them one copy.' I spent the day reviewing the information, and sure enough that evening I received a visit from two men in dark suits. They introduced themselves and

I gave them the copies of the documents. They said they would return them the following evening. The next day I went to see Ali at the ministry and reported the meeting of last evening. He and I had become good friends. 'That was quick! Normally they take a few days. Your project is a high priority for the government. But, as I said, there are people who want you to fail.'

I asked Ali to book my return flight to the United States and retrieve my passport. On cue, one of the men arrived with the set of documents I had given him. He apologised for the inconvenience. I perused the documents to see if they were intact. They were not. Some of the maps were missing and others had been partially blacked out. I had a dilemma: if I took the original documents out of the country, would I be in trouble at the airport? I consulted Ali the next day. He wasn't much help: it was my choice. He gave me my tickets for my flight home the following day, and I said goodbye to him.

I spent the afternoon in the hotel, packing my bags and contemplating my trip back to Tulsa. I had been away eight weeks and had had minimal contact outside the country, a couple of telexes. I went to the airport and held my breath. It wasn't as if I had stolen the documents, but I didn't have much moral support from Ali, my only real friend. Our team had shrunk to one, myself, and I was disappointed with both Robert and Salim, who had basically left me holding the bag. I was surprised that they had acted the way they did.

I tried to look nonchalant at the immigration desk and was waved through to the waiting lounge. I sat down relieved but still vigilant. I would only relax when I was in the air. I looked around and saw nothing but a sea of robed Arabs, it was primitive, with no signage. A PA system would periodically announce something in Arabic and people would rush forward to the only door onto the tarmac. I waited and waited. A large businessman in flowing robes translated the announcements for me and eventually the MEA flight to Beirut was called, two hours late. It would be a tight connection to Zurich on Swiss Air. As we took off, I heaved a sigh of relief and fell asleep.

I awoke as the plane was approaching Beirut airport. I glanced out the window. There was another aircraft on our runway. Our pilot gunned the aircraft and we swooped up over the airport and made a tight left turn as mountains loomed. We seemed to skim the buildings and flew out to sea. Our second approach was okay, the other plane had gone, and we glided to a stop, taxied and parked on the tarmac. I was met at the bottom of the steps. 'Mr. Campbell?' I nodded.' Please wait here. I will get your bag.' I handed over the tag and he ran off. The other passengers disembarked and disappeared. I stayed by the steps and surveyed the scene. The airport building was festooned with sandbags and machine guns. I started to feel very lonely and vulnerable.

It seemed like an hour passed, but it was probably only ten minutes before my man reappeared with the bag. He pointed to a nearby aircraft and I followed him at a jog. 'They are waiting for you.' I looked at the plane; it was Scandinavian Airways (SAS). I yelled, 'It's the wrong airline! I'm on Swiss.' 'No, they are expecting you.' He took my bag around the other side of the aircraft as I mounted the stairs thinking I was being hijacked, but at least leaving Beirut was good. The steward waved me forward and I found a seat at the back. The plane was almost full and the main group resembled Turkish clerics with their red fezzes and black robes. A steward counted the passengers and suddenly I realised I had no boarding pass or even a ticket for this airline. The steward counted us again and after ten minutes closed the door, and we taxied to the runway. We took off and the pilot announced our flight time to Istanbul was two hours. I slept.

At Istanbul airport I found the Swiss Air counter and introduced myself. 'Ah, Mr Campbell, we were expecting you. Sorry for the inconvenience. Our flight left Beirut before you arrived and our agent rerouted you here. We have tagged your bag to Zurich, but you have three hours before your onward flight. Can we invite you to the lounge?' He gave me my boarding pass and

I found the lounge. It was mid-afternoon and I hadn't eaten. It felt good to be in a clean, refined room.

I arrived in Zurich and had an overnight layover. It was my first time in Europe and I wanted to explore the city. It was cold, overcast and drizzling. I walked for a while, but it was miserable. I found a cosy bar and settled in. I ordered a beer. I sat there and thought, 'I don't know one person in Europe. All this culture and I have no idea what to do.' I felt homesick. I returned to the hotel and, very tired, went to bed. The following day I visited some galleries before my flight that evening.

I arrived in Tulsa to freezing conditions. The boys ran to hug me and Margaret prepared a big baked dinner to make up for Christmas. It was good to be with my family. Tulsa doesn't have an attractive winter, little snow but ice storms and wind. Our friends, Bob Perry and his family from Canada, shared dinners and outings and I felt comfortable again.

I had a lot to do back at the office. I briefed my bosses and set about getting the engineering department working. I called Des Plaines to find out if Salim had returned. Negative. Salim had quit. I arranged a meeting in Chicago to review our position. It would be easier to do the work in Tulsa, we had the skill, but we had won the work with Procon, a process specialist. Bob Bain was the senior engineer in Procon and we went through the plan. I suggested they provide concept designs and Williams Bros could detail the work so that it integrated with the production design work in Tulsa. Bob apologised for Salim's behaviour, and understood my position. We agreed on a plan and I returned to Tulsa. The next step was to call Robert Blake in Denver. We chatted on the phone. He seemed well and I told him the outcome of my final meetings with the minister and said I would send him what I needed to complete the work. I appreciated his help but regretted his abrupt departure from Bagdad. My next task was to get better maps, if possible. I talked to our land people and was directed to the Central Mapping Bureau in Washington. I wrote a letter setting out my requirements. A few weeks later I received a letter stating it was not the bureau's policy to release maps of sensitive areas.

Two weeks later I received a large roll of maps by courier. There was a note attached from the Central Mapping Bureau. 'We understand you have recently returned from Iraq. We believe you may be in a position to check details of installations in the north Iraq oil fields. We would be pleased if you could check and advise.' I was very nervous about it, but they were great maps. I decided to accept the maps but ignore their request.

The team began to scope the work and I was feeling pretty good about our progress. David Williams, the owner of the company, came by to check on things and receive a full briefing. Meanwhile, I received a visit from a fellow who said he was with the US State Department. He enquired about my Iraq visit and wondered if I had experienced anything interesting. He was very relaxed and I was very nervous. I gave him an outline of our task and recounted our visit to Kirkuk and Mosul. He asked about the level of troop movements and I replied I was not military minded and couldn't help him. After about an hour he thanked me and left. I didn't hear from him again.

Two months into the work I received a telex from Iraq. They wanted to send a team of engineers to Tulsa to review the status. Our marketing liaison made the arrangements and three Iraqis I had never met were ensconced in the Hilton. I took the drawings down to the hotel, as they had said we could work there. We met in the lobby and they indicated the bar was the best place to talk. I started to drag out the work we had done, but they waved it away. 'We can look at that later,' said one of the visitors. 'First we have some shopping to do. Then we need to find some good night spots.' It was clear they had no interest in the project – more fool me. By 9pm we were at the Crystal Pistol. Nahib had chatted up a waitress and wanted to take her to Acapulco that night and was trying to convince his colleague Qasim to take the waitress's friend along with them. The third Iraqi was sick back at the hotel. I told them Acapulco was out of the question. We had a project to review and, by the way, they'd need visas – 'It's another country' –

so there was no way they'd be able to go tonight. Nahib was only slightly fazed. 'Well maybe we could go to Las Vegas?' I took the girls aside and said, 'Tell them it's Acapulco or nothing.' I needed the Iraqis to sign off on our plan, even if they hadn't studied it. It wasn't easy, as they wouldn't come to the office. Formality seemed to get their attention, so I asked divisional manager John Grinter to arrange a lunch at the Petroleum Club, where we would sign an accord. This did the trick. They signed and I was able to get on with the design.

Some weeks later another telex arrived asking that we expand the work to cover a plan to provide Baghdad with a distribution system for a natural gas domestic supply. This required a return to Baghdad with a distribution expert. Lloyd Evans, a Canadian, was our in-house authority and he accompanied me. I now knew the ropes and Ali made the arrangements in Baghdad. Lloyd was older and had come from a retail gas marketing background, but he had never been out of North America. I felt like the old hand. Soran was to be our guide again and Lloyd gave him a list of what he needed to see. The town plan was important, and he needed to get an idea of the demographic. The ministry needed to set down the standards that were to be followed and data for current usage. Most households used kerosene, but many were switching to LPG. The water table in Baghdad is quite high and the salinity of the soil was an issue.

Soran drove us around Baghdad. We looked at housing styles and found a good restaurant for lunch. Wherever we went, Soran greeted people as old friends. I couldn't believe anyone could know so many people. In the restaurant he pointed out a man across the room who he said was a general in charge of troops near Basra, in the south. I challenged him to bring the general over. 'No,' Soran said, 'he's too important. I'll take *you* to him.' We crossed the room and he introduced General Abass. 'You are lucky to have such a good guide. We are best friends,' Abbas said, beaming at Soran. I was floored; they were fighting the Kurds in the north. Back at the table Lloyd asked Soran how people would accept natural gas when they were just switching to bottled LPG. Soran replied, 'It will be seen as a status symbol. The rich people will embrace it and it will grow from there, but it will take many years for full development.'

I met Ali in the ministry and briefed him on the Iraqi team's visit to Tulsa. He smiled and said the engineers rarely got out of Iraq and when they did they tended to go a bit crazy. I explained our progress and asked to speak to their production people, to relay to them some questions from our process group. Lloyd was happy talking to the marketing group. I consolidated the new information and felt another trip to Kirkuk would be helpful, to check more questions that had been raised. Everything was so much easier this time, as the ministry had decided that we were competent and that progress was being made. I asked Lloyd if he wanted to come to Kirkuk, and he agreed. I said we could go back to Mosul and he could see how the LPG distribution was working. We set out a couple of days later and noted the military movements. Lloyd was having second thoughts. 'Is it a real war?' he said. 'As far as I can see, yes,' I replied. 'It gets more obvious when we're in the Kirkuk area.' Lloyd sat quietly and looked out at the desert. We took a different route this time, and passed large aggregations of military equipment parked off the road in the desert. There were tanks, armoured vehicles and aeroplanes stretching for kilometres. We tried not to notice.

I met the managers of the different oil fields and we were invited for a special dinner in the camp mess. They had a separate room and six members of their top team were gathered. They were interested to be briefed on our progress. I had not prepared for this, and ad libbed a response which seemed to satisfy them. I was interested in how they kept the oil production going when they didn't seem to be drilling more production wells or using any secondary production techniques. 'Allah provides' was their response. Later when I had the opportunity to talk to them one on one I discovered they were using a primitive water flood on one of the fields. They were hungry for new technology, but only had access to Russians, who were not particularly helpful. Otherwise, they were happy and we drank lots of scotch.

When I asked why they didn't drink *arak*, they said it was for the lower classes.

We returned to Mosul and endured the same chaos we had experienced at Christmas. There seemed to be more military movements and Soran thought we should return to Baghdad the next day. I asked if anything was wrong, but he only replied that it would be better to return. I showed Lloyd the town with our guide and we had an early night. The trip back was uneventful and we arrived in Baghdad in the late afternoon. The secret service surveillance was not present this trip. The weather was pleasant. Summer could be oppressive in the capital. We had achieved all our goals and headed for home.

Back in Tulsa, the pressure was on to complete the feasibility study. Keplinger had finished its work and Procon had agreed to my plan for them to do only the concept work. Nearing the final draft stage, I needed to arrange a review with our senior management and my partners. Bob Bain flew in from Chicago and one of the partners at Keplinger came; apparently Robert was sick. With some minor suggestions everyone felt the result was excellent and we launched into final production. It was a multibillion-dollar endeavour and I felt proud to be associated with it. I was lucky to have had a top team who warmed to the underlying ideas. There were gas gathering, transmission and distribution systems for three major oil fields, amounting to a billion cfd and 150,000 bpd of LPG, with some associated gas liquids, covering half the country. We couriered off the packages and waited.

A couple of weeks later they telexed to ask that we present the report in Baghdad. My boss, John Grinter, and Lloyd came on the trip with me. We were greeted warmly in Baghdad by Ali and escorted to the Baghdad Hotel, which was starting to feel like home. Ali hosted a dinner with a couple of his colleagues at a nearby restaurant and said the presentation would be at the university. At 10am next day we arrived at the campus and were led into a large lecture hall. There were around 150 people seated. I was taken aback. I had thought we would present to the senior management of the ministry, maybe ten executives. I had no idea who these people were. After introductions and setting up some slides and overheads I started my delivery nervously. I didn't know if the audience was technical or commercial. After an hour of talking I turned to Ali and asked what he wanted to do. Questions were then fielded, mainly to Lloyd regarding the gas distribution in Baghdad. The audience didn't seem interested in what I thought was the main event. After another hour, the head of the ministry called a halt and we packed up. I was congratulated and felt relieved; it had been an ordeal. Our trip home was uneventful as we went via Bahrain to avoid the Beirut war, which had escalated.

Once back in Tulsa I felt both elated and flat. I wondered what was next.

The family were well integrated into the local community and I spent time attending family events with our friends. The county fair was a big show and the boys raced from pillar to post keeping us busy. I was very happy.

Over the next months I reviewed JV Ray's Dome pipeline and did some work on the Fairbanks gas project. There was no word from Baghdad. They had paid the bills and there was no more contact. A month later I was called to the Tulsa boardroom, where a senior vice-president, Ray Bryant, and John Hathaway, the president, were present. I had met John when I arrived in Tulsa, but had had little exposure to him since. Ray relayed discussions he had had with Brown and Root, a Houston-based contractor. B&R had been working in the south of Iraq and had received a request to provide a study of the potential to export natural gas from Iraq to Europe via pipelines. However, the request had come through the ministry of health. They felt it might be a conflict of interest, and wondered if Williams Bros would be interested. I said I could study the concept.

A few days later Ray told me a meeting had been arranged in Houston and asked if I was available. He picked me up the following day with one of his colleagues and we went to the airport. B&R had sent their private jet to pick us up and we had a pleasant flight south. A limo waited on the tarmac to speed us to the Petroleum Club for the meeting. It felt very mafia inspired to me, but everything I experienced in the USA was another movie episode. We were met by four people in a private room. The lead guy was a rotund bald man. He was an American, Charlie Zimmerman, but had been brought up in China and now lived in Switzerland. Charlie told us all this as we had coffee. They had a presentation which described the overall scheme.

Halfway through I whispered to Ray that it wouldn't fly. The pipeline costs and their projected volumes would make it too expensive. Ray said, 'Let's hear him out.' At the end I voiced my concerns, which the B&R people thought were a bit premature. They outlined the commercial arrangements. Basically US$10 million was set aside for the work. We would be paid half for our report and the rest would be paid to an offshore drilling operation run by the Barudi Bros in Beirut. I assumed B&R would be involved in some of that. Ray said we would think it over and get back to them.

Over lunch Charlie showed his true colours when he related a story of an experience he had in Algeria. 'The lion can attack you, but if you feed it regularly it will be on your side to do your bidding.' I thought, 'This guy is totally bent.' We went back in the limo and by agreement did not speak of the project. After boarding the Lear jet we were offered scotch, but kept our comments to sport. I arrived home at six. Margaret asked how the day had gone. 'Well, it was a bit different. I think I was in a movie, but I can't think of the name.' 'Did you go out?' she enquired. 'Yes, way out!' I gave her the outline of the day and she frowned, 'You be careful.'

We met in the boardroom the next day at 8am. John Hathaway joined Ray and me. Ray opened by saying, 'I think it's a great opportunity to build on Grahame's work in the north. They're willing to give us $5 million for the study. I think we could knock it off for $250,000. How did you read it, Grahame?' I said, 'Why isn't the oil ministry doing it?' 'Well, there seems to be some competition in the cabinet.' 'Ray,' I said, 'it's a fraud. It's a way for the health minister to get his hands on four to five million dollars. I could prove to you this afternoon that the plan has no merit. I think the oil ministry would see through it, and we'd have egg on our face.' 'I'm not saying we twist the outcome,' said Ray. 'Maybe it is a pile of shit. We can still do a good job and be well paid.' I turned to John and said, 'I won't be working on it and it would be good for the company in the long run to steer clear. That's why B&R aren't in.' I left them and went back to my office. I heard on the grapevine later that Ray did go to Beirut and meet with the Barudi Bros, but nothing came of it.

15. My career takes a turn

My plans for London are dashed.

Forbes Wilson was planning to set up a London office and suggested I might be interested in helping him. It sounded just right for me and I talked to some of my friends in the office. They said it was a growth area, with the North Sea starting to fire, and that offshore engineering had a big future. I still had work on the Dome pipeline and I was keen to take a trip into the Rockies with the family. I arranged two weeks off work for the holiday. My boss was happy to oblige after the success of the Iraq work. It was good to spend time with the family.

I was finding the business environment stimulating. I formed great friendships and started to understand the production side of oil and gas business. Forbes Wilson called me from London and said everything was arranged for my new role there. I was looking forward to exposure to North Sea oil and gas projects. The world was changing quickly, with new projects across the globe and the price of crude escalating seven or eight times.

Then I had a call from Sydney. The Moomba pipeline construction had hit some snags and the management was being changed. I was being offered the job of project manager for the eastern half of the project. In one sense I felt very proud to be offered such a role. The project was the biggest in Australia at that time. The eastern section comprised the third part of the main line through the mountains and the Wollongong and Newcastle pipelines. The timing was bad – I desperately wanted to go to London to extend my training in the industry – but essentially I had no choice; the decisions were being made at the highest level. John Hathaway, the president, called me into his office and congratulated me. He complimented my work in Tulsa and wished me well. The family was keen to go back to Australia, so it was a done deal.

Although cut short, my international exposure had changed my view of an engineering career. I had realised that an Australian could compete on the world stage. My training as an undergraduate gave me a basic education, but the postgraduate work had given me a maturity that came with project experience mixed with a higher technical outlook. It made me realise that engineering excellence came from a deep understanding of the culture of the world that supported it. I had been lucky to meet several mentors who were willing to spend the time answering the myriad questions I threw at them. I was now about to experience possibly the worst year of my life.

16. Project manager blues

Every day is a grind.

I had missed the turbulent political events of November, when the Labor Government was dismissed and Malcolm Fraser had become the new prime minister. I caught up with the events leading to the change of government. The Labor minister for minerals and energy, Rex Connor, was the main trigger. The media had uncovered his unsanctioned attempts to source funds for the government from Pakistani banker Tirath Khemlani. The seeds of the disaster were sown with the national grid studies I had performed years before. Conner had proposed billions be spent on a massive pipeline network that was totally unfunded. Connor's subsequent resignation brought down the government. None of this changed our pipeline project, but business was nervous.

I went to the office in my new elevated position and found a totally different mood from when I'd left. Steve Harrison was the managing director of the joint venture. Andy Meyer was back in the States. I was very pleased to work under Steve. David Evans was project manager for the western section, and I would be replacing Ken McGlynn as project manager for the eastern section. Ken had been terminated at the request of the client, which had lost confidence in his ability to do the job. The construction had not gone well; there had been major union disruption to the project. Section 2 had been awarded to a joint venture of Hornibrook, led by Corbet Gore, and APC, led by Carter Johnson, an American. Carter had upset the metal workers in Victoria when he built the ethane line across Port Phillip Bay. The metal workers had threatened reprisals and saw the current job as a good opportunity to wreak havoc.

The second major problem was the inspection regime. The pipeline codes had been written around X-ray techniques that had been superseded. The use of internal crawlers to perform the X-rays improved the quality of the checking significantly, but meant that satisfactory welds were being rejected. As an added problem, the welders were complaining that Australian steel was inferior to Japanese. This was because of the use of rare earths by BHP to achieve the required notch ductility of the steel. The union claimed that this led to faulty welding. Japanese steel did not use them due to better 'controlled rolling' techniques. Also, the pipeline was coated in coal tar enamel. In the western section this was done just before the pipeline was lowered into the trench. The eastern section was too hilly to do this and the pipe was pre-coated in a yard and transported to the site. Again, union disruption had made the process difficult, with some of the coating being more brittle than was ideal after being reheated several times due to work stoppages. This was only discovered after the pipeline had been completed through the Nepean and Cataract Gorges to the south-west of Sydney. It was feared that when the hydro testing of the pipe occurred, the coating would crack and the pipe would need to be replaced. This would cost tens of millions of dollars and set the project back many months. I had walked into a minefield.

My first meeting with TPA was catastrophic. Five Authority people sat opposite seven of my staff in a tense atmosphere. Tom Baker, the deputy managing director, pounded the table for answers. He had been told a solution to the coating problem was due. I had reviewed the reports, felt we needed to do more testing and thought it would take two months to come up with a recommended strategy. He stormed out of the room, banging the door behind him. My team sat silent for a minute, seeking direction. I asked if Jenny Grimm, our receptionist, could come in. She had been one of the earliest members of the team. Her first words were, 'What did you do to Tom? He was swearing blue murder at the lift.' I asked if she could go across the road to the TPA office and 'calm him down'. We then set about constructing a clear plan to develop our recommended strategy and make an informed decision. Tom Baker had the revised plan the next morning. Over the following months I established a warm relationship with Tom, who had appreciated my quick response after months of obfuscating from my predecessors.

Later that day I had a call from John Robinson at AGL. It wasn't friendly. He wanted to know what I was doing about the pipe coating for the 20-inch pipe that was falling off in the yard at Kembla Grange. There was 190km of it. Hoechst Chemical had provided the polypropylene to Shaw Pipe Protection, but had omitted the UV protection chemical. They had sprayed the piles of pipe with white paint, but it was too late. I met with the Shaw bosses, who dramatically threw the keys to the factory on the table and said we could have the plant, as they had no money to fix the problem. We agreed to find a compromise.

I arranged to visit the Cataract area, as it was close and I needed a day out of the office. Bob Young, the chief inspector, met me at the site office, near Wilton, southwest of Sydney. He was a big Canadian, with strong views on everything. Newham Techint was the contractor and I met the spread bosses. Bob expressed his views on the management, client and contractor and generally they were uncomplimentary. Late in the afternoon we pulled into a pub and he bought some beers. 'And what the fuck is your job on this mess?' he asked accusingly. I could tell that he thought I was some new engineer, out to make his life miserable. 'Bob, I'm your new boss.' He stared into his beer for a minute. 'Fuck,' he said, possibly regretting what he'd said earlier.'

I established a routine for the day. At 7am I would call the spread bosses to get an update on the operations. At seven thirty I would go through the mail and draft replies if necessary. At nine, Jock Telfer, the AGL supervisor working for John Butters, would come to my office to chat. He didn't seem to have much to do. Around ten I would walk around the office and chat to the section heads, and deal with any issues. At lunch I would catch up with my superiors and keep them up to date. In the afternoon I would review reports and check schedules. By 5.30pm, people would gather in the boardroom for informal meetings. Once a week I would spend a day on the various sites, to keep in touch with the operations. Every two weeks there were formal meetings with AGL and TPA, but almost every day I would receive calls from both, complaining about some aspect of the project. It was intense, and wearing on the morale.

Essentially I was supervising two pipeline contractors and other contractors building the receiving facilities for the gas at Wilton and Wollongong. This was on behalf of two clients. My main task was to form good relations with all the participants, so that problems could be resolved quickly. I had come to know that deferral of technical and management decisions quickly complicated progress.

I heard that Bob Young had been making disparaging remarks about one of the AGL managers. I called him and said he was to be in my office in two hours, about the time I figured it would take him to get there. I put down the phone before he could make a reply. Two hours later he appeared. 'I'm busy out there, this better be good.' I told him about the complaint, said if it happened again he'd be dismissed and sent back to Canada. I told him to leave. He stared at me, said nothing and left. He was my best chief and we got on well after that.

Controversy was never far away. John Butters, the AGL project chief, was currying favour with the politicians. He organised a site visit and I suggested that I go and that we leave the outspoken Bob Young out of it to avoid problems. John insisted that Bob would be OK, and I left them to it. I heard the next day that Bob had dominated proceedings and led the pollies on a merry ride. To top it off, they had retired to a pub where John hoped to push his political barrow, but Bob spent the evening telling dirty jokes, much to the chagrin of John. I received an indignant call from John, suggesting Bob be sacked. I pointed out it was his call to invite the Canadian. A week later, John Robinson received a letter from the politicians, praising the pipeline progress and particularly praising chief inspector Bob Young, who was one of the most informed people they had met. They added that Bob's suggestion of establishing a welding school would be pursued. Bob had that effect.

Harry Butler who had provided help with the environmental enquiry but quit in frustration was brought back to certify to quality of the restoration work on the right of way for all the pipelines. This proved very difficult as various government agencies gave conflicting instructions. The fire and water authorities wanted trails maintained for access but fitted with gates to deter trail bike riders. The environmental authorities wanted them all eliminated and covered in slow growing native plants. The mines department wanted fast growing vegetation to reduce the danger of erosion. Harry was the right man for the job.

He had become a celebrity with his TV show *In the Wild* and was named Australian of the Year for his down-to-earth approach to the environment. The environmental movement was dead against him, of course, because he didn't have a university degree. Vincent Serventy had been the darling of the movement, but had no understanding of how to strike a balance between development and good environmental practice.

Harry came to the house for a barbecue one Sunday and attracted a dozen of the local kids who'd poked their heads over the back fence and spotted the TV star. At one point Harry invited them in and gave an impromptu show. It was amazing – for the next hour he had them all in thrall about the bush, in our backyard! It was a great example of how intelligent teaching can capture young minds.

It was 1976; I marvelled that I had started on the pipeline in 1971. WB-CMPS had been engaged by AGL for a project to bring natural gas from Bass Strait to Sydney and to be completed in thirty months. The state government had blocked supply from Victoria and the federal government had basically nationalised the project in 1973, causing long delays as the new terms of reference were thrashed out. Severe floods and union bastardry had caused further extensive delays. Major problems with weld acceptance caused the codes to be rewritten and brought into line with the improved inspection techniques. These issues, and the contractual disputes that arose, would go on for many years after initial operation. It would evolve into Australia's largest court case up to that time. My job was to knock off the daily problems and hope the team stayed focused. I was starting to feel I could see the end of all this, and felt confident that gas would arrive in Sydney at the end of the year.

We were approaching the end of construction of the main line and had set in motion a series of commissioning tasks. Within this was the critical hydro testing of the pipe, which would validate our theories regarding the integrity of the coal tar enamel coating. In this testing, the entire pipeline would be subjected to a pressure of 10,000 kPa, which represented the minimum yield strength of the steel. We were aware that the manufacturers incorporated a factor of safety, but this stress would be the highest that the pipe would ever endure. Any weakness, however small, would be revealed. It was on this basis that we could then confidently operate the pipeline at 80% of this pressure. A completely new team was mobilised to commission the pipeline system and provide initial operations beforehand over to the owners. Steve Harrison had far more experience than me and his support was invaluable.

Before we went into operation, a 'smart pig' with accurate measuring equipment was inserted into the pipe, to determine if the pipe wall was sound, properly round and had no dents. After the hydrostatic test, the water would be drained and the pipe dried with glycol, to allow the gas to travel in the most efficient way. Various pigs are used to achieve this. Block valves are inserted in the pipeline about twenty kilometres apart, to isolate the gas in the event of a pipeline failure, and pig launch and retrieval devices are located about every 100km. The pipeline is protected from corrosion by an electric current which works with sacrificial anodes, that is, zinc rods that corrode before the steel. Monitors are placed along the pipeline to measure gas flow, temperature and pressure. These are connected to a SCADA system and a microwave communications system, to allow valves to be operated in the event of unusual events or unauthorised external interference. All the systems and devices needed to be tested before normal operations could commence. The custody transfer and odorisation of the gas occurred at Wilton, south-west of Sydney, and represented the most sensitive management problem for me. My two clients, AGL and TPA, were not on the best of terms.

The pipeline traversed the whole gamut of land use possibilities – forests, farms, water catchments and semi-urban landscapes. Other utilities and services were intersected, including railways, roads, water pipelines, power lines and sewage systems. All the authorities who operated these facilities needed to be convinced that the gas line operations wouldn't degrade their services; also, access to key points along the line needed to be maintained for emergency operations. Often these objectives are at odds with each other and acceptable outcomes require the wisdom of Solomon. This is all overlaid with the requirement to restore the ROW to its original condition, to satisfy the environmental laws.

AGL had decided to announce the arrival of natural gas into Sydney on New Year's Eve. That became our overriding target. A gas flame would be lit at the Sydney Opera House.

In the months running up to year's end there were flooding rains and rolling petrol strikes by the unions. We were forced to buy large quantities of petrol drums and locate them along the line to keep our fleet of vehicles moving. Generally, the operations worked smoothly. However just before Christmas I had a call to say the results of the pig runs revealed several significant dents in the line. The pipe would need to be excavated to discover the causes. I called George Cameron, our field supervisor, to arrange equipment, and the contractor, Cleary Bros, to do the work. George could not be contacted. I rang Bob Young, who told me Cleary Bros had been dismissed by George, and had left the site. The Campbelltown motel which had become our centre for commissioning operations only had a part-time telephone switch operator and couldn't cope.

I sat and wondered how we could sort out the developing mess. I went to the men's room, past reception. Jenny Grimm the receptionist remarked, 'You look worried.' I turned around and stared at her for a moment. 'Jenny, could you go to Campbelltown for a couple of days?' 'When?' 'Right now.' 'What do you want me to do?' 'Man the switch at the motel and be the communications centre for the commissioning. You know all the people.' She looked at me for a second. 'All right. I'll need a car.' 'No problem, and I'll give you one of our two-way radios as backup.' In ten minutes she had gone. When she arrived in Campbelltown two hours later she negotiated with the motel owner to manage the switch and rent some additional rooms. She hauled George out of bed and on the phone to me, when I instantly dismissed him. He did not respond and left the job immediately. Bob and I rehired and then turned around Cleary Bros, the contractor. Jenny on the ground gave me reliable feedback about what was actually going on.

It was raining steadily and businesses were closing for the Christmas break, so it was hard to motivate the support we needed to learn the extent of dent damage. I was getting calls every couple of hours from AGL management about the opening ceremony on New Year's Eve: would the deadline be met? Finally, the news was in. By removing the rocks that were causing the problem all but one of the dents had 'popped'. We could not operate the pipeline with dents beyond a certain limit. Bob said I needed to come out and make a decision – a 'responsible person' was required. I arrived a few hours later and stood on the edge of a large crater. Bob drew a picture for me of the problem and we discussed alternative strategies. Finally it was decided to increase the gas pressure to a point where the pipe might yield and we could certify that the pipeline met the specification. We had a 3m straightedge and an offset device to measure the deflection. This would take a couple of hours. I was the only person who could take the measurement and certify the result.

I climbed into the hole and we started. Lying on my back, I could hold the devices and make the measurement. The rain didn't stop. After an hour I reported it had improved, but was still out of spec. Bob said we were approaching maximum pressure and I became acutely aware that the pipe could burst and we may all die. I had been staring at the deflection and tried to imagine it looked better, but until I actually took the reading I didn't know. I adjusted the equipment and read the dial. Water was dripping in my eyes and I had to squint and and wipe my face with the back of my wrist.

'Okay!' I yelled up to the group on the edge of the hole. 'She's right.' Bob pulled me out of the hole and I hugged him. I then realised that I was soaking wet and very dirty, but I didn't care – we were ready to roll. All the men congratulated each other. It looked like the end of a rugby game that we had won.

I went to the motel and called Maurie Williams, the AGL CEO, to say the pipeline was ready for operations. Maurie had recently taken over from John Robinson who had retired. I still needed to put the data together and sign the forms for the government certifier, but I knew that was just a formality. The paperwork done, I thanked Jenny and the team. She had been there four days straight without a whimper. We all went home for Christmas and Boxing Day. On the 27th, I reviewed the operating performance and our teams signed off on the TPA/AGL interface protocols. Aside from some clean-up work, the job was done.

I sat in my office and stared out of the window, reflecting. I felt empty in a way. The job was largely done but at what cost? I had done nothing else for a year with hardly a day off. What had I achieved?

We still had major work on the Wollongong and Newcastle pipelines and there were many challenges ahead, but the crisis issues that presented on my arrival back in Australia had been overcome, and for the first time I had a chance to take a step back and assess my life, and think about my future direction. The London assignment was a distant memory. I felt empowered by the successful conclusion of the main line project. I also felt exhausted by the non-stop grind of the seven day a week hammering I copped from my two disgruntled clients.

I had passed a huge test with the completion of the Moomba to Sydney Pipeline. For many years I had been given challenges that had stretched my capabilities. I had no real feeling for what I could achieve but I reflected on my childhood and the self reliance that had been instilled in me by my parents and our local community. The words of my father, 'Don't expect too much in life, life is hard,' rang in my ears. My greatest fear in life had been that I wouldn't have the opportunity to do what I wanted in life. I now began to realise that I could create my own future. I decided to take a break. I sat down with a map of the world and plotted locations where friends were working; I'd visit them.

Part IV
Reflections and choices
1977

17. World trip

I become a businessman but I don't desert music.

Early in January my original employer, Eric Mansfield, one of the partners, ran into me in the street in Chatswood on his way to lunch at the Chatswood Club, a popular haunt. 'Hi, Grahame. How's it going? Congratulations on the pipeline commissioning.' 'Thanks, Eric. It's been a tough year. I think I'll take a trip around the world and take a breather on the company for five or six weeks.' He knotted his brow and replied 'Has that been approved? I haven't heard about it.' I was taken aback 'No, it never occurred to me that I'd need permission.' 'Well, we can't have our chaps just buzzing around the world willy-nilly.' And off he went. I puzzled over this and realised that he and I, and probably the entire board of the company, were on totally different wavelengths. My objective in taking a break from work was not to lie on a beach, but to meet people in the industry and bounce ideas around in a relaxed atmosphere. I resolved not to seek permission from the board. If problems arose on my return, I would deal with them then.

My first port of call was Los Angeles. I had a friend there, Ray McGraw from Hood Corporation. He was a welding expert and knew of two companies doing advanced research for welding techniques based on nanotechnology, called TIG welding. It was being used in nuclear plants and might be adaptable to the pipeline industry. We visited the Astro-Arc and Dimetrics plants. Their senior technologists took us through the research work underway. Over lunch I recounted my experiences in Australia over the past year and we talked about new opportunities. It was refreshing to discuss the next generation of welding with experts.

Back at the hotel, Ray asked if I would like to meet some senior executives at Pacific Gas and Electric (PGE) the next day at lunch. He felt they would enjoy an update on Australia. We met in the PGE boardroom and I recounted our success with the pipeline. It emerged that they were scouring the world for supplies of LPG for their business. I told them that the Cooper Basin could meet their needs. They said they had checked that out, but there was no way to get the material cheaply to the coast. I then explained that due to by-law entry of oversized pipe, the Moomba to Sydney pipeline had spare capacity and was available, as it would be hugely underutilised for some years. LPG could be injected into the line and recovered in Sydney with a receiving plant. The pipeline owners would jump at the opportunity. Their eyes lit up. 'Can they deliver 12,000 bpd?' 'Sure.' Before we finished lunch I had given them a contact and two of their executives flew to Sydney that night. I hardly had time to alert Steve Harrison of their arrival.

I was staying at the Bonaventure Hotel in downtown LA. It was a brand new hotel which had opened only weeks before. It had five towers bursting through a large atrium filled with ponds and gardens. To get to your room you had to find the right tower, and a lift which looked like a bug on the side of the circular tower took you to the top. It was a strange sensation as you rose about 25m inside the atrium and then continued outside the wall of the tower to your room level. They had over 2,000 staff, most of whom were learning the ropes with me. I had lunch with a contractor friend in the lobby area. We were led through the ponds and fountains to a booth with a beaded curtain. He looked around, contractor fashion. 'This is where you take someone else's wife, I think.'

Dizzy Gillespie was playing that night in South Central LA, at a place called the Golden Dragon. I asked the concierge how I could get there. 'You can't… It's very dangerous, because of the race riots. There have been major fires and gangs control the area.' I was disappointed, but not totally deterred. I spoke later with the doorman, Larry, to get a sense if there might be a way. I reasoned that if Dizzy was playing it couldn't be too bad. He said no taxi would go in, but he might take me. 'You'll get in OK, but how do you get out? … I'll tell you what, I have a friend who lives not too far from there. He might pick you up at an agreed time. I'll call him.' I came back that evening, as he had left a note in my room sounding positive. He clocked off work at 9pm, and we went to the club. He said his friend would be outside at 12, but he wouldn't wait long. 'OK,' I said, and went in.

The venue was completely deserted. My heart sank. It must be the wrong night. A waiter came over. 'No, he's on about eleven. It's a bit early yet.' There were a number of round tables with about eight chairs each. 'Where can I sit?' 'Anywhere you like. I'll get you that beer.' I sat and wondered what I'd do for a couple of hours. Meanwhile, my ride was coming at midnight; it all didn't fit. After an hour a few people drifted in and it felt more homely. I'd had a couple of drinks and finally a suave black guy accompanied by five beautiful women headed straight for my table. 'May we join you?' 'Of course.' He introduced himself and then the women.

Donnie sat with one of the women between us and ordered drinks all round. 'What brings you here, my good man?' I explained my interest in jazz and that Dizzy was a hero in Australia. 'Well, you've come to the right place. The room is full of the best musicians.' His eyes roved the room. I explained that Ray Charles, Count Basie and Duke Ellington had toured Down Under and enjoyed the experience. The name of the late Sydney-based American promoter Lee Gordon came up, and we talked about his enthusiasm for the music. People kept leaning over and embracing Donnie, who responded warmly. I chatted to the girls, who told me Donnie was the black equivalent of TV talk show host Johnny Carson in LA. They obviously admired him. Every now and then Donnie would introduce me to a musician as Lee Gordon's friend. The room had filled and I noticed I was the only 'honky' in the room. Suddenly a big black guy came over, booming, 'Who de cat who know Lee Gordon?' I looked at him and introduced myself. 'He was the kindest man in the world. I loved that cat. I'm Sonny Cohn with the Basie band.'

The music started. Dizzy fronted a young Brazilian band playing fresh Latin-inspired tunes. It was fabulous. After an hour the band took a break and Dizzy headed straight for our table, 'Hi, Donnie, how's it going?' He was very relaxed and clearly happy with the performance. Donnie introduced us all and I felt I was with family. The room was buzzing. Dizzy had recognised three heavyweight world champions during his first set, and the whole Basie Orchestra seemed to be in the room. In no time Dizzy was up for the second set, and the night rolled on. About 2am I realised I hadn't gone out for my lift. At 2.30, Sonny Cohn came over and started reliving his Australian visit. Donnie stood and embraced me, said, 'Thanks for the table,' and left with the girls. I started to move with the crowd, with Sonny guiding me to the door. As we hit the pavement I saw a large crowd waiting for cars. I looked around and a taxi drew up. Sonny yelled, 'Make way for de man who know

Lee Gordon.' The sea parted and I was ushered into the cab with a grand gesture. As we sped away I suddenly realised that I had not been presented with a bill. The whole night had cost me nothing. My head was spinning. I asked the driver if he knew where to go. 'They told me it was the Bonaventure, is that right? This is one of the Basie cars, Sonny said to look after you.' He dropped me off fairly quickly, as we were not that far away. I went to my room feeling very indebted to a lot of people – what a night!

I awoke in the morning to remember that I had a schedule to meet. Tulsa was my next stop, to catch Ed Robinson, my first mentor in Australia. He had the best computer models for oil and gas transmission in the country. We had lunch at the Petroleum Club and he shared his current problems. 'I'm doing a review of the new 56-inch gas export line in Iran,' he said. 'It's a three-month job in Paris and I have no one qualified and available to go.' I thought for a moment, we may be able to help in Sydney. 'What do you want?' 'Six people with big inch skills.' he replied 'Done,' I said. 'I can do it from Sydney.' 'Really?' he stared at me hopefully. In an hour I had given him a plan nominating the team members. Our Sydney team would enjoy a trip to Europe. Ed studied me carefully, 'Grahame, five years ago I came to teach you how to design pipe systems and now you are working on a world-class project where we can't put a team together. You've come a long way and I am very proud.'

When we were back in the office I telexed Sydney and then caught up with some friends who were visiting from Sydney, Joe Metka and Chris Sutton. I told them I had met a girl on the plane from Dallas who was involved with the concert that Lightnin' Hopkins was giving that night in Tulsa at Cain's Ballroom. We were having a drink in the 'Chances Are', and I talked them into going. We drove in Joe's car to the venue at north Tulsa, the black area. A large crowd was milling about outside the hall. Not many white people, but people in a good mood. We walked up the stairs and Joe asked a policeman, 'Can you get a Coke?' He replied, 'Coke on the left and grass on the right!' Seemed like it could be an interesting night. Joe came back with some drinks. There was a rock band on stage playing to what looked like a thousand people jiving about. The band finished and a guy jumped on stage calling for revolution. He wasn't very coherent, but I picked up that he wanted to burn down the town hall. In a while an announcer boomed, 'Lightnin' only strikes once and it's gonna strike now'. Drum roll... The rest of the band started a riff, but no Lightnin'. After ten minutes of riffing, the announcer came back and went through the routine again. More riffing, and finally Lightnin' appeared. Two people were holding him up. They trundled him across the stage and sat him on a stool. A guitar was strapped to him and they stepped back. Lightnin' was mute. Minutes passed;

the band was still riffing. Lightnin' hit the strings of his guitar. He did it again, with a bit more vigour, and again, and again. We were off – the groove was established and suddenly there was a wail. Lightnin' started to rock and the band lifted, the crowd roared and we were on a wild ride. Ninety minutes later it was all over. Lightnin' was helped off the stage and we left euphoric – another great night.

Chris Sutton was on a fact-finding tour of multi-product pipeline technologies. His expertise was control systems and it was at the heart of this process. He invited me to join him on a visit to the Explorer Pipeline Terminal and the DX refinery in west Tulsa. Explorer was the domain of Andy Meyer in his Shell days. I was constantly seeing cross-links in the industry and felt grateful that so many people were willing to share their experiences. Dinner was in Clint McClure's house, a Tex-Mex extravaganza. Clint had been a hit in the Australian office, with his purple plastic suits complete with cowboy boots – lizard skin, of course. He was the complete Texan 'good ol' boy', chewing on chillies. He was always cheerful and had become a good friend, along with Jake Cheeves.

On the Sunday I drove down to Jake's place, near Okmulgee on the B line. I followed his instructions, but needed to stop at a store for directions. 'Cheeves? Never heard of him, not around these parts.' I left mystified, and just drove around looking for a sign. There it was – 'Pipe Woods', Jake's property. I pulled in and was met by the dogs – his wife had fifteen Afghans. She had brought them over from Australia. We had lunch and I asked if he knew the store owner. 'Yeah, Jed. We're huntin' buddies.' 'Well, he wouldn't tell me where you lived.' He laughed, 'You had the wrong accent, coulda been a federal agent.' Jake told me he was retiring as he couldn't stand these Harvard graduates telling him how to build 'papline'. I reflected that as generations move on, the youngsters don't listen to their elders enough. I could see that there was a clash of cultures as the systems and technologies emerging drove the 'good ol' boys' out.

At the last minute I decided to catch up with friends in Houston, and made a side trip. I went for a day and stayed a week. Forbes Wilson was running the office and Hank Brolich, my tennis buddy in Tulsa, was there. I began to realise how many friends I had made a few years earlier. I called Bob Young in Sarnia to see how he was going. He had signed up to go to Tehran with the construction team associated with the group I had organised for Paris. He mentioned that his nephew, Dr Gary Gregory, was a two-phase flow expert in Calgary. I should look him up. My visit was proving hugely productive. I visited CRC-Crosse, the leading automatic welding company in the world, with Ted Bruno of MCI. Ted had worked with me on the main line in Australia.

This was followed by a visit to Exxon's Baytown refinery, the biggest in the world, and the Phillips polyethylene plant, which manufactured 400 million pounds a year. It was a busy time.

Back in Tulsa I had dinner with Andy Meyer, my boss in Sydney in 1973, and Fred Bruch. Andy had big ideas for the company in the Mid-East. He wanted the group to invest in a major export scheme from the Red Sea. Also, Syrian oil was to be developed; the Saudis were backing it, and Fred Bruch – the oil pipeline expert I had worked with in Adelaide, and a great mate of Andy's from Shell days – tossed these ideas around over dinner. It became clear that David Williams's grand scheme for a world energy engineering powerhouse had some cracks.

Morgan Greenwood had been appointed CEO under David, and would not invest in these schemes until they developed a stronger cash flow. The nuclear business under Holmes & Narver was stagnant, and cross-cooperation had not occurred. Everyone was going their own way. I reflected on the broad sweep of engineering and particularly the energy industry which had absorbed David Williams' life. No one in the USA and probably the world would contemplate building a major pipeline without consulting David first. He was a giant in the industry.

I was off in the morning to Calgary to rendezvous

with Bob Perry, an old friend from Tulsa. We'd been the best of friends. Bob is a backwoodsman and we set off in his pickup into the Rockies to find an oil drilling rig he thought I needed to see. On the way back it started to snow. It was getting dark and we seemed to be in the wilderness as we negotiated the twisting road. We rounded a bend and saw a minibus in a snowdrift. We stopped. Six people were huddled beside the vehicle. Bob asked if we could help. They waved their arms about. They were deaf and dumb. We rigged up a tow and got them back on the road. Bob restarted the van and they climbed in, after hugging us. Bob said, 'We better be getting on. It's cold.' I laughed. 'It's freezing, but I feel good.'

The next day we had lunch with some oil buddies and chewed the fat. It was good to be in the thick of the boom. Oil was king and we were part of it. After lunch we went to the university to meet Bob Young's nephew', Dr Gary Gregory, who was studying two-phase flow for oil and gas. This was a new area for me and Alberta was leading the charge. I spent a couple of days working through Gary's research as it was useful for the North West Shelf production design.

In the morning I was off to London for more adventures. I was met at Heathrow airport by a short, fat, fast-talking New Yorker named Bill Atteridge. I had worked with Bill in Tulsa and admired his enthusiasm. He apologised that Barney Moreau, the current boss of Williams

Bros in London, was not there to meet me, and said I needed to rush to the train for a trip to Cambridge. I had asked to meet the leading welding expert in the UK, John Harrison, but didn't know where or when. In the taxi to the station Bill told me I had to disembark the train at Dunphy End, where a man would meet me for a short trip to the Welding Institute. He took my luggage and said I should return to the Intercontinental Hotel that night, where I would find my bags. It was the day before Good Friday. I had been travelling all night and I sat on the train looking across at my fellow travellers in a closed cabin. I must have looked a mess in my cowboy boots and jeans. I stared back at them, thinking that I hadn't the slightest idea which direction we were going, and wondering how far it was to Dunphy End. After an hour the station was called and I went to the end of the carriage. There was no door handle. I panicked. There must be a button? No. I pulled the window down and was preparing to dive through when I saw the handle on the outside. The train was about to leave as I opened the door from the outside and stepped out. No other passengers alighted. I looked down the platform and saw a man in a suit standing alone. I walked up to him. He said, 'Mr Campbell?' 'Yes.' 'Follow me.' I obeyed and we climbed into a Vauxhall and sped through the hedgerows. Very James Bond.

We arrived at a walled set of buildings and at reception I was asked to sign in. I waited a few minutes and a confused John Harrison appeared. 'I didn't know we were due to meet. I'm off on holidays in 30 minutes. What's it all about?' I didn't know what to say. 'I've come from Australia to talk about our welding problem on the Moomba–Sydney natural gas pipeline. It's built, but the government is challenging the welding quality.' He sighed and led me through a maze of corridors to his office. It was surrounded with bookshelves filled to the ceiling. His desk was covered in reports.

We sat and I outlined the state of play and the current issues. He became absorbed and we exchanged points of view for more than an hour. I asked about his holiday commitments and he gasped, 'Oh Christ! Oh well, it can wait. This is important.' We continued talking for another hour and then went to the laboratory to see the methodologies he used to test weldments. He was developing a new acceptance protocol called crack opening displacement (COD) testing, to overcome the code/radiography impasse. This was a turning point in the industry. Basically, we had been rejecting welds with a very minor undercut for a short length. He proposed that a weld cracked to half the thickness of the steel and the entire circumference could be certified as 'fit for purpose' if the COD test was positive. That was such a strong statement it couldn't be ignored. This was a most valuable meeting.

We finished and I noticed that the place was deserted. He asked how I was getting back to London. I had no idea, but I had a rail ticket. 'OK, I'll take you to the station.' We went out to the car park. It was snowing as he dropped me off. I thanked him warmly – or as warmly as I could: I was freezing, hungry and tired. It was 4pm and dark. A train arrived after 20 minutes. I jumped aboard, hoping it was an express. Once seated I surveyed my fellow passengers. They were Scottish, mainly, very drunk and rowdy. I went to look for food and found a small counter. I could have a cheese sandwich. I took a beer to get it down and retreated to my seat. The sandwich was almost inedible, but I hadn't eaten for 20 hours.

In London I caught a cab to the Intercontinental. I was exhausted. At reception I announced myself and the clerk suggested I might have the wrong hotel. I had a confirmation telex in my briefcase and angrily swung the case up onto the desk, accidentally knocking over all the marble ornaments holding pens, etc. After rooting around I found the telex and closed the lid to find the front manager looking at me. 'Can I help you?' I handed him the telex and said my bags were somewhere. He smiled, welcomed me to the hotel and gave me a key. 'We can sort the details out later, in the morning. You look tired. Why don't you go to your room, you'll find the bags there.' I thanked him and went to the lifts. I woke at 11am and couldn't remember where I was.

I relaxed over the weekend and reflected on my trip so far. My North American travels had been amazing. I had bounced from place to place and had fruitful meetings when I had no expectations. I had kept my mind open and had no time constraints. I'd also enjoyed the repartee with friends who were generous with their time and I felt relationships had been deepened.

On Tuesday morning I met Barney Moreau who was running the London office. He gave me a rundown of the operations. We shared experiences and he organised a dinner with his team before I flew off to the continent. It was interesting to get his take on Williams Bros (WBEC). He felt Tulsa management had little understanding of Europe and that the Mid-East was the focus. I also met with King Wilkinson (KW), a project management group working on the Total refinery in Sydney. Their main office was in Amsterdam, my next destination.

LNG was on everybody's lips and Shell IPM was the technical partner of Woodside for the North West Shelf. I made a pitch for the WB-CMPS team to make a proposal. The engineering chief listened, but it was clear he thought that any engineering would be done by them. Well, I'd tried. Later I met with the KW team, which was productive as they realised we had strength on the ground in Australia. This would lead to work on the Total refinery. I then ducked over to Paris to talk to the oil companies who were operating in Australia. Total and Elf were very active, and we had useful discussions at La Defence, on the outskirts of the city. I now had useful contacts to close the loop for further discussions back home.

My old buddies from the WBEC marine group were in town for the Mediterranean gas crossing near Gibraltar. This was the same project I had worked on in Tulsa in 1975, two years earlier. Bob Aldridge was running the project, supported by Bill Brownfield, and he invited me to the briefings with the client, SEGAMO. It was a typical French arrangement, with a complicated management structure; around eight companies were involved. WBEC had bid for the job, but the French wanted WBEC's expertise without paying too much for it; hence, they had a supervisory role with Sofregas, who resented the intrusion. For me, it was a window on the cutting edge of marine engineering. I spent two days with the team. They proposed that twenty parallel pipes be laid on the sea floor, at depths of up to 1,600m. They had used submarines to map the sea floor. Dredging runs and cone samplers were used to determine material strengths for the sea bed. It was a magical interlude for me. They took me to the oldest restaurant in Paris, Le Procope, apparently frequented by Robespierre during the French Revolution – a great cultural experience.

Next stop was Zurich, Switzerland. Forbes Wilson had organised a meeting with Frank Popoff a friend of his. Frank was head of Dow Europe and would go on to head the global company. This was important, as Dow was contemplating a petrochemical plant in South Australia, which was the recipient of the liquids from Moomba via the pipeline that I had worked on. We had a productive meeting. He explained that politics drove Dow's decision making. It was studying projects in the Balkans, the Middle East and South-East Asia. Australia was fourth on its list. The key for Dow was what the government would provide for infrastructure and what tax breaks it was give to improve the viability. It was my first exposure to high-level business strategy. Technology was not an issue. Pitting governments against each other was the name of the game.

Forbes Wilson had also given me an introduction to the boss of ElectroWatt, a leading European engineering company involved in major infrastructure. Herr Schneeburger presented himself as my guide for the visit. He put a car and driver at my disposal and said he would take me anywhere in Europe to see his company's projects. I was impressed. We first went to ElectroWatt HQ, where I met the president, Forbes's friend. We discussed the Australian scene and world engineering in general. After lunch I felt like a million dollars and vowed to take advantage of the hospitality. I decided to go to the major tunnel that was being constructed through the

Alps from Switzerland to Italy which would carry cars and trucks at speed deep under the mountains. I was privileged to have a front seat watching the massive machines drilling and creating the tunnels.

Next I was off to Tehran Iran via Beirut and Bahrain. The Gulf Air flight took me to Shiraz, where I boarded a flight on Iran Air. In Tehran I met the Williams Bros team. It was like old home week. Leo Kenyon, the engineering manager in Australia, was the project manager and Bob Young was the chief inspector, along with the team I had organised in Tulsa earlier on my trip. Leo took me aside and asked, 'How can you keep Bob under control?' I smiled. 'With a four-by-two.' Apparently he had suspended our local partner by his ankles out of an eighth floor window to get his agreement on an issue. Leo had never had to deal with someone like Bob. The economy was red-hot and locals were milking it for all they were worth. It was difficult to find a hotel room and getting staff for projects was well-nigh impossible. I stopped in on the CMPS office. John Oxley was the boss and very happy to have the oil and gas office up the road. He had struggled to build a business in the mining area and had now won a job building telecommunications networks for IGAT, the local gas company. I was pleased that many of my team from the Moomba main line had fitted in so well in Iran. The 56-inch gas transmission system was a world-class project.

It was time to go home. I headed for Bali to meet Margaret for a few days. The trip had been for six weeks, but it felt much longer. I had achieved so much, with so little effort. By taking the time to visit friends I had opened up vistas I didn't know existed when I set off. It turned out to be a hugely successful business development trip. The returns far outweighed the cost. I also felt liberated, for I had crossed a line from project leader to business strategist.

18. Wollongong or bust

The unions test our resolve.

I prepared a report of my trip and sent it to the board. I had almost no feedback and no comment on my expenses. The future work I had generated kept our operations busy for months. I had time to play with the kids and decompress after my whirlwind trip. Fitting back into the daily work grind was hard but the pipeline to Wollongong needed to be finished.

We had mapped a route from the mainline to Wollongong but needed to solve the problem of descending the escarpment. The coast south of Sydney was well known for its suitability for coal mining – and equally well known for the unstable scree that had occurred over millennia spilling from the cliffs. The rail line had a long history of landslips and mining's disposal dams had created hazards.

Our initial route was discarded as unstable. I quizzed the team about alternatives and was greeted with a blank stare. 'We may have to follow the coast from Stanwell Tops,' volunteered the surveyors. 'Why don't we bury it deeper?" was another thought from the surveyors. Many alternatives were put forward and finally someone piped up, 'What about a tunnel through the ridge, that seems to be stable?' We pondered on this and finally a member of the team asked, 'What do we know about the mine workings?' This brought the meeting to a halt and we adjourned to research the area. It was a difficult assignment. The mapping was sparse and unreliable. There was a risk we could intersect old workings and our tunnel would be compromised. One of the worst mining disasters in Australian history had occurred close by in 1912, It was a gas explosion in the mine. We did more work to narrow the downside and decided to go ahead and design the tunnel. This was outside normal pipeline practice as pipelines are rarely put in tunnels, but if successful would solve our dilemma. AGL agreed with the concept and we set about detailing the design and called tenders for the tunnel construction. A specialist constructor gave us a good price that we accepted. We engaged an Austrian tunneller to supervise the constructor.

An adit (tunnel entrance) was built and we held our breath while the operations progressed. The tunnel proved a godsend and a major obstacle was overcome. I documented the progress and wrote an article for the Oil & Gas journal in the US to show how innovation can work. Always look for the solution from a different angle.

The pipeline contractor Lucas-Hood was struggling with the welding of the pipe. There were similar problems to the 34-inch mainline pipe that was Australian made. Andy Lukas was the project manager having left Williams Bros to join his father's company. He had written to AGL complaining about the pipe. A meeting was called and we gathered at the Haymarket, where I hadn't been since before Tulsa. John Butters opened the discussion in a conciliatory tone and Andy produced a large computer printout of the project schedule. It must have been six metres long. An American named Bill Burgess, the Hood senior manager, interjected, having just arrived in Australia. He looked like a middleweight fighter and had a contractor's toughness about him. He asked Andy to put the paper away and stated that he had come from the States to build pipeline. He apologised for Andy's behaviour, and said he was the new project manager. With that he stood up and left, with Andy in tow. John closed the meeting and I spoke with him outside. He was a bit perplexed. 'I wonder how Andy feels.' They were very good friends. I said I hoped Bill could get the project back on track. I had objected to Andy providing a bid for the project as his recent role in Williams Bros created a conflict. John had overridden my complaint.

A couple of days later Burgess invited me to tour the job and we spent the day together. He was impressive. At one point he jumped out of the car and went across to a dozer driver and took his place. He did some manoeuvres and showed the driver an easier way to work. We drove further down the right of way; Bill was focused on the road, his brow furrowed. Finally he said 'What can we do to get this thing off top dead centre?' I was pleased he asked the question. I admired his determination. 'You're in charge. We're here to help. Call if you want me to clear a roadblock.' He drove for ten minutes without a word, then he uttered one: 'Thanks.' We ended up in Port Kembla and I felt we had formed a bond.

Family life brightened my otherwise beleaguered existence. Corinne was born in July. Her brothers were unsure how to react to such a small baby. We all needed to adjust our lives, although Margaret had the biggest load to keep the three kids organised.

Sadly, our joy was short-lived as the unions had stepped up their pressure and made life a misery. They couldn't have cared less if the project was ever finished. We signed a completion agreement for the Wollongong line on the basis they didn't strike. They struck! We withdrew their completion bonus and they struck again. I ordered the contractor to fill in the open trench and abandon the project. BHP had been in the press, planning the expansion of Port Kembla, based on the arrival of the gas. I issued a press release saying the unions had refused to complete the job. Within hours, a call came from the metalworkers boss. 'What are you up to? We're in negotiations.' 'No,' I said, 'it's over.' 'Are you crazy? The steelworkers are depending on it.' 'Yes,

I'm crazy. Piss off.'

The next day the unions returned to work, and the job was completed in four days. I had a call from AGL, from Jock Telfer. 'I heard a rumour you stopped the project.' 'No, Jock,' I was able to say, 'it's finished.'

The Newcastle pipeline was the next challenge. A French contractor, Spie Capag, was in charge, but it had little experience with our unions. The project was the only one underway in Australia, and the metalworkers' union was fixed on soaking it to the limit. It was a relatively short job but quite difficult: you had to cross steep terrain and avoid population centres. We were in union heaven, but the industry was dying. There was little on the horizon for the following year. The Newcastle pipelines were finished very late, and the unions had won. The industry was shut down.

CMPS was struggling. The 1970s were a flat period for Australian development, largely because of inflation and uncertainty over government direction. The dismissal of the Whitlam Labor Government in 1975 had resulted in a do-nothing Liberal government led by Malcolm Fraser. All the excitement of my trip was wearing off. I was ready for a big challenge.

I had a call from Ted Peacock to come to his office, a rare occurrence. He offered me a seat and with no preamble said 'Grahame, we want you to go to Melbourne to run the Southern Region for the company.' He waited for my reaction. I didn't know how to respond. I wanted to stay in the oil and gas industry, but this was a big promotion. 'Thank you,' I said. 'I appreciate it.' It was exactly ten years since I had joined the company. CMPS was the largest consultancy in Australia, and I was returning to the place I had started. I discussed it with the family and the five of us headed south. There was great reluctance on their part as new found friendships would be lost.

19. Building a business

I return to the lion's den

Our office was on the top floor of Clunies Ross House in Parkville, between the university and the zoo. Having flown to Melbourne the previous evening I walked in the door and looked around. I couldn't see anyone, but I could smell failure. A large room to the right ringed by filing cabinets hosted the typing pool. Straight ahead was the principal secretary's corner, to the left of the manager's office; she had left the previous week. It was exactly as I had left it ten years ago. I went into the manager's office and sat at the desk and stared out over the parkland. Where to start?

John Clinch, the chief engineer, popped his head around the door. 'Grahame! I heard someone come in. Welcome! We were told you were coming.' I asked him to sit. 'What's been happening?' He hesitated and stared at the floor. 'Where do you start? It's been a bit slow.' He talked for half an hour about the staff numbers, projects, possibilities and recent history. I didn't interrupt and watched him closely. Finally I said, 'Let's go and look around the office.' We went into the general office which could accommodate about 100 staff. I greeted five people, all familiar from my earlier stay.

They were keen to talk and seemed happy that I had arrived. I noticed that not all the lights were on. I said, 'I want all the lights on regardless of who's here. It's depressing otherwise.' By morning tea, a dozen people were at their desks as the tea lady did her rounds. I smiled to myself. Gotta have the tea lady in Melbourne.

I sat with John and outlined my plans. 'First, take all the filing cabinets and put them in the back. I want the main entrance to be cleared of clutter and all the pictures on the walls to be removed. Finally, I want Nairn's desk to be put in the small office in the back.' John bridled at this. 'Mr Nairn won't like that. He's still a partner.' I said, 'Nairn may be a partner, but he's not a partner here. If he comes, he's a visitor. He works for Sydney as an international operator.' I was determined to cleanse the office. Ted Peacock hadn't had the guts to fire him, and he was in Africa working for the federal government on an aid project in Tanzania. I asked John to get a couple of the guys to help move the desk; it was a cleansing operation, very symbolic. Jane, the lead typist, temporarily became my secretary as I set about hiring one. I went through the recent monthly reports and the financials. I needed to learn how we ran the banking, and the chief clerk helped me with that. I then called all the staff to my office individually and chatted with them for about an hour each. They had no plan; everybody was waiting for work to materialise. I asked Sydney if they could give us something to do.

They came up with some bits of project work. I then spoke to the other offices in Adelaide, Perth and Brisbane to see if I could place some of the Melbourne staff temporarily to ease the cost burden.

I then set about examining the work we had done in the last five years, and listed clients we might call. Additionally, I needed to find a home for the family.

On the Friday, I called all the staff into the boardroom for a drink after work and a chat about the future. It was an open discussion, and I recorded their ideas on the whiteboard. The first week had been tough. I had no real idea what we would do, and was relying on feedback to make a start. I felt if everyone was busy doing something, even if it was cleaning out the office, it would lift morale. We had some good section leaders and young engineers who were keen to make a go of it. I managed to hire a good assistant, Janet Ryan, who started to pull the administration together and get reporting and time sheets in order, but we needed work. I made calls to a list of potential clients. They were interested in my plans, but my background was oil and gas production, and there were few companies doing that in Melbourne. After the first month, I was no further ahead. Melbourne had a different way of doing business than Sydney: Melburnians seemed more conservative, or maybe my being from Sydney put them off.

Out of the blue, I received a call from Tony Webster, head of the Dairy Corporation, who asked if I could come and see him. I took John Clinch with me for moral support and was offered tea in the boardroom. Webster reminded me that my company had designed and built the Dairy Corporation's facilities in Asia. Now the corporation had two more to build, in Indonesia and Thailand, and he would like us to start immediately. Could we manage that? I leapt at the invitation. 'Of course. I'll put the team together.' Back in the office, I rang Sydney and asked when it was that we did the last work for the corporation, 'About fifteen years ago, in Singapore.' 'Fine. Who does them?' 'John Stone. He's in Adelaide.' I called Adelaide. 'No problem,' said John, 'I'll be in Melbourne in the morning. I was waiting for the dairy board to approve these facilities; I keep in contact with them regularly.' I was amazed and wondered how many other potential projects were brewing.

Basically, the corporation was charged to sell Australian dairy products into the Asian market. This wasn't easy, as Asians generally didn't drink milk. Much to the concern of the UN health people, the main product was sweetened condensed milk for babies and children. I now had the chance to land a significant project for the office. John arrived the next day and briefed me on our history with the Dairy Corporation. What became clear was that we needed project people, because all my staff were design engineers. During the next couple of weeks, I hired Frank McNamara, a young engineer from Dow Chemical who had worked in Indonesia. He, John Stone and I went to Jakarta to meet the local client staff and scope the project.

Don Gillies was the dairy chief, and I got on well with him. He was a devotee of Scottish culture, although his family had been in Australia for many generations. After a business dinner, he took me to a famous bar, the George and Dragon. In the early hours of the morning, we discovered that his mother and my grandfather went to the same kindergarten at Ulmarra on the Clarence River, just outside of Grafton, in 1896. It was a mystery as to how we got onto that subject; Don thought it was the scotch. Next we went to Bangkok and repeated the exercise with the Dairy Corporation staff there. I was starting to feel good about the operations. On my return to Melbourne, I learned that APM, a large paper manufacturer, had asked for help on their new paper mill, and Esso in Bass Strait was responding to my feelers. By the end of the second month, we'd employed thirty project people.

Our connection with the paper industry flourished. Les Patterson was a respected industry figure. He had been with CMPS for several years, but not been able to secure work until we demonstrated project skills beyond the engineering design work. ANM in Hobart were contemplating a newsprint mill in Albury. It was a major expansion for them, and they needed to find a company to engineer and manage the development. We put together a strong bid with the Sydney office and Ted Peacock received a call from their chairman to say we'd been successful. I was ecstatic – this was hundreds of millions of dollars in investment and a major win for our company.

My world crashed the following day. I received a call from the managing director, Brian Gibson, to say his chairman had been out of line and the project could not be financed with an Australian engineer manager. He said a Canadian firm, HA Simons, would be the lead, but we could work with Simons in joint venture. I was shocked. Brian went on to say that he had arranged a meeting on Saturday to facilitate a splitting of the work.

Les Patterson and I met with their project leaders, Sven Boirdal, a Swede, and Keith Potter, an Englishman. They basically offered us the mill's perimeter fence and the gatehouse; I was seething. On Monday, I called Brian Gibson and told him they were clowns, mercenaries. I pressed him on why we had failed. He said it was the banks and particularly the investment bank Australian Investment Development Corporation (AIDC), which had blackballed us. I spoke to Peacock about this, and he undertook to investigate.

A few weeks later a meeting was arranged in Melbourne with the AIDC investment banker responsible for blackballing us. Peacock came down from Sydney and we asked him over lunch why CMPS was not bankable. 'You don't have the project management skills; no Australian company has. We have to learn from North America.' I told him about my Tulsa experience, where I had shown them how to do it. Peacock chipped in with our Kurri Kurri smelter experience and other major projects. I asked the banker if he had read our submission. 'No, I don't go into that much detail.' 'Well, you've set Australian firms back a few years with this decision.' It turned out that the banker had been with SMEC, the government engineering group originally responsible for the Snowy Mountains Scheme. Afterwards I said to Peacock, 'It was our fault. We need to canvas the banks and let them know what we can do.' It was clear that in the age of project finance, the banks pulled the strings. We had just been blindsided by an ignorant investment banker, and it was our job to correct that.

During meetings with the Canadians over the next few months we were subjected to humiliating questioning of our skills, but we clawed a sizable amount of work that they couldn't manage back into our office. This was a pivotal period for me, as I had not been directly exposed to the rough and tumble of international competition. These people would destroy us for commercial gain; to hell with the client. Brian Gibson became a good long-term friend and he began to realise that the success of the project lay with our performance, not these foreigners.

After six months we were at capacity in the office at a hundred people, and making good money. I was proud of the team and wondered what I could do next. However, there was a fly in the ointment: Nairn. He had returned from Africa and was surprised to see all the activity. He was also upset about his desk having been moved and let it be known that he was a partner and was due respect. He made demands on my secretary for money from petty cash and expected her to run his errands. I had instructed her to be pleasant to Nairn, but to give him nothing and not let him order her about. However, I was not always in the office, and he always seemed to appear when I was out. I finally had a showdown with him in the corridor. I made it clear that he was a Sydney, not a Melbourne, operative, and I would 'knock his block off' if he upset my secretary. He threatened to report me to the chairman. I said, 'Fine; the sooner, the better.' That was the last I saw of Nairn. He resigned a month later to join the government.

Despite the fact that we were in Melbourne, very little of our work related to Melbourne. We were not part of the establishment. I wasn't sure if this was important, but I wondered whether I should tackle the issue. A lot of government work was handed out, but we received none, in spite of now having a sizable office. I visited the state instrumentalities and was listened to politely, but I wasn't a member of the Australia or Melbourne Clubs. I hadn't gone to school in Melbourne.

We were approached by Coors brewery in the USA to work with them on a new aluminium can production line in Ballarat. They had heard from Alcan about our work on the smelter at Kurri Kurri in New South Wales. Our lead industrial man working on the paper mill went to Golden Colorado to develop a proposal. We were bidding against Bechtel. After a couple of months, a proposal was submitted and warmly received. The feedstock was coming from Alcoa's smelter in Point Henry. After clarification meetings, Coors indicated we were the preferred tenderer and negotiations were commenced. About a month later, I had a visit from the Coors chief. He invited me to lunch to say they had been instructed by the government to deal only with Bechtel, as Bechtel was Alcoa's and the government's manager for the smelter work. The Victorian government didn't think an Australian company had the skills. Once again, ignorance dealt Australian engineers a black eye.

I was approaching the end of my first year in Melbourne. I felt I had achieved quite a lot, but had an empty feeling in my stomach. I longed to work again in the oil and gas industry and to be back in Sydney, my home town. Our work in South-East Asia had progressed well, and the office was buzzing. I had no real connection with Melbourne and had made no friends outside of the office. As an engineer, I was learning nothing, and the management challenge was waning. We could make money, but it was all outside of Victoria. I attended monthly management meetings in Sydney and again felt alienated in trying to share experiences. The other regional managers were focused on their own problems and saw no bigger picture synergies. My success in Melbourne was not being replicated in other parts of the company. Sydney seemed to be the major problem. It was clear that the head office was not performing, and it was growing more expensive by the month as Peacock was trying to follow new management trends rather than returning to basics. The board thought that business was cyclical and that poor performers would eventually rise again. To me, this seemed a suicidal approach. No one was challenged, and there was no plan to find new business models to take advantage of our market position.

I received a call from Steve Harrison, the former Williams Bros boss in Sydney. He had moved to Houston to work for Roy M Huffington, a successful independent oil producer. By accident, Roy had discovered the largest gas field in Indonesia and built an LNG plant at Bontang. They were planning another in Trinidad in the West Indies, and Steve enquired if I would like to be the country manager, based in Port of Spain. Now, this would be a radical change. He suggested I think about it and if I was interested, could I fly to Houston in the next day or so to discuss the prospect. I sat there looking out over the park; it was raining and cold. How did this stack up against a tropical paradise?

Two days later I was in Houston. I met Steve, Roy, Roy's son Michael, and George Spear, the world guru of LNG. Roy asked if I'd been to Trinidad and I said I hadn't. He said, 'Well, stop by on your way home.' The next day I was in Port of Spain. I met the Australian trade commissioner, Graham Hargraves, and in eight hours he organised visits to schools and local businesses, a swim at Maracas Beach and a cocktail party in my honour at his home to meet his friends. That evening Graham put me on the plane to London to connect to the Australian flight. I went around the world in five days.

Back in Melbourne, I collected my thoughts. If I accepted, my pay would be tripled, and I would be on full expenses for food and lodging in my new home in Trinidad. Taking the job seemed an obvious choice, but I needed to discuss it with Margaret and the kids, who had just about become used to Melbourne. They were understanding, and I emphasised the warm tropical beaches, but it was another major disruption to them.

A few days later, I flew to Sydney to tell Peacock. I explained that I was happy in Melbourne and appreciated that he had trusted me to run the southern division, but this was a great opportunity to develop my international experience. He offered me more money to stay. I said, 'It's not about money,' and returned to Melbourne.

The last few years had been tumultuous. I had been

in the USA and Iraq, and spent a difficult year back in Sydney finishing the Moomba pipeline. The trip around the world had been pivotal. I realised I could communicate with my peers in the oil and gas industry and create successful outcomes. My engineering training combined with the project experience had made me confident. The year in Melbourne had made me realise running a business was tough but rewarding. I seemed to be on the path I had always envisioned, but the fights with Nairn had dragged down my spirits. I loved the project work, but the petty corporate issues I found distasteful. My new adventure would put me back in the oil and gas world, and on the other side of the fence: the client side. I was very excited about the prospect.

Part V
Around the world with energy
1979

20. On island time

Where Calypso sets the rhythm of the day.

We decided to rent our house in Melbourne to keep a base in Australia. I had no idea when we would return or to where. Our new life overseas, now we were a family of five, was another adventure, a leap into the unknown. Margaret was left to cope with school issues and packing up the house. I flew off to Houston to acquaint myself with the new company. I relied on Steve Harrison to point me in the right direction. On my last day in Melbourne, David Giddy, the finance director, flew from Sydney to make a last-ditch effort to turn me around. Giddy was an old naval man and a confidante of Peacock. I was starting to understand the nature of the organisation. It was a mark of respect for me that they went to so much trouble. I think he understood where I was coming from, but the other partners clearly thought I was turning my back on what was a privileged position at my age in the organisation, and resented my leaving. I said I might return, but made no promises. I knew I might not be welcome back, but that was a risk I was happy to take.

I arrived in Texas to a red-hot economy. Oil was king, and Houston was the oil capital of the world. It felt so good to be back in the oil world. Huffco, as it was called, was in a downtown office connected by a bridge to the Hyatt Regency hotel, which was my home for the next couple of months. I shuttled between there and Port of Spain in the process of setting up the operations. Huffco was a different company to what I'd expected. They had completed the world's biggest LNG plant in Indonesia with a staff of thirty people. Roy Huffington believed that a core staff could achieve more by outsourcing most services, as long as the managers kept in close contact and worked in a collegiate fashion. There were few written instructions and the key executives met in his office every other Saturday for a catch-up meeting. It didn't matter where you were in the world – you *had* to be at that meeting. People were expected to travel at short notice and be available at any time. I met with Roy when I arrived to discuss the company's policy on setting up new operations. Roy looked and talked like John Wayne. 'Grahame, everybody speaks well of you, and I trust you'll do a great job in Trinidad. When you make decisions, just reflect: "Is it reasonable?" That's our policy. Welcome aboard!'

I quickly met the team, which consisted of the development group and the exploration team. Roy Huffington was an independent oilman. He had come out of the Humble Oil Company, which was eventually bought by Exxon. A wildcatter was an explorer who drilled in new areas. Roy's view on wildcatting was: never drill further than you can see a producing well. He believed he was smarter than the big corporates, and reasoned they missed a lot of the good pools through poor interpretation of the geology. He had gone to Indonesia looking for oil and discovered the largest gas field in the country. To an oil man this was poison; at that time there was no market for gas. He ran into George Spear, who suggested he look into LNG, which was in its infancy in the world. George had successfully developed the Brunei plant for Shell and had built a team which became available for Bontang in Kalimantan. The chance to build a new plant in Trinidad arose when Huffco was appointed by the government to be the operator for a consortium comprising Tenneco, Peoples Gas of Chicago and the government itself. Steve Harrison was the project director; he was based in Houston to direct the small project team supervising King Wilkinson. KW was retained to do the feasibility study. I had met their representatives on my tour in 1977 in Den Hague. My job was to set up an office in Trinidad and coordinate the local engineering and government requirements to get the project ready for development.

Steve Harrison organised a series of meetings to acquaint me with the status of the project and how I should organise my work in Trinidad. We had three partners with divergent goals. Tenneco and Peoples Gas were primarily interested in acquiring a new source of natural gas. Tenneco had fought very hard to be the operator, but the Trinidad government had recognised Huffco's success in Indonesia and Tenneco's failure in Algeria and Canada. Tenneco resented Huffco's success. King Wilkinson had the senior role in producing the feasibility study, but much work was required in Trinidad and the government, our third owner, wanted to maximise the work done by local firms. Steve believed I could bring this all together, both from a cultural and technical point of view. He thought an American would be less effective in that country. Years earlier I had been on the team to select the site for the Australian LNG project on the North West Shelf, and I was familiar with the key issues that needed to be addressed to achieve a cost-effective design. In many ways, Point Lisas in Trinidad was an easier location. Our plant would have a protected marine terminal in the Gulf of Paria. The only downside was the potential for seismic activity, and earthquake design was critical for the sandy foundations. Several existing gas conversion plants in the estate and the current construction of the steel plant next door were excellent reference projects for me. Trinidad had a long history of oil-field development and oil refinery operations. The workforce was experienced, although highly unionised.

Staying at the Hyatt Regency in Houston opened my eyes to the high-powered oil clientele. Booths around the lobby were filled with businessmen hosting their Arab guests in the evening before heading for private dinners in nearby restaurants. They were entertained at a piano bar by an Australian pianist, Julie Hibberd. Julie introduced me to the local jazz scene, and I discovered her sister was about to marry a geologist, Bob LaRue, who worked for Huffco – small world! Bob was about to be posted to Balikpapan in Indonesia, to support Huffco's operations. Houston was the centre of the world for oil and gas development, and 1979 seemed to be the peak of the oil boom that had triggered rampant inflation around the world. I went to the Houston Petroleum Club several times to be in the swirl of oil tycoons doing deals with the OPEC chiefs, and many hopefuls including Trinidad government officials wanting to cash in. After my time with the Iraqis in 1974, when it was just getting started, it was intoxicating for me to see the frenzy.

In Trinidad, I stayed at the Hilton Hotel, which was unique – an upside-down hotel. It was built on the side of a steep hill, with the main facilities at the top and twelve floors of rooms descending to tennis courts at the bottom of the hill. The floors were numbered going down. It overlooked a large park called 'the Savannah', popular with the locals for morning runs, walks and general fitness activities. Beyond this was the dockland area and the Gulf of Paria. You could see Venezuela on a clear day. The hotel was the business heart of the country, which was experiencing a boom based on oil and gas production. Everything was in short supply, making house hunting hard. Homes for rent were rare and, if available, were expensive. New cars were only obtainable after a long wait.

The tennis club at the hotel was the best place to meet people; many locals were members. I played every evening and met a broad spectrum of future friends who gave me an understanding of the culture. Every Tuesday evening the hotel hosted a cocktail party for guests to connect with local businessmen. I met the bankers, lawyers and accountants who would be my contacts in establishing our operations. My best friend was Peter Baillie, a food importer from Canada who had married a local girl. Peter played tennis and was a keen sailor. I found a totally different attitude to life here than I had ever experienced. The locals all had jobs, but many other things lit up their lives. There was a bond of friendship that made me feel that I was important to them and that I could seek help if occasions called for it.

On my second visit, I put some of my newfound friendships to the test. The exploration guys in Houston needed to register with the government their interest in exploration permits, and had asked if I could I get the documents and bring them back to Houston. It sounded simple, but I had one day, a Friday, to do it. I went to the oil ministry and discovered I needed $25,000 to pay for the documents. I had no bank account or money. I remembered a banker from Barclays at the hotel cocktail party and found him. He was polite, and we discussed opening an account. No problem. I then asked if he could give me an overdraft for $25,000. He said it was illegal for foreigners to run an overdraft, and I had no credit rating. I said I had an hour before the ministry closed and I was on the plane that night back to Houston. Could he see his way clear to cut some corners? He looked at me for a few seconds, then said, 'I'm sure it can be sorted. I'll draw the bank cheque right away.' I thanked him and dashed across the way to get the documents. Two weeks later I was back with several hundred thousand dollars to set up the accounts correctly. Barclays became our bankers.

Several things happened during those early times to make me realise that trust is a very strong thing. I had run up a large bill at the hotel and was leaving at 4am to go to the airport to fly to Houston. The hotel ran a fleet of taxis, large left-hand drive American cars. I had struck up an acquaintance with a driver, Hamid, whom I generally used. As I was checking out, the clerk said my American Express card had a limit, and I was well over it. I retorted that there was no limit on Amex. He corrected himself: it was the hotel that imposed a limit on how much one could spend using an Amex card. He threatened that hotel security would not allow me to leave the premises until I paid my bill another way. I became angry, for I had no other way to pay. Hamid, the driver, came in and said we must leave or I'd miss the plane. I explained the situation, and he immediately peeled off a couple of thousand dollars and gave it to me. 'Pay me when you get back, in US dollars.' I couldn't believe a taxi driver would carry that amount of cash. Hamid was full of surprises, I subsequently found. He ran several businesses and used the Hilton taxi job as an entrée.

One day, when I was in the market for a car, I became aware that a local who was moving permanently to Toronto was trying to sell his vehicle. He wanted to do the transaction in a week's time for $20,000 cash. The snag was that I was going to Houston the following day and would not be back for a couple of weeks. So I asked my friend Peter Baillie to hold the $20,000 for a week, give it to the car owner and store the car for me till I got back. The arrangement went off without a hitch, and I had solved my car problem. I was grateful to Peter and discovered a lot of business was transacted like this. I had Roy's dictum in the back of my mind: just be reasonable.

However, I very quickly discovered that outside the Hilton hotel environment, few things worked in the Western way. The hotel was a cocoon that protected the foreign businessman – at a cost, of course. Outside, there were no guarantees. I found Trinidadians to have a great sense of humour. It seemed that to them failure was fun. They loved to recount stories about people trapped in lifts for hours, traffic jams caused by truck breakdowns and shortages of foodstuffs in the supermarkets. Music dominated their life and Carnival lasted from December to February. Trinidad Carnival is one of the biggest celebrations in the world. Half a million people don costumes and participate in the parade. This is half the entire population of the country. It follows the Christian tradition of Shrove Tuesday prior to Lent and the events surrounding that. It takes months to organise the music, costumes and dance routines. The hills rang with steel band practice and calypso was on every street corner.

Office space was facilitated by Tenneco, which was drilling offshore and had its operations in the Tatil building across the Savannah. Bob Cooper was in charge, and he helped me establish my office suite on his floor. I managed to hire a secretary, Gail Campbell, a local who turned out to be invaluable although unconventional. She was as bright as a button and made me realise there are no problems, just things to do. Her sense of time was different to mine. If I asked her to type a letter and later asked how it was going I would get one of several responses: 'Oh gosh' meant she had totally forgotten it, 'Just now' meant she would start soon and 'It's coming to come' meant I would probably have it the next day. It was always an experience trying to organise tasks and schedules.

It was time to return to Australia and bring my family over. Trinidad must be the most distant place on earth from Australia. It takes a couple of days to travel by air. In fact, it takes a day to get from Port of Spain to Houston. I had been making the trip every two weeks, to follow Roy's Saturday meeting in Houston edict.

1979 was a pivotal year for the world. The Shah of Iran was deposed, and the peak for oil prices had been reached. America was reeling from high prices for energy imports, but the early signs went unnoticed in Houston, as business was still booming. Nothing happens in Trinidad without social interplay. I needed to spend more than half my time meeting people who seemed to have no connection with my job. Gail kept me tuned in. We had started site geotech studies and needed to investigate possible earthquake activity, as we were situated on the 'ring of fire'. The site was sandy, and liquefaction was an issue. We had hired a Texan company to do the work. They needed to import a large drilling rig. That was the start of the problem. Gail came to my office. 'Errol wants to see you.' 'Errol? Errol who?' 'He's the head of immigration' 'Could you make an appointment for tomorrow?' She came back a few minutes later. 'He'd like to see you today.' 'OK, I'll go this afternoon.' A few minutes later she was back. 'I think he'd like to see you now.' 'Is he mad or something?' 'Yes.' I wondered what it could be about; I had no issues with their office and had set up a protocol for our people visiting. I called

Ron Cottee at the Energy Board to help. He was my liaison with the government; he always had a smile on his face.

We arrived and were shown in. Errol was a big man wearing a safari suit and a grim expression. He motioned us to sit and started shouting at me. I was transfixed. I couldn't understand him because he was shouting in patois, all I was able to make out was, 'We have him in jail. He works for you.' I turned to Ron. He asked if I had a drilling operation going. 'No, we have people on-site doing preliminary work, but the rig hasn't arrived.' Eventually, it transpired that a subcontractor to our contractor had breached his visa. He came in on a tourist visa; it ran out, and he had tried to have it extended. 'Why?' they asked. 'We haven't finished the job.' Bang! They arrested him. I said to Errol, 'He doesn't work for me.' Big mistake! Errol launched into another tirade. I hung my head and finally promised never to do it again. Errol stood, and we were dismissed. As we walked out, Ron said, 'You should have introduced yourself when you arrived. He was mostly upset by that. Have a barbecue and invite Errol and all the department heads.'

Back at the office, there was more trouble. I found that the drilling rig had arrived on the boat with no papers, and customs wouldn't allow it to be unloaded. It was Friday afternoon, and the ship sailed over the weekend; it would set us back months. It wasn't a good day. Gail came in to go for the weekend. 'Yo lookin' so sad. It's the weekend. What's wrong?' 'Nothing, I'll see you on Monday,' I said, but she wouldn't leave till I told her. She jumped up and left, and I wondered what I could do. Then the phone rang. It was the drilling contractor. 'You're a genius. The rig is being unloaded. Thanks!' I'd had no idea. On Monday I quizzed Gail. 'Sarah down the hall did it all. Her brother runs Customs. I just mentioned you were sad.' Gail performed many similar miracles over the next months. Doing business in Trinidad was different, but when I thought it through, it made sense. In a country when nothing works, everybody has to help each other to get through the day. I was beginning to like it.

The airport was the biggest challenge. It was halfway across the country and more than an hour's drive, with difficult traffic. Flights were always full, because the locals made many bookings on the off chance they might travel. Everybody knew this, but the airlines did nothing about it. You just went to the airport and hoped to get on. I never failed to find a seat on a plane, but it was a bit nerve-racking. Eventually, you find everybody is related or knows someone who is. So when you go to transact something, from air bookings to buying LPG for the house to the most trivial transactions, you must spend time establishing the network. I think Trinidadians just like the social interaction, and it can be fun.

However, it's not behaviour relished by hard-headed Texas oil men on a mission.

I participated in the first joint venture meeting for the LNG plant, where the Trinidad minister for trade and our US partners were trying to agree on the sales plans for the project. I was appalled by the Americans' behaviour. Their attitude implied they were doing the locals a favour by building the plant and they should realise it. The minister listened patiently and left for another meeting, with the New Zealand Cheese Board for the import of cheese. Both meetings were of equal value to him, but the second was more pleasant. My debriefing with the Texans was feisty. I gave them my impressions and said the locals were sophisticated and would not be bullied. The contracts would be drawn up under English law and in T&T currency, among other things. They harrumphed and left. I spoke to Steve Harrison about our strategy, and we agreed that that type of meeting was counterproductive.

Dr Ken Julien was a university professor but drove Trinidad's industrialisation. The country had oil, but the large gas reserves were being utilised as feedstock for fertiliser and methanol plants. About eight had been constructed at Point Lisas, down the coast in the Gulf of Paria. Julien had set up an industrial estate, where the LNG plant was to be located. A direct reduction steel plant was under construction next door. Nothing happened without Julien agreeing. He was chairman of the National Energy Board, the steel company and the LNG consortium, along with many other roles. He was an engineer and had been the founder of Trintoplan Engineering, our local partner designing the site works. I regularly visited the office to monitor design progress.

The coastal engineering was of particular interest to me, given my role on the North West Shelf LNG project. When I approached Rafael Maraj, the leading engineer in the field, he was suspicious that we were not serious, and wondered if he would get paid. It was clear that engineers had a tough time. I reassured him and gave him the brief. His work was exemplary, and I made sure he was paid on time. However, Trintoplan displayed all the bad characteristics of the locals: time and cost were flexible. There was a plane load of executives arriving from Houston to review the site engineering, and the Trintoplan report was key to the review. A couple of days before the meeting, I called to get an advance copy to review. The woman I spoke to said they were all in Miami for meetings and would be away a week. I blinked. 'What?' I drove out to their office near the airport and discovered that the senior managers looking after my project were gone, but the engineers were there. I set about mobilising them to produce the report. I was back in my role as a consultant. The meeting went off without a hitch, and the Houston boys complimented me on the report. 'We didn't believe the locals could produce such quality.' I chuckled. 'Thanks, I'll relay the comments.' The following week the Trintoplan senior managers called and apologised for their absence, and thanked me for my help. In Australia, they would have been sacked, but we had no alternative here.

The site needed large earthmoving works to prepare it for construction. The obvious plan was to secure fill from the hinterland, and we had costed the haulage alternatives. I was paid a visit by executives of a Japanese construction company, which owned a dredge that had just completed some work. They proposed to source the material from the bay and pump it ashore. I asked if they had discovered suitable sand, as the gulf was mainly fine sediment from the Orinoco River in Venezuela. They stared impassively at me, perplexed; then one replied 'No, we will find some. You need not worry we are expert and will solve all your problems.' Pressed them. Do you have costings? Have you done tests on the settlement characteristics of local material, as time is an issue for us.' Again they stared at me impassively. 'We solve all problems.' I thanked them for their time, thinking they would leave as it was clear to me we couldn't use them. They produced a draft contract and asked if I would sign a memorandum of understanding. I said no, I didn't think they were in the ballpark. They protested that the prime minister of Trinidad was backing them and that we had no option. I said we had plenty of options, and none of them involved their plan. They were insulted, stood and said I would be hearing from the prime minister. I shrugged my shoulders and showed them out.

The Japanese were interesting. They had several companies operating in the country and seemed to be successful. I regularly visited the steel plant construction next to our site, to see how the contractors were performing. It was an ant's nest of workers. I watched a ship loader that had been delivered from Japan being installed. It was fascinating how the teams worked together. On the other hand, a Japanese civil construction firm struggled to pour concrete and get the embedded holding down bolts in the correct position. I noticed they welded the bolts to the steel reinforcement, rather than suspending them on an independent frame. Their method was cheaper, but eventually more expensive when you had to cut out the bolts and redo them. It was totally cultural. In an enclosed environment, the Japanese worked very well. When there were externalities, the system fell apart. I never did hear from the dredgers again or the prime minister.

The US energy scene was changing. Surging prices were being overseen by the federal agencies and the policy of 'rolling costs into the rate base' was being challenged. Essentially, gas companies could spend any amount of money efficiently or inefficiently and still recover their investment through government-approved tariffs. The government was suggesting that incremental gas would be charged at the incremental price. I ploughed on, oblivious to this, trying to unravel the mysteries of Trinidad life.

Peter Baillie introduced me to Francis Pau, a relative of Charmaine, his wife. Francis did many things, but mainly ran the most popular restaurant in the Caribbean, La Cocrico. People came from Europe and North America to taste his French-inspired cooking. He was a perfectionist and spent three months a year in France keeping abreast of trends. Francis also played the French horn in the Trinidad symphony orchestra. We became friends, and he suggested that I audition for the clarinet seat, as they were short at that time. My audition was successful. Several times Francis invited members of the orchestra to his restaurant after hours, to jam and savour his lime soufflés. I met many locals at the rehearsal sessions, including Alan DeFreitas, a singer who also read the news on TV. My colleagues in Houston were bemused by this development in my life. Our marketing director, Byron Applegate III, asked, 'What does it do for Huffco?' I replied, 'The president is the patron of the orchestra.' 'The president of what?' 'The president of the fucking country!' He shut up. I continued, 'You know those exploration permits we're after? Well, the president knows I run Huffco here, and a word is always welcome on behalf of friends.'

On a subsequent visit, Byron insisted on meeting at the Hilton to discuss his meeting with the oil minister, Errol Mahabir, who had a reputation for corruption. I suggested we deal only with Ken Julien, but Byron was determined. He insisted that we hold our conversation in the bathroom of his hotel room, with the shower running to muffle the sounds in case the room was bugged. I despaired. 'Byron, you're overdoing it.'

The following evening I drove him to Mahabir's home in San Fernando in the south part of the country, where we met with the minister. I was totally unimpressed, he didn't seem to know much about the oil industry and mainly spoke about arrangements that needed to be in place. He was a rotund man who obviously liked his food.

Trinidad prided itself on its racial integration. About 40% of the population was black, and the same percentage Indian. The rest were Chinese, Syrian and there was a small white residual. The Indians were mostly rural – a hangover from the indentured labour period which filled the gap when slavery was abolished. The blacks became the city dwellers and took the top government jobs. The Syrians and Chinese were the merchants. On the surface, all was well, but the Indians resented their rural status and wanted a bit of the action. Mahabir was at the forefront of that pressure, and San Fernando was his base. The blacks, on the whole, were very relaxed, and Carnival was their thing. Prime Minister Eric Williams was black and had held office since independence. He was a noted historian and had a strong approach to keeping the peace.

Carnival was coming up, and Gail encouraged me to sign up. She was playing with Peter Minshall, who had the coolest masquerade band, and was popular with women. Peter was a designer with the New York ballet. I went down to Edmond Hart as directed, and decided to dress up as a goblin, along with 250 others. The costume was minimal, which was good as the weather is often very hot and humid. The band was divided into several sections, all connected by an overriding theme. We needed to practise a few times to get some dance routines set, and then would turn up on the Monday afternoon before Shrove Tuesday for a full rehearsal.

On the weekend, the king and queen of Carnival were proclaimed, and the clubs hosted non-stop parties. The Country Club in Maraval, with its large clubhouse and extensive grounds and sports facilities, was our place. The staff all seemed to be over 70, and it hadn't had a facelift since independence, but any blemishes disappeared under the Carnival bunting. After the Sunday night party, Peter took me to the Jove Festival, the 'dirty Carnival'. It traditionally starts at 4am, and centres on your favourite steel band. Ours was the Trintoc Invaders. It felt eerie to be to walking the streets quietly with hundreds of others. We arrived at the site to find people covering themselves in oil and mud. I had my wineskin for refreshment because I knew when the sun rose the temperature would hit the high 30s and the humidity would be a killer.

Peter introduced me to some of his friends as a novice. Everybody was in a high state of excitement as they prepared for the fray. A girl started rubbing oil on my back. She laughed when I jumped and put some more oil on my arms. Suddenly the band started: it was right on 4. A hundred steel drummers hit their instruments, spread over fifty metres. The percussive impact was enormous. They wailed and started moving out, with some 200 people trailing. Another girl rubbed her body against mine. I looked around for Peter, but he was gone. She grabbed my hand and took me along with her in the wave of people shimmying down the road. It was intoxicating. Then the girl disappeared into the crowd. I felt alone and exposed. Where was Peter? What happens now? Another girl rubbed against me and we blended into the swirl. The music throbbed and the entire crowd was grooving. I felt another woman on my right side put her arm around my waist; we were swinging hips together. I looked across and a couple seemed to be having sex while dancing. I'd heard of 'wining the woman down', dancing behind her and pulling her almost to her knees. Maybe I should be doing that? I wasn't ready for this.

Peter reappeared. 'You OK? I like your girlfriend.' 'What?' The band drowned out normal speech, so we had to yell. Both girls had disappeared, and Peter was grinning. 'Just go with the flow.' I was shuffling along in the middle of a crowd who seemed to circulate at an astonishing rate. Time was not linear; I had no idea where we were or how long we had been dancing. I fell in and out of love every two minutes. I noticed we were entering Independence Square and that the horizon had a slight glow. I was exhausted and paused for a swig of wine. Two bands intersected and I was confused about which way to go. I paused again to try to find a familiar face. A third band approached, and the music became mixed. Then, as the music receded into the distance, I wondered what I should do. The sun was rising, and I sat in the gutter and waited for the band to return. I was filthy, tired and had blisters.

A swig of wine revived me, and I squinted around. Another reveller flopped beside me, looking even worse than me. 'Thirsty?' I asked. He looked at me quizzically, and I squirted a stream of wine in the direction of his face. Some went into his mouth. He perked up. We sat there surveying the scene and a band passed in full throttle. I gave my friend another shot of wine, which he swallowed, and I jumped up to join the group.

Once the music got my feet working, the pain eased. I felt I had gone through a barrier. We travelled along

Fredrick Street, and I knew I was heading in the right direction. My companions were jolly and we boogied arm in arm, oblivious to the surroundings. I was beginning to feel I was a local and started being less self-conscious. We were back at the Savannah, and I broke off to figure out where I had left the car.

The sun was a killer, and my spirits slumped again. I was alone and trudged towards the car. When I arrived home, the family looked at me and wondered if they should call a doctor. I fell into the shower and realised I had two hours to make the rehearsal for the main event. I slipped into my goblin costume, much to the delight of the kids. The whole idea of Carnival is anonymity. Gail had explained that she didn't play 'mas' with her husband; he was in another band. The masquerade makes you anything you want to be. At that moment, I wondered if I would last the distance. Some 5,000 of us met by the Savannah and the marshals took us through the routines. I had put two pairs of socks on to quell the pain in my feet and some wine helped.

After three hours was back home to get ready for the Country Club party. The club was the No.1 place to go on the eve of Shrove Tuesday. Margaret and I set off in our finery. We met Peter and Charmaine and some of Peter's friends who were sharing a table which was decorated to the hilt. Everybody was dancing and drinking. I paused for a minute to catch my breath when my gutter friend of that morning came over and thanked me for saving his life; he looked much revived and vaguely familiar. Peter told me I moved in grand circles. 'What do you mean?' 'That was *Mick Jagger*. Is he a mate?' I laughed. 'I'm hopeless with faces, but his voice was familiar. No, I just gave him some wine in the square after I lost you this morning.' 'Well, he seemed pretty grateful.'

I was feeling much better on Tuesday morning after a few hours sleep. I slipped into my costume and headed for the Savannah. Brian Page had organised the drinks and the road band with his friends, and the 5,000 masqueraders were gathering in their sections. By 4 o'clock I was done. The costumes were ragged and couples were supporting each other. It was time to prepare for the final dance at the Country Club that evening. Logic told me I should go to bed, but I was determined to go the whole hog. On the stroke of twelve, everything stopped. It was Lent. In the eerie silence, we made our way to the car and drove through the streets strewn with cast-off costumes and quiet groups sitting on the ground or making their way home. It was over, what a party! We reached the house and I collapsed. Sleep consumed me till midday when I woke and stared at the ceiling.

Partying was over for now; I needed to go to Houston to coordinate the design developments with our work on the site. Final layouts were fixed, and the marine terminal had to be integrated with other shipping movements. Huffco was growing, and people were working on the Bontang expansion and moving to Turkey for a new venture. I was feeling very much a part of the team and enjoyed the camaraderie.

The US energy scene was changing, and our project was in the firing line. Our schedule was slowed, but we pressed on. A major part of the plant was the giant compressors and their gas turbine drivers. The turbines were similar to those used on jumbo jets and Rolls-Royce was hoping to win the contract for we would be as big a customer as the national airline BWIA (known as 'bee wee'). Rolls-Royce sponsored a conference to tout the benefits of their products. It was well attended, and scholarships were handed out to students. I attended and was impressed with the organisation. Alan DeFreitas, the news reader and singer, came up to me. 'What are you doing here?' He only knew me as a clarinettist in the symphony, not as an engineer trying to develop an LNG plant. I explained the connection with the turbines. 'Could you do an interview for me for the news?' he asked. 'You seem to know more than anybody.' I said the R-R boys were paying the bill – they should do it. 'You'll be more credible.'

In the morning, Gail rushed in all excited. 'You're on the morning news!' I smiled and said we might be buying Rolls-Royce engines. 'Not off the planes!' she exclaimed. 'No,' I said, 'they make special ones for us.' She ran down the hall to tell all the other girls. Gail spent about half of her time out of the office 'networking'. I didn't complain, as she had demonstrated great skill in sorting out administrative issues. She'd say to me, 'Why you worry so much? You just get vex if you plan everyt'ing. Relax, boy, an' de t'ing come.' (It was my ambition to say 'boy' to one of the big black guys down at the energy ministry, without causing offence. When I could do that, I knew I'd be totally culturally integrated.) I started to realise I was a bit of a workaholic and that it wasn't helping in this place. Gail was right.

My parents made the trip to Trinidad to visit us, but it was a tough trip for my mother. She had been fighting breast cancer and seemed to be on the mend, but the trip took it out of her. She was thrilled to see the kids, and we were proud to show her around. A couple of months after the visit I had a call from my father to say Mum wasn't well. I asked, how bad? He was non-committal, and I decided to go home with the family. We left the next day and had an arduous trip as we were late leaving Port of Spain and only just made the connection in Miami by running to the gate. We caught the flight and finally arrived in Sydney to be met by my father. My mother had died while we crossed the Pacific. I sat in the gutter and cried. My father said it was OK to cry. That upset me. It was unnecessary for him to say it.

The funeral was strange for me. Having been so far away, I felt remote from the proceedings and that I had failed my mother in some way. It's the price of living on the other side of the world. She had been a great inspiration to me with her positive attitude and encouragement. I didn't know how to act at the wake, and carried on like it was a normal party. I hadn't seen a lot of friends there for a while, and they were keen to find out about Trinidad. I felt really bad afterwards, as I felt I hadn't shown enough respect. For many years, I reflected on this moment and still today have not resolved my feelings. We were only back a short time while I tidied up issues with the family. My father had watched his wife battle cancer for several years and seemed stoic about her passing. I had no idea what he was feeling.

Back in Trinidad, I was busy coordinating the design work in Houston with the government procedures in Trinidad. We were organising contracts for the site works. I was still going to Houston for the bimonthly management meetings. The mood on Trinidad had changed a lot, and it was generally felt that the US would not allow us to import gas in the normal way. The consumers would have to pay the marginal price of that gas, and that would probably kill the project. This was very disappointing for me, as the major project issues had been resolved and our project was in an excellent position to be constructed. The marine side was set and facilitated fast turnaround for the ships.

The gas supply was available and the plant site ideal. I was totally immersed in the society and well connected to the government. I felt very proud of our company profile in the country.

21. Helping Huffco

I spread my wings and fly to Asia.

BONTANG AND SANTAN

Shortly afterwards Steve Harrison called from Houston and asked if I could go to London to meet one of the development people about a new potential project in Bangladesh. This was typical of Huffco: fly to London to be briefed about Bangladesh. I needed a visa for Bangladesh, so I went to the High Commission, which happened to be a terrace in Knightsbridge. As I walked in, I saw bullet holes in the wall of the terrace next door. It was the Iraq Embassy, where they had had a shoot-out the previous week. At least I was done with all that. The clerk told me that my visa would take a week and I needed seven copies of the application and seven photographs. I said, 'Look, *I* don't want to go Bangladesh, but my boss and *your* boss, the president, would like me to go, so I'll be back tomorrow. You do have two copies. It's your choice.' He looked at me blankly and I left.

In the morning, having collected my passport and visa with no fuss, I went to see the commercial attaché upstairs to get details of the area in the south of Bangladesh where the proposed LNG plant was to be sited. I was told that the attaché didn't turn up till noon and then only stayed 30 minutes before going to lunch. I asked if I could wait in his office. This didn't seem to be a problem even though there was no secretary. I looked around the office and found pretty much everything I wanted, so I bundled up the documents and left, telling the receptionist not to worry. As I went down the stairs and out, I noticed a Rolls-Royce pulling in with several Bangladeshi officials; I assumed he was one of them. I walked right past them and went on my way. I met with the Huffco representative and ran through the proposed development. I showed him the documents I had obtained from the High Commission and we spent a couple of hours sketching out the fundamentals of a development.

That night at the hotel Steve called again and asked if I could help with a problem in Bontang, Indonesia, on the way. He explained that the storage for the LPG in Santan was almost full, and ships were not scheduled to load in the near future. They were looking at re-injecting the LPG into the formation, as a way of keeping the LNG plant going. This is a dangerous process and one to be avoided. Steve asked if I could assess the situation and suggest another solution. I arranged to go to Jakarta and meet the Indonesian manager. Once there, he briefed me on the issues and we arranged for a visit to Santan and Bontang. This would need to be via Balikpapan in Kalimantan on the east coast.

I was looking forward to catching up with Bob LaRue and Paula, as they were living in Balikpapan. I was given VIP treatment and put into Roy's apartment. Cocktails with Bob and Paula was a treat, as I was able to get acquainted with the local scene. It's always the best information when you come to a new site. I mentioned I was taking a chopper to Santan. Bob asked, 'Why do you need a helicopter? It's only a twenty-minute drive on the new road.' I said, 'I have no idea, Jakarta arranged it.' Obviously, Jakarta was not coming to the site enough.

The next morning I cancelled the helicopter and we drove to the camp, where the local manager was expecting us. Santan is a large storage area for many companies. It is the main export point for gas liquids, with more than eighty tanks behind the export marine terminal. My guide pointed out the Huffco area and I made notes about all the tankage. We spent most of the day documenting the layout and naming the owners of the various facilities. I could easily recognise the different types and got confirmation from people on the ground. It all seemed to be according to what I had been told in Jakarta, until I asked about an area in the back that nobody seemed to notice. It included an obvious LPG tank. My guide had no idea who owned that area. I met some people from Total Petroleum, who told me that it was fairly new and they thought it was owned by Huffco. We went to the main tank and I looked at the inscriptions. The tanks had been manufactured by Chicago Bridge. Back in the office, I sent a message to Jakarta to check the validity of the information. The message came back quickly: they had been built for Huffco. It seemed extraordinary that nobody seemed to know they existed.

I called a friend in Bontang to confirm whether he had any knowledge of it. I asked how it was that nobody seemed to know that they were our tanks. He laughed. 'You know head office – they don't seem to know what their left or right hand is doing.' I was amazed. My job was over.

I went back to Balikpapan to find a major party was in progress and I was invited. Paula had organised a fancy-dress celebration to farewell one of the senior geologists, who was leaving after a long stint. It turned into an all-night affair, and we ended with lobsters for breakfast. Later that morning, it was tough sitting in an *attap* hut in the heat and humidity of the Balikpapan air terminal, waiting for the charter flight to Singapore. I'd had no sleep, but was happy with the work I'd done.

LNG in the Third World

I was off to Dhaka to meet our local agent, Ahmed Rahman. Many years before, Shell Oil had discovered a large gas field in Bakhrabad, in the north-east of the country. Shell was not interested in gas and had abandoned the discovery. The emergence of LNG had stimulated the government to explore options. Roy Huffington had met the national president and our visit was a follow-up to assess the viability. Two Huffco engineers, Bob Drake and Alan Gale, also came to give me a hand.

Dhaka is a miserable place. The people are downcast and poorly dressed. Litter in the gutters chokes the drains. Everything seemed damaged, with footpaths broken and street signs twisted. Our host owned a steel fabrication plant that produced steel reinforcement for concrete and insisted we visit his facility. Hundreds of people were outside the perimeter fence, waiting for a job. This surprised me, because it was the most dangerous plant I'd seen. The equipment was old, and safety screens were minimal. 'Do you have accidents?' 'Yes, unfortunately,' Ahmed replied, 'but there are many people who will fill the places of the injured.' I couldn't get out of there quickly enough and took an instant dislike to Ahmed. However, the port was picturesque, and I took pictures of the colourful sailboats. I saw a cement barge being unloaded and again realised safety was of little concern. A line of fifty men carried a bag each, which was filled in the hold before they trudged to the waiting trucks, where they emptied their bags and began the task again. Each time they passed through the hold, they inhaled cement dust. They would all be dead in a couple of years from silicosis. I wondered how we could build a modern, sophisticated operation and run it when these activities were tolerated.

We had to plan a visit to the fishing port of Cox's Bazar, which was close to the proposed site for the LNG plant and terminal. It needed to be that far south to allow an LNG tanker to dock in the shallow waters of the Bangladeshi coast. IMEG, a British consultancy, had performed a preliminary study suggesting a plant could be located behind a large inlet to the north of the town. At dinner, we met our pilot, Hasan, who was the chief flight instructor for the country – a good sign. I explained to him that we needed to overfly the area around Cox's Bazaar to see the pipeline approach landscape, the plant site and the marine environment. I said we would take photos along all the runs. He agreed quickly, but seemed more interested in the whiskey we provided. He paid little attention to our discussions and finally collapsed in a drunken stupor – not a good sign.

The team and our agent took a local flight to Chittagong and boarded an old Wiley's jeep for the journey south. It was very uncomfortable, as Ahmed and the driver sat on the front seat and the three of us were on seats facing each other in a separate cabin behind. It was difficult to sit up straight, and we bounced as the back wheels hit ruts. On arrival into Cox's Bazaar, we were greeted by ramshackle buildings spread along a wide, long beach. After checking into the local hotel, we immediately went to the local airstrip to find our pilot. Hasan, the pilot, was very jolly and seemed to have recovered from his hangover. We boarded a small four-person Cessna. Bob and I got in the back so Alan could take photos from the front seat. There was a man lying on the floor under my feet. I said to Hasan, 'What's this?' 'Oh, he's a trainee pilot just getting up his flying hours. Is he in the way?' 'Yes, don't be crazy.' The man crawled out of the plane. Hasan started the engine and we were taxiing in seconds. He didn't seem to check any of the instruments. We passed a burned-out small plane, which Hasan acknowledged was the result of pilot error, and we readied for take-off. As we cleared the perimeter fence, Alan took out his camera to be ready for his shots. Ali turned and said there could be no photos; we had no permission. Hasan and Alan argued, and I told Alan to put the camera away till we reached a few thousand feet, as Hasan seemed to be more interested in arguing than flying the plane. At altitude, Hasan and I discussed the plan. He said we were too close to the Burmese border to take photos, and anyway, we did not have a permit. I said, 'Why don't you fly the plane where we tell you and don't look at the camera. Pretend it doesn't exist.' He finally agreed, and we continued. We made it safely back, but I could have killed Hasan.

The next day we went across to the proposed LNG plant site and met the local villagers. We sat through a welcome ceremony and ate and drank the local fare of offal and rice – quite an ordeal. The chief led us through paddy fields to the inlet river bank. At one point he stopped and put his finger to his lips and then pointed just in front. A large krait snake was sliding from one pond to the next; it seemed to be about 2m long with red, black and white bands. I was glad I was wearing cowboy boots. That afternoon we hired a tinnie to travel the river to get soundings. As we made our way downstream and out to the sea, I noticed a strong current taking us out. I saw the sandbar in the distance, with large waves. It reminded me of my horror when the three children died at Brunswick Heads all those years ago. I asked the boatman to start the engine and held my breath. It fired up and we started back against the current. When we were nearing the jetty, I asked the boatman how much fuel he had left, as it had been a slow return. 'Almost out, but we here.' This rammed home to me that I had put my team at risk: if the motor had failed or the fuel had run out we might have drowned, as the current would have dragged us to the raging offshore surf.

The hotel was half built, as were most of the dwellings in the town. Cox's Bazar is touted as the Riviera of Bangladesh. 'See Cox's Bazar before the tourists discover it!' spruiked the ads. A mini boom had triggered a building spree, but it had fizzled out. No one came. It was mosquito-infested, but the 145km beach was a highlight. Millions of small red crabs moved like a wave

Bangladesh jeep

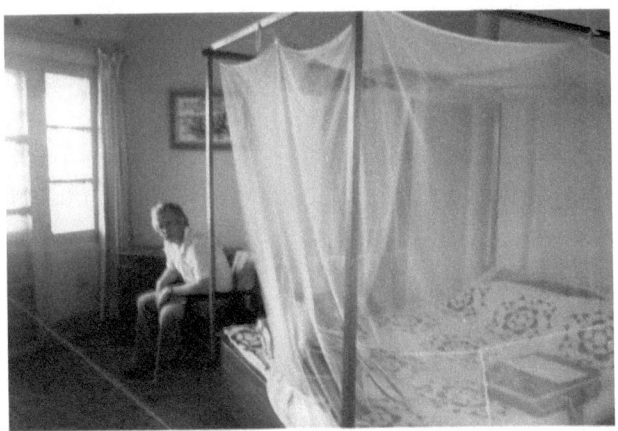

Bangladesh hotel

as you drove along the beach – extraordinary!

On our drive back to Chittagong in the jeep, we continually stopped to fill the radiator with water. We had two swampers (labourers) just for that. We entered a forest and on rounding a bend were confronted by a stone wall across the road. The driver slowed and Ahmed started screaming at him to accelerate. We crashed through the wall and people ran out of the forest towards us, waving rifles. As we hunched over in the back of the jeep thoughts flashed through my mind. We have no weapons, do we fight? I had no idea. We accelerated more and rounded another bend till we were out of sight. I yelled at Ahmed 'What was that!?' No answer. 'Are we still in danger?' Ahmed finally said 'Hill tribesmen'. It meant nothing to me. We were unaware of the local uprising of the Shanti Bahini of the Chittagong hill tribes, and would have had no way of defending ourselves. We stopped at an army outpost about 8km further along, and Ahmed jumped out to talk to the officer. The soldiers immediately sent a truck south to investigate the stone road block as we resumed our journey north. Nothing more was said.

Back in Dhaka, we were scheduled to meet the head of the petroleum ministry. It was raining, and we entered a building whose windows hadn't been cleaned in decades. The large spiral stairway inside the entrance concealed beggars who stretched their hands towards us as we passed. The clerk greeted us and we were seated in a large, dingy room looking over the street, which was all but invisible through the filthy windows. Our host Zahir Patoyari arrived and invited us to order tea or coffee with his aide. Zahir was nattily dressed in a pin-striped suit with highly-polished shoes. Just then, the power went off, and it became gloomier. Zahir ignored this and we discussed the LNG project. He enquired about our findings in the south, and I said the lack of infrastructure was the main issue. Also, the various bureaucracies might prove hurdles for development. He was optimistic and asked his aide to provide copies of government initiatives that would help our understanding. We chatted for half an hour, but no tea arrived and neither did the documents. Apparently there was a problem with the printer. The power was still off. We rose to leave, and Zahir assured us that the documents would be sent to our hotel when they could be printed. We were back on the street, and the rain teemed down. For the locals, being poor was bad enough, but huddling under a piece of plastic to stay dry must have made their poverty immeasurably worse.

The team assembled in the hotel to review our findings. The overriding issue was the lack of access at Cox's Bazar for LNG tankers. The IMEG report glossed over this with a statement that a channel could be cut through the offshore bar and maintained. But we had experienced the volume of water that moved with the tides. Access was impossible, and my coastal engineering training reinforced this. Mounting a large project in this environment was fraught with difficulty; also, the bureaucracy would drown you in paper. My instincts told me to report negatively back to Houston.

22. The USA gas bubble bursts

Energy prices crash back to earth.

Back in Houston, I submitted our report and Steve thanked me for both missions. I went on to Trinidad, glad to be home. Life was more relaxed as the project was basically on hold but the partners were happy to keep the meter ticking over. We continued engineering and site studies, to be ready for a change in the US regulatory rules.

I reflected on my recent assignments and realised I had felt totally competent to complete the tasks. I had a good appreciation of the industry and worked well with the people assigned to help me.

The orchestra was about to perform its first opera of the season, *The Magic Flute*, with the opera company. The concert hall seated 500. Rehearsals were interesting for me, as I had never been exposed to a top-flight conductor. The BBC sent a team from London, comprising some principals and the conductor, to boost the standard. It was wonderful. I found playing clarinet with a classical conductor not too demanding, as my experience in the big band had taught me counting time and reading. Sometimes the conductor confused me with his arm waving. I thought his counting wasn't too good on occasion, and when he beat four for a 2/4 section I was lost.

Our opening night approached and the tempo increased, as everybody tried to concentrate. We settled into the orchestra pit and 15 minutes before curtain I could smell burning. All the lights went out. People started running about with matches. Our lighting cables had fused on the music stands. Amazingly, it was fixed in a few minutes, and we were ready to go on as the curtain rose. I was aware of family and friends in the audience and hoped for a good performance. We played the overture and it all went to plan. On the second night, I got tangled with the 2/4 thing and held a note a fraction too long, in an unintended solo. At the interval, the conductor barked at me, 'What are you doing?' I retorted that he had to count it in two, not four. 'You ruined it,' he said. I think only he and I knew what had happened. It went well in the later performances, and he was very friendly at the end of the season.

The *Trinidad Guardian* had a policy of headlining the government's latest mess-up, and the paper had plenty to choose from. Like when the government bought a new wide-bodied aircraft, the Lockheed L-1011 Tri-Star, which was not licensed to fly to London, the most common route for West Indians. And when the government purchased a ferry in Venezuela to ply the Tobago route, but it was only suited for river service and nearly sank on its maiden voyage across the ocean. On Fridays, 'The Bomb', a weekly paper contained salacious stories about politicians and businessmen, half of which were correct. With great merriment, everybody tried to figure out which half. Trinis loved gossip. When I asked politicians why they put up with the constant criticism, they said I didn't understand the Trini humour. They were right.

For several months I drifted along, tidying up reports and keeping ready for a return to the schedule. I went to Houston twice a month and felt embarrassed, as everybody was busy and I felt I wasn't pulling my weight. Roy told me not to worry as the company was being paid handsomely to hold the fort in Trinidad.

Finally, on one trip I was leaving Houston to go back home and Steve asked if I wanted to go to California that afternoon instead. He said they were looking at building an oil refinery in Bakersfield. I said I didn't know anything about refineries or the downstream industry. 'Come anyway, you'll enjoy the trip.' We flew to Anaheim, where Fluor Engineering had its base, and they presented their concept for the project. The Kern River oil fields had extensive oil reserves, but it was very heavy oil – about 12-gravity crude. It had to be steamed out of the ground and was hard to manage, as it needed to be coked and refined locally to be commercial. The proposed plant would coke the oil and produce a series of light products that would be piped into Los Angeles for final processing.

Fluor put on a cocktail party for us at a resort on Balboa Island that evening after the presentations. One of the Fluor managers congratulated me with, 'I hear you're the new boss of the project.' It was news to me. I found Steve and asked what was going on. He smiled and said, 'You can have it if you want it.' I stood there open-mouthed. This was out of the blue. 'Christ, I'll have to think about it. You know I know nothing about these things.' 'That's why you'll do a good job – you have no baggage. We'll go and have a look at one tomorrow.' I didn't know what to think. I was settled in the Caribbean and happy, but I knew it couldn't last. Was California the place to go?

The next day we crawled over a similar refinery, with Steve giving me a rundown of the processes. He was a good teacher and by the end of the day I had the basics. I told him I needed to talk to the family and think about my future.

It was a totally new direction for me, but a great honour to be considered for such a task. Only a few years earlier I had come to the States to learn the business, and now I was being asked to head a new project in California, not in some remote site in a third-world country. I must be doing something right. I returned to Port of Spain and told the family the news. They were disappointed, but finally accepted that we were moving. As with our departure from Australia, there were several months of overlap as I established the new scene and Margaret was saddled with packing up the old location. At the time I realised that I was putting a huge load on my wife to manage the kids' expectations and deal with being so far from friends. I probably didn't discuss these issues enough as I felt I couldn't explain my career path to them as I was grabbing opportunities as they appeared. It would be easy to say I was selfish but I was providing for my family the best I could.

23. The good oil in Bakersfield

Oil and agriculture jostle for land.

The only accommodation available on my first scouting trip was a tennis ranch to the east of Bakersfield, in the foothills of the Sierra Madre mountains. In some ways, it was a relief not to live in the oil-field-surrounded town of Bakersfield, for the local motels were basic. Bakersfield is unattractive – there is no other way to describe it. It lies in the San Joaquin valley, 200km north of Los Angeles. The oil fields have a long history of operation and remnants were evident across the district. Rusting tanks and pipework had not been removed and stood as a stark reminder of civic laziness. Our refinery site was covered in abandoned pipework and operating oil wells. It contained buried pipelines which might be still operational – there was no certainty – and considerable time was spent cleaning up without rupturing pipes which might leak oil into the sandy soil.

I needed to establish an office on the construction site and hire a secretary to anchor the communications. I managed to find one with some staying power, Glenda Gaines from Georgia. She asked where her office was. I explained she had to work with the contractor Fluor and mapped out our requirements. 'What about the furniture and equipment?' 'You'll have to buy that. Just be reasonable,' I said, echoing Roy Huffington's instruction to me. In the early days, I needed to be in Anaheim to set up a separate office for my team in the Fluor complex. Design development was advanced, and I wanted to get on top of Fluor's procedures so we could provide a seamless interface for approvals. I planned to have about six people in my group. The refinery would be subject to the tightest environmental regulations. It would have zero emissions.

Bakersfield's demographic mix was unusual. The farming community attracted a large Hispanic group, mainly from Mexico; historically, the Oklahoma dust bowl influx had brought a cowboy flavour; and there was a Spanish influence with Basque sheep-herders. The oil industry was host to Occidental Petroleum, which had its headquarters in town and Shell Oil also had a major operation. There was a music industry, with *Hee Haw*, the country and western TV show with Roy Clark and Buck Owens being made there. Unfortunately for me, there was no jazz. With travelling between Bakersfield, Anaheim and Houston and trying to keep the family happy, I was pretty busy.

I got into a routine of four days in Anaheim and three in Bakersfield. It was a long drive, and I learned all about the LA freeways. There were ten possible routes and the traffic reports told where the traffic was lightest. It was interesting having Fluor as the turnkey contractor. Fluor had its systems, and some were good. I don't think they had ever had a client like me, who understood their business as well as they did. They needed up to 400 people in the office to get the specs and drawings out. There was a senior core team, about ten of whom were permanent staff; the rest were contractors. The USA was experiencing a boom in alternative fuel development, and Fluor was at capacity, even in its new facility. We struggled to get people.

The project manager was old school, and I was not impressed. When I asked about certain details, he would fob me off with platitudes. I spent quite a bit of time getting to know the supervisors. Though keen to impress, the Fluor people were surprised that somebody in my position would be looking at the detail I did; little did they know that oil refining was all new to me and I was on a fast learning curve.

As I became familiar with the processes I decided that their procurement could be one of the issues to be solved. I was hearing rumours that it was difficult to obtain refinery equipment in a reasonable amount of time. The procurement group was separate to the project and almost impenetrable. 'Its system 5,' I was told. 'What's that?' 'We don't have any control over that part of the operations.' I said I didn't believe it and at the next review meeting I asked for a plan which showed how we would contract the major equipment. Fluor came up with the idea that we had to pre-order all the heat exchangers. There were about forty of them and they constituted a major part of the refinery equipment. I said, 'How can you provide a competent order when you haven't worked out the duties?' They said we were in the hands of the manufacturers, who were mostly in Oklahoma. I asked for a full review of the heat exchange program. They came back the following week, saying, 'We've improved the program by 20%.' I went up in their estimation and they were embarrassed that they hadn't done it themselves earlier.

I then refused to place the orders for the exchanges until we had completed the design. They said I was putting the project at risk, as the schedule would suffer. I acquired a list of the suppliers and, with the buyer, went to Oklahoma to talk through the problem. It was a valuable visit, as the suppliers had not been apprised of the project in detail. When I explained our schedule and key supply dates they were happy to fit the design output.

This alerted me to a serious problem within Fluor. One of the key parts of the refinery design was the control system. Honeywell were the only people with a competent product and we were in their hands. When we bought the TDC 3000, I noticed there were severe restrictions in the contract. I asked them about this and was told basically that they could rape and pillage our contract if they felt like it. It was a sellers' market. Honeywell advertised to the world that it was a new company with its clients' welfare at heart. We didn't seem to be experiencing this bonhomie. I wrote to the chief executive, attaching the correspondence and asking if this was the way they did business. He replied that he was surprised and was sending his district manager to discuss our relationship. The district manager arrived the following week and told me that if I was not completely satisfied with their performance, he would lose his job. I replied, 'No problem. We'll work together, and assuming we keep in contact you'll keep your job.'

Fluor appointed an Englishman, David French, as the construction manager. David and I became firm friends; it seemed that the Commonwealth was building this refinery. We spent many hours poring over the construction plans and he came up with some very novel ideas. The whole site was basically sand, with a variable water table. The water table seemed to be controlled by the California canal people. If we could convince them to keep the table low for a couple of months, it would be possible to excavate the entire site, construct the foundations and put it all back again. We would need more carpenters, but David had another plan to utilise them. Normally in a refinery, all the pipe racks are made from steel. He suggested that we use concrete, which would utilise the carpenters. This seemed like an ambitious plan, but I was willing to go along with it.

There was a large vacant block next to our site. David asked if we could use it, as it was owned by Huffington. I hadn't been aware of this, but did confirm it. David contacted Huffco's property department, but was informed that it was unavailable. I said to David, 'Leave it to me.' I called Roy in Houston to update him on progress and said the project was going very well. I said it was fortunate we had learned the adjacent property was owned Huffco, and using it would save us more time and money. Roy was pleased and wished me well. Problem resolved. I told Dave to go ahead and forget about the property department, and he did as I instructed. A few weeks later I had a call from Houston, from someone who introduced himself as the head of property. 'I understand you're in charge of the refinery development.' 'Yes.' 'Could you tell the contractor to remove all the equipment.' 'Why?' 'We may want to use it over the next couple of years. We're working on some plans.' I said we'd be out of there in six months. He replied, 'I can't take the risk.' I said I would not remove the equipment and he could talk to Roy about it if he liked. That was the last I heard of it.

I was most impressed with the unions and their ability to read the plans to avoid any demarcation disputes before the start of work. In Australia, that would never happen. I don't think they *could* have read the plans.

The supervisors were supplied with dune buggies to get them around the site quickly; they also had two-way radios. When the workers were moving about, they did so quickly and with purpose. It was a joy to watch them. I also noticed quite a few female tradesmen, which would have been unusual in Australia. The project was going like a dream.

However we still had some big hurdles, as the main decoking vessels needed to be transported from Japan, and the trip from the San Francisco area to the site would require much coordination between police and local authorities. These would be the biggest vessels transported along the road system in Californian history.

My other big problem was the new refinery manager, Dub Crawford. Dub was of the old school and had worked in refineries all his life. When he came on board he started making suggestions to improve the refinery design. I had a system where if the change was essential for the refinery to work, then we'd do it; otherwise it could be part of the budget after the refinery was completed. Every week he'd send me letters outlining his changes. I think I processed maybe one in a hundred. As the refinery was starting to take shape, he was looking at the as-built drawings. Every now and then he would come in and query me on what I was doing about his suggested changes. 'Well, Dub, maybe a few of them didn't get into the system, but that's something you can schedule when you're running the show.' He looked at me strangely. 'There's a lot to do,' I said, 'and sometimes things get lost in the shuffle.' I was very quickly making an enemy, but I had a job to do and I knew I had the backing in Houston.

John Wright was the engineer who had brought the project to Huffington. He had his own company and a small interest in the equity of the refinery. He came to site every couple of months from Houston, to review progress. He quizzed me about some of the unusual techniques we were using and I showed him the cost and time benefits. 'Grahame, you're not tackling this in the time-honoured way.' I said I had come from the upstream oil production industry, where we could use the more progressive, cost-effective methods. 'Well, I can't fault you on that and I'm happy to go along.'

About this time Ted Peacock, the CMPS CEO, visited with his wife Marie, who we discovered was related to Margaret. We had dinner and I took them around the refinery site the following morning. Ted was impressed. I also showed them the oil-field operations; the steaming of the oil from the reservoir was unique in the oil industry. The field produced about 1 million barrels a day of fluid: 900,000 barrels was water and 100,000 barrels was heavy oil. They burned 35,000 barrels of oil to raise steam for the operations. That left only 65,000

Bakersfield house

Bakersfield refinery construction

barrels of saleable product. This was our feedstock for the refinery. It was clear that if they could get cheap gas rather than burning oil, it would be a big improvement for the environment. No solution had been found at that time; gas was in the area, but old habits die hard. Fluor was preparing the project for commissioning and I needed to work closely with Dub Crawford to agree a handover schedule. Everything was coming together and I started to think about the future.

Ted Peacock called from Pasadena a couple of months after his earlier visit and asked if I could meet him there for dinner. We had a long night. Ted wanted me back in Australia. After much wine, he offered me the job of running the oil and gas division of the group in Sydney. This would involve becoming joint managing director of the Williams Bros joint venture – essentially Steve Harrison's old job. Several things preyed on my mind. Huffco was suggesting I could run the next expansion of the LNG plant in Bontang, Indonesia. It was the biggest job they had, and I'd receive a big salary increase – very attractive, but I was feeling homesick. The boys were in high school, and a move to Indonesia would mean boarding school for them. The freedom and trust that Roy Huffington had shown me was very strong, but I had a decision to make.

After several discussions with Steve Harrison, I opted to accept Ted's offer and return to Australia. The family was happy. Steve was disappointed by my decision and suggested I consider being the refinery company president, but I couldn't see myself being Dub Crawford's boss and having to reject all his suggested changes again. I really wanted a new challenge and the idea of going back to Australia was very attractive, even though the oil business there was spiralling downward.

On my final round of goodbyes in Houston, Roy said he would buy Delhi Petroleum in Australia if I'd run it for him – what a compliment! I thought he was just being nice. He put in an offer, but was trumped by CSR, which went on to lose a lot of money before it was eventually on-sold to Exxon.

Steve Harrison was sorry to see me go and we remained good friends. He had been a great mentor for me, and I appreciated the opportunities I had been given. For the first time in my life I was putting my family before my career trajectory. Relocating in Australia was not a backward move, as it landed me back in my comfort zone, even though it would be much tougher from a business point of view. Project life is an itinerant existence that pays well and leads to bigger projects. My new life would be as a businessman even though I would be leading engineering teams. As our plane made it's final approach into Sydney I glanced out the window to see Kyeemagh approaching below. I could see my childhood house and the beach I had grown up with. Unfortunately the sandhills had gone and a Pizza Hut fast food outlet surrounded by by bitumen car park stretched across the landscape. The gypsy camp I had visited was under the airstrip we were about to touch on. It all rushed back to me and I glanced back to my family beside me hoping I had made the right decision.

We were lucky to find a good family home in Neutral Bay, and the boys were accepted into the academically selective North Sydney Boys High School. Corinne attended Neutral Bay Primary. Margaret was glad to be back among family and friends after a tough time in the desert. If you mention Bakersfield to any Americans they react instantly with, 'Poor things, how did you survive?'

My father had become friendly with a neighbour in his apartment block in Mosman who was a widow. They got married a few years later. He spent a lot of time with the grandchildren and was pleased we had returned.

Part VI
Pipelines in Australia
1982

24. Home turf: 1982

Living with $5 oil.

I had been out of the scene for several years. It's amazing how your thought patterns change when you have a different job. My first task was to sit down with Don Brown, my co-managing director and former boss in Tulsa, to understand the state of our business. It turned out to be quite poor. We basically had no major projects and were surviving only on study work. The scope of the business had been expanded to include New Zealand and South-East Asia. We agreed I would look after South-East Asia and Don would handle New Zealand. Our technical scope had also been expanded to include oil and gas production and processing. Our partners expected the operation to provide a full service: oil and gas engineering and management delivery.

Very quickly I realised that Don had a totally different view of how to win business. He relied totally on personal contacts. I preferred to understand the client's business and find the most appropriate people to talk about our skills. To confound my theory, Don met an old friend who was working with Delhi Petroleum and had contacts in Dallas, Texas. They were looking at developing the liquids – that is, ethane, propane, and butane – in the Cooper Basin. The gas fields had been in operation for many years and they had been storing the gas liquids in anticipation of a project related to petrochemicals. The plant would be located at Redcliffe, in South Australia. It was a great platform on which to start building the business.

By now my relationship with Don Brown was not too good. I found it impossible to be a joint leader. Two people can't be responsible for one operation. Don had no feel for the local culture; he was straight out of Texas. I shared this thought with Don and we agreed to seek help for our dilemma from the joint venture committee. To Don's surprise, he was asked to go home. It was all up to me now.

I spent a lot of time in Adelaide, establishing relationships with senior Santos and Delhi management. They had totally ignored our early work on a multi-product pipeline, as Davy Engineering, a large English company, was a plant specialist and Santos had appointed an ex-Fluor chief, Brad Kern, to overview the whole liquids program. I went to a Friday night after-work drinks party in the office. John Squarek, the Santos engineering manager coordinating the Delhi work, had invited me, and there were about a dozen executives present. Brad Kern came in and poured himself a beer. He looked around and on seeing me snapped, 'What the fuck do you do?' He thought I worked for Santos. I replied that I was the director for the liquids gathering project, working with Delhi, and we were well on with the design. 'Well, thank God some fucker is making progress. Not much else is happening.' I asked John what Kern's problem was. 'He's just arrived and doesn't like Davy. He's ex-Fluor. They were doing the work in Houston and the coordination was poor.' I asked why they didn't use the separated products concept we had proposed a decade earlier. 'They don't understand it, and believe they can manage the separation at Redcliffe.' It wasn't my problem, but smacked of old thinking.

Business for oil and gas was slow in the early '80s, after the oil price crashed. Exploration had stopped and companies weren't investing. We were very lucky to have our Cooper Basin work, but it wouldn't last forever.

CMPS were having many problems with the business downturn. They decided to appoint David Evans as the new managing director, with Ted Peacock remaining as executive chairman. I thought this was a big mistake, as Ted had been running the company for several decades and David had no chance to define his own direction. I was invited to join the board and accepted, which was a great honour, but I found it depressing. It should have been a highlight, similar to when I had been appointed an associate, but they were bogged down in analysis when they should have been out talking to their potential clients. The industry had changed. CMPS had had a good run, but had finally become moribund. A new suite of services was required, and I tried to explain why the oil and gas business had had success. It fell on deaf ears. 'Our business is different' was the recurring refrain.

The only difference was that CMPS was trying to win work with its outdated consulting engineering concepts. I pointed out that only about 20% of the work we were winning was traditional engineering. The other 80% comprised project services which may or may not be performed by professional engineers. The charging arrangements under the contract with the client had evolved with lower margins but a much broader base. Overhead costs generally adsorbed by consulting engineers were charged. This was totally foreign to the traditional consulting engineers but driven by the large American contractors. Our clients were attracted to the low margins and tolerated these charges. The growing use of individual contract staff gave greater flexibility to build project teams quickly and also disband quickly at the end of the work.

We were nearing completion of the Moomba facilities, and the team was looking for the next opportunity. It was during this period that CSR wanted to exert more influence over their new acquisition and organised an opening ceremony at Dullingari, one of the fields servicing the gathering system. I was invited to join the CSR management, which included their deputy chairman, Jack Campbell, the operations manager, Gavin Campbell, and Greg Swindon, the new Delhi boss. As we flew over Broken Hill, the pilot said the area was experiencing a dust storm, and we would have to divert to Birdsville and wait. Jack was writing his speech and became upset. 'What's the point? I can't give it at Birdsville! We may as well go back.' Gavin tried to settle him down, and eventually the pilot said the dust storm was over, but he was lost and asked for directions to Dullingari. I told him to follow the river system going north-west, and we might cut across some roads. Eventually, we found it and landed safely. Jack gave his speech, and we were soon on the way back. As soon as we reached altitude, Jack produced a bottle of scotch, which was quickly demolished. Gavin had another and we went at it. Suddenly Jack asked the group, 'Who's going to the Gathering of the Clan?' The Clan Campbell was to meet in the highlands at Inveraray in October, so I piped up: 'I'll go.' Jack told me to call Burns Philp, as it had organised a tour.

It turned out to be a great trip for Margaret and me. We hadn't been to Scotland, and the idea of 10,000 Campbells descending on the south-west of the country was exciting. The festivities were held over three days and started with a visit to the Inveraray Castle to meet the Duke of Argyll, who was the head of Clan

Campbell. It was interesting viewing the paintings of earlier generations. I was sure I could see likenesses of myself there; it must have been my branch of the clan. The next day we attended church services and toured the area out around Robbie Burns' house. A Highland Games event was the main focus of the Gathering, and everybody was dressed to the hilt in kilts, all Campbell tartans, of which there are four. It was a great day, and the duke sold a lot of his personal brew. Margaret and I experienced a wonderful trip.

Back at work in Australia, there was the constant grind to find more work and expand the business. We had opened an office in Jakarta and formed a joint venture with two local companies. It was hard work to align our cultural objectives. We had a good product to sell, but the locals were focused on relationships. To build the business, they were willing to give away the product. This was fine, but they were giving away my product at my cost – easy for them. We managed to win some small production work in the first few months and were on our way. Frank McNamara, who had worked on the milk plants when I was in Melbourne, came back to run our operations. He had married an Indonesian girl and was keen to work in Jakarta. Cash flow was a problem in Asia, as clients were slow payers. I never understood this trait, as they had the money, but felt we were servants and it was our lot to wait. It drove me crazy, as we had limited cash resources.

I found Indonesia fascinating; I had watched the country climb out of a dark hole in the early '70s and prosper for the last decade. President Suharto had done a great job keeping the country on a growth path during the oil boom, which was now waning. I attended the Oil Exposition at the trade centre in Jakarta and found the Huffco stand manned by Roy Huffington himself. He greeted me warmly and said he was standing in for Dexter Roberts, who was on a meal break. Roy asked how I was going in Australia and said it was a pity he had been unsuccessful with the Delhi acquisition, as I could still have been on the team. A multibillionaire, he was still working hard, punching holes in the ground, as he called it. He was flying that night to Germany to stitch up another deal. Dexter returned and Roy was free to go. I watched him trudge off through the crowd to catch the plane. I had learned so much from him. Humility was the main thing.

I was keen to get a foothold in Malaysia, and through the help of the Williams Bros chairman in Australia, Sir Eric McClintock, we were able to hook up with Malaysian Mining Corporation (MMC), who wanted to break into the oil business. Tan Sri Ibrahim was a dynamic young businessman with political ambitions from Sabah. We formed a partnership to bid for the Malaysian north–south national gas pipeline. The Australian government, through Austrade (the Australian Trade Commission), was supporting our bid to the exclusion of other Australian bids. This was the first time Austrade had done this. I had included Transfield and Tubemakers, a contractor and pipe supplier, to broaden the team. According to Tan Sri, we were certain to win, as the finance minister had endorsed us.

Just before Christmas, a very upset Tan Sri called to say it was all off. Apparently the Australian trade minister had made an unscheduled call on the Malaysian finance minister *en route* to Hong Kong. The trade minister had been drinking heavily on the plane and on being asked by the finance minister if he supported our bid, replied that he couldn't say one way or the other. This was as good as saying no. We were out. A Canadian bid succeeded, and they held the central position with pipelines in Malaysia for the next ten years. The Austrade chief was livid – years of work wasted. Our relationship with MMC faded, although we continued with smaller projects. Another lesson learned: beware of government help.

My next task was to develop a marine oil and gas business. Williams Bros had established a group in Houston under Tom Labiosa and we had begun bidding for work in Asia. My relations with the struggling new management in Tulsa were strained. Larry Fisher, the new CEO formerly of Exxon, was keen to get into downstream processing, which didn't much interest me. I believe he regarded Australia as a poor cousin, even

APIA conference dinner with Harry Butler and Chris Sutton

Tulsa: me, Sir Eric McClintock, the WB CEO, David Evans, and Ted Peacock

though we were technically superior in many areas. Williams Bros had a bigger pool in which to play and my calls for help were not often answered. David Williams' cancer diagnosis put paid to his dream of a global engineering behemoth. He was putting his affairs in order, and the group was sold to US Filter Corporation. The vision from the top was gone. CMPS had signed up for ten more years. Larry Fisher had fixed ideas about the future, and none of it fitted my market. Its best management systems were the ones I had installed a decade earlier, and Mitch Schwarz was still running them. My only hope was to get the Houston offshore group behind me. If I'd had the financial acumen, I could have bought Williams Bros, as US Filter was uncomfortable with an engineering company.

25. Oil from western Queensland

Bjelke-Petersen kicks sand in the face of the southern socialists.

My ears pricked up when I heard that Delhi Petroleum had discovered a significant oil field at Jackson in the south-west of Queensland. It was a great opportunity for us, having had a good experience with Delhi on the liquids program. Santos operated the gas fields and Delhi the oil fields. Delhi/Santos decided to integrate it with the liquids collection project at Moomba in South Australia. Preliminary design work started on a pipeline to Moomba. Queensland Premier Joh Bjelke-Petersen had other ideas. He wasn't sending oil to the socialists in the south! The oil would stay in Queensland and be processed in the Brisbane refinery. His government issued expressions of interest to all comers to build, own and operate a new pipeline to Moonie, a length of 780km, to connect to the existing oil line to Brisbane. The oil-field operators would have to compete with others to deliver their product. All the major players submitted bids.

I wondered where we could fit but did not want to be aligned with any one bidder: they might not succeed, and we would sink with them. I put a design package together and offered it to all the bidders. I would charge a lower fixed price to each. I needed governmental approval and pitched the idea that all bidders would be treated the same. Our credibility carried the day, and the bidders were happy. We sold eight packages. The caveat was that we would offer no further advice, but answer questions if they were asked. Commercially we were on a winner and well placed to support whichever winning bid emerged. Only one bidder declined to avail itself of our offer, RedRu, a small contractor based in Crows Nest, west of Toowoomba.

In a surprise move, the rights were awarded to … RedRu. The contractor was run by Ron Nicholas, a former welder who had formed a joint venture with a Korean contractor, Kukji-ICC. The oil-field developers were dumbfounded. They were in the hands of a junior, untried pipeliner. How could the government do this? Ron Nicholas was a close friend and supporter of the Premier. That could be a clue. The Koreans realised quickly that Ron had little chance of delivering the project. Project finance and management were foreign to him. I called Ron to offer assistance. His response was that engineers and managers were the bane of his life and this project would be built by the 'true' pipeliners. I asked, 'How can you order pipe and valves when you have no engineering?' He told me not to worry; he knew some blokes who understood that stuff and she'd be right.

Ron had a young daughter and during one of our conversations earlier I mentioned I had a daughter about the same age. Ron had started calling me on a Sunday morning to discuss our 6-year-old daughters' weekly activities. He became very animated and excited to learn and compare their activities. Each time I'd slip in a comment on the pipeline – 'How's it going?', 'Have you got the engineering nailed?' – and always received the response, 'Don't you worry about that. I know you're an engineer, and you seem better than most, but you don't understand pipelines.'

The Koreans, meanwhile, were scouting the landscape for a new plan. They had leverage and were promising the premier lucrative resource deals if they could work with others. Joh held firm: RedRu was to be in charge. Deadlines passed and no structure for a plan having emerged, the operators pressured the government to intervene. Santos secretly put a plan together with the Koreans to take over. The Koreans had realised that RedRu was not capable of delivering the project and Joh was being advised along the same lines. Joh's loyalty was waning, but he tried to keep RedRu in the picture.

One Sunday, an agitated Ron told me the Koreans were white-anting him. He said they wouldn't put their money in and he couldn't buy pipe. I said, 'Have you put your environmental application in to government?'

'Don't you worry about that. Joh will fix it.' Next Sunday he started our phone chat with an outburst: 'The bastard Koreans have done a deal with Santos and Joh has taken the project off me!' 'Can I help?' I responded 'No, I'll still build it, and Santos has said they'll commission it on the original date. I told Santos it'll be finished when I finish it. You'd better get cracking – Santos will announce tomorrow that they're in charge, and they'll seek bids from engineer managers that day, for submission four days later. They'll select the successful bidder the next day.' I put the phone down and thought, 'We're the only people who can win this! I called my core team to a meeting that afternoon. We had the concept plan and the work we had performed during the original government inquiry. A lot of the team were on hand, as there were no other pipelines under development in Australia, but my key project manager, John Balint, was not interested in going to Brisbane, for a swag of personal reasons.

As expected, the Santos document arrived in the morning. Santos' key imperative was that construction must start in 30 days from award of the contract. I said to the team, 'Let's assume that we're in RedRu's shoes,' and worked up a schedule that assumed we had access to all the data accumulated by Ron over the past year, though in John's opinion the data probably wasn't any good. I started writing the bid response. Normally it would be a hundred-page document for a project of this size, with a lot of researched details. But they wouldn't be able to read that in the time, so ten pages would do – only the essential stuff.

I was due at an APPEA (Australian Petroleum Production & Exploration Association) dinner on Thursday night in Melbourne, the day the bid went in. I signed the bid and jumped on a plane. All night I was thinking about our new project. I had a bit more to drink than usual and went to bed with a spinning head. Failure would be a major problem for the company. At 4.30am, my secretary phoned alerting me that Santos had called. The company had been ringing the office since ten the previous evening, but the switchboard was unmanned. My secretary told me Santos wanted to meet us at 9am in Sydney. I leapt out of bed and called a taxi. After some hassle buying my ticket, I was on the 6.30am flight, trying to collect my thoughts. I arrived in my office just before nine. They were already there!

John Squarek and his team had just one question: could we start construction in 30 days? The government, giving Santos the ownership rights, would take the project away if they couldn't meet this condition. Gaining environmental approval would be the biggest hurdle to achieving the 30-day deadline, along with the availability of pipe and access to the ROW. They asked again, 'Can you do it in 30 days?' 'Yes!' I shot back. 'Well, sign here and we'll let you get started.' When he was vetting the contract, our lawyer recommended we not sign because it contained severe penalties for non-performance. I countered that we had a lot of protection against the penalties written into our bid and if we attached it to the contract we should be safe. At 10.30am, the deal was done, and I briefed the team under John Balint, who still hadn't agreed to do the job.

I flew back to Melbourne for the APPEA lunch. I was floating. Luccio Lussu, the boss of Saipem, a leading pipeline contractor, leaned back in his seat and congratulated me. Wow, *I* hardly knew I had won. Further across the room as I searched for my team our leading competitor, Bruce Andrews from Pipetech, who obviously hadn't heard the news, grabbed my arm and smiled. 'I bet you're wondering what Santos is thinking.' I concealed a smile and enquired if Pipetech had received a call. 'No,' he said. 'We only put the bid in yesterday!'

My first job was to persuade John Balint to accept the project manager role. He said his family came first and he didn't want to relocate to Brisbane. I argued, 'It's only for a year, and you can commute. Leave the family in Sydney and at the end of the job you can all go to Europe for a month on me.' He looked at me for a moment. 'All expenses paid, for the whole family?' 'Yes.' 'Well ... OK.'

John and the team flew to Crows Nest to negotiate with Ron Nicholas on the documents. Ron basically threw them out, with a, 'You can all get stuffed.' I called Ron on Sunday. By then he'd calmed down. We discussed our daughters for a while. Finally, I asked him about the pipeline documents. He paused and said, 'If you don't send an engineer, you can have the landowner files and the survey work.' I thanked him and called Bruce Winterford, our land guy, and he arranged to fly up the next day. Our next hurdle was getting pipe. Tubemakers had done work with us before, and we had the specs completed. It could make the date, but where did we want the pipe sent?

The construction management people had spoken to all the contractors who could participate. They asked, 'Isn't RedRu going to do this?' They had called Ron Nicholas, and he had told them all to bugger off. Ron called on Sunday and we talked kids. Eventually, I asked where he would source all his equipment, as his spread was too small. He replied, 'Those Koreans are still there, so I'm not going to do it. I've washed my hands of the whole mess.' I didn't think I was getting the whole story, so I let it slide. Back in the office on Monday, I briefed the team. 'Get the environmental assessment together and submit direct to the minister, Russ Hinze. Bruce, take it in and talk him through it.' We had the background of having been involved in several major completed pipelines and experienced the environmental restraints that had been imposed. Pipeline construction is a tight, clean process when done by the top contractors. The likely contractors had successfully worked with Harry Butler, the highly-regarded environmentalist, on the Moomba to Sydney gas pipeline.

Obtaining the main block valves in time and ordering the control system were the next priorities. We had a new control solution: distributive control, which utilised many small computers talking to each other – much cheaper and fully redundant. The system could be assembled quickly. We talked to Santos who said it had never been used before and that Honeywell, its preferred supplier, maintained it would be five years before distributive control could be operated properly. But time was of the essence, and we assured Santos it would work if they backed us.

The main construction contracts were due to be reviewed in Adelaide, and I headed for Brisbane to the Pipeline Industry Dinner, where senior government people and the industry would gather. It was a volatile meeting, as the energy and mines minister was the speaker and was laying down the government's ambitions for energy development. Late in the evening, I was approached by a leading contractor who said that the Koreans had claimed to him that if they didn't join with them, they would not win a contract. He was very upset and wanted to know what was going on. I said to ignore the call and that I would guarantee them a fair hearing in the contract review. A little later another contractor came to me with the same complaint. I gave him the same advice and told him to tell all interested contractors to hold their fire and wait for the outcome the following day. Near midnight, I called John Balint and got him out of bed. I relayed my discussions with the contractors and told him to carry on as usual. If the Koreans attended the bid review meeting and had offered a bid, then he should ask them to leave. If they refused, he should then leave.

At breakfast, I received a few side glances from the contractors. This was the only pipeline contract going in Australia, and a win would put them back in business. We had structured the sections to get the project built in the fastest time. The eastern section near Moonie was more difficult, with more hills and rock sections. We had made this shorter. The other two sections were of equal length, but construction would commence at either end. The final meeting point would be wherever it occurred. I had a call from John mid-morning. He said the Koreans were at the meeting, and he had asked them to leave when they said they had submitted a bid. They had refused, and John had told the Santos reps that he would not participate. Santos met with him outside, and he explained the events at the Brisbane meeting. Santos went back into the meeting. John waited, and 15 minutes later the Koreans trooped out with their bid. The evaluation process proceeded quickly, as all the major contractors had been prequalified and there were no questions on their ability to deliver.

The next day the winning contractors assembled in Brisbane and an overall plan was agreed. We had had a major win with the unions. Under pressure from the welders, they had agreed to allow 'piece' work. That meant that welders would be paid per weld. In the past, the unions had determined that a welder could only perform twenty welds per day. More than that, they insisted, would cause strain and possibly poor workmanship! The stage was set.

Premier Bjelke-Petersen decided he wanted to declare open the start of construction, thirty days from our appointment. A gala day was arranged at Jackson, a desolate place with gently undulating open red plains stretching to the horizon and little vegetation. A hut with a generator that had been left from the exploration well was the only building within sight. A small group of Aborigines looked on as twenty-two corporate jets arrived, along with Joh and several TV crews. Beryl Young flew the premier's plane and when it landed he strode across the red earth in his pith helmet straight to where I stood. 'Joh's the name, he said, and shook my hand. Clearly he had been briefed on my role as project director. 'Well, I'm glad it's getting underway on time! I always knew it would. That Ron is a great chap. Where is he?' I looked at him in amazement. Joh knew Ron had been removed, but was taunting me, trying to get me to tell him what I thought about the way Ron had been treated. Before I could respond he was jumping up and down like a chimpanzee. Again I looked at him in amazement. He babbled on, 'There's oil down there, you know!' It seemed he was testing the 'drumminess' of the ground. He then strode up to the lectern and seats that had been been set up by the hut and declared, 'Can't do it here. Too much noise from the generator.' Down the hill he went, towards the oil well, trailed by other government officials and a young lady in a light red dress carrying the lectern.

Suddenly Joh stopped, looked towards the sky and announced, 'I don't see any F-111's. Those socialists in Canberra are not going to force me to send the oil to South Australia.' And like a cloud of bees the acolytes gathered. The lectern was placed and the TV cameras arrived, and when a sufficient number of the attendees had gathered he surveyed the scene (his pith helmet still in place). The Franklin River dam controversy – when the federal government sided with environmentalists to stop the damming of the Tasmanian wilderness river – was in full swing and attorney-general Gareth Evans's decision to use F-111's to overfly the dam area and take surveillance photos had inspired Joh to attack the 'socialists'. 'Queensland for Queenslanders!' he crowed. 'We have the resources and skills to develop a great state!' His rhetoric resounded around the landscape.

Suddenly he strode off to the backhoe that was standing ready to dig the pipeline ditch. His knowledge of farm machines allowed him to start it and launch into digging as the cameras whirred. Joh was in his element.

Later we tramped back up the hill to find large tables festooned with lobster, prawns, salads and an array of Queen Adelaide chardonnay chilled for the crowd. In half an hour most of it was gone and people started heading for their private jets. The three Aborigines by the hut looked on and I wondered what they were thinking. In a few minutes only the caterers were left to clean-up. I hurried to our plane which was lined up alongside twenty-one others on the dirt strip, preparing to leave. Gerald Minson, the boss of one of the contractors, collared me. 'Which is the Santos chairman?' I pointed him out and Gerald left his briefcase beside me. It became very dusty as planes made their way to a take-off position. I tried to get into my plane as another fired a blast of dust in my direction which blew Gerald's briefcase into the bushes. I could see Gerald holding his hat, trying to make a point to the chairman of Santos, Alex Carmichael. Suddenly Carmichael turned on his heel and strode up the stairs behind me. As we sat down he remarked, 'Who the hell was that idiot?' I glanced out the window to see Gerald looking for his briefcase. Gerald had wanted to introduce himself as a leading contractor in the industry but it appeared that Alex considered him a minnow.

As we winged our way back to Sydney, the conversation with our small group of four was about politics. I tried to steer the subject to the difficulties of construction but received no response. You come to realise that everybody has a different perspective on development. Environmentalists worry about what ifs that generally never happen. The media concentrates on potential scandals of any colour. Business leaders try to maximise the commercial imperatives. The politicians try to second-guess the lot. The builders try to get it done.

Within a couple of weeks, southern Queensland had the largest flood in living memory. It inundated 80% of the right of way. In an emergency session, the contractors all cooperated, and we rearranged start points. Resources were shared to get construction started quickly, and we were able to make up some lost time. Once things were in full swing, the work rate skyrocketed. Rather than twenty welds per day under union control, we were achieving 100. The defect rate was about the same and the crews were elated, as they were making record money. The construction went magnificently. As the two main spreads converged to the centre, competition was at its peak. Quality was maintained because going back for repairs was a real drain on resources. Our target of nine months for the 780km was in sight – a potential world record.

As the final commissioning was underway, everybody involved felt tremendous pride in their achievement. The Australian pipeline industry was back on top and investors realised that new pipelines could be cost-effective. This was after a calamitous project, the Sydney–Newcastle dual pipelines, had shut down the industry for five years, due to union madness.

Santos, meanwhile, had been training a team of liquids operators, as its main expertise lay with gas. Relations with Delhi, which operated the oil field, were not good. CSR, via its subsidiary, Delhi, was new to the oil and gas industry and were arrogant about their ability to run the operations. A feature of the Jackson oil was its high wax content. Wax causes the oil to solidify if it is not treated with a chemical diluent [thinner] or kept warm. It was Delhi's responsibility to condition the crude oil for transport to the refinery in Brisbane. As we were commissioning the pipeline and starting operations, our team was training the operators to understand the unique issues for this material. The control system was innovative and untried but proved to be a winner. As both the oil field and pipeline groups were new, and not totally cooperating as we had hoped, extra effort was required to get it right.

A couple of months passed. Premier Bjelke-Petersen wanted a big celebration in Brisbane to honour the parties for what had been a wonderful achievement –

an oil field and pipeline brought into production in world record time. We were feeling pretty good about the rebirth of the pipeline industry in Australia. Then, out of the blue, we had a phone call from Santos: 'The pipeline is turning into a 780km candle!' We were stunned. 'It's not our responsibility – we've signed off!' Santos pleaded to us, 'Can you help?'

Alec Dietsch, our head of engineering, asked some questions. 'What and where are the pressure build-ups? What are the temperature profiles?' It quickly emerged that freezing conditions in the mountains west of Brisbane was the main problem. Alan concluded that the diluent had not been added correctly and a section of pipeline was immediately at risk. If one section failed and stopped flow, the whole pipeline would eventually effectively freeze, never to function again. Santos asked 'How long have we got? What can we do to fix it?' We needed additional pumping capacity, which was only immediately available from exploration mud pumps. Several were sourced and commandeered. We needed to deploy them to inject energy into the line without over-pressuring the pipe and causing a rupture.

Alec and his team started running mathematical models using the control data pouring in from the site locations. He predicted that the operations had about 48 hours to get the sluggish oil moving normally to avoid disaster. Helicopters were used to fly mud pumps to the sites nominated by the design team. They needed to be cut into the line at the block valve locations. The team worked through the night, relaying information and receiving operating data. Beds were set up in the office to keep the team together for the next couple of days. We held our breath as the pumps kicked into action. Pump failure at kilometre 620! Switch to upstream pump and restart cycle. The team reacted quickly and our control systems worked beautifully. After three days we felt the crisis was easing. Another two days was required to be sure.

The premier's celebration was held two days after we had stable flow. Only the direct operatives and some senior managers were aware of the crisis. It was decided to keep it like that. No point in causing alarm. The field operators were aware of the dangers, and all teams were operating harmoniously. It was a tough way to get cooperation!

The celebration was a great success. The investors danced the night away; Joh speculated on drilling the Barrier Reef. 'You have to feed the chooks' was his catch cry. He was baiting the media, and we all knew it. With the successful outcomes, we looked to the Northern Territory for new projects. Australia was in a decline in the mid-1980s and CMPS were struggling. The oil and gas group were doing well, but we needed another big project.

This project reignited the pipeline industry and showed that pipelines could be built economically. The unions realised that the new productivity was significant and did not interfere. We looked to the future with great enthusiasm.

26. Gas from the Red Centre: 1984

Our friends at Tubemakers were keen to win more business and mentioned to me that development of oil west of Alice Springs was a possibility. A pipeline from Mereenie to the Alice could hook up with the rail going south to Adelaide. We put a proposal together and I called a friend, Graeme Lewis, whom I had met at a conference. He was the president of the Country-Liberal party (CLP), which was in office in the Northern Territory. He agreed to set up meetings with the chief minister, Paul Everingham, and the energy minister, Ian Tuxworth.

This was my first visit to Darwin and I arrived with a heightened sense of excitement. Trevor Hammond, the Tubemakers manager and I flew up on Sunday to get a feel for the place and drove around the area. The frontier feel came through strongly. On Monday morning we met Graeme Lewis and he took us to the chief minister's office. 'I can't stay,' said Graeme. 'You two are meeting with him without me. I'm sorry, but it was all I could do.' With that he left Trevor and me in the waiting room. Then Ian Tuxworth arrived and introduced himself. 'Good timing! I want the chief to hear what you have in mind.' I was a little puzzled, as I didn't think Tuxworth was aware of our plans. The secretary ushered us into the boardroom and shortly afterwards Paul Everingham came in, brusquely telling us he didn't have much time and asking what was it all about? Tuxworth launched into an outline of a gas pipeline from the Alice to Darwin for the new power station. Paul turned to me and asked what was my interest in this? I said none; I was here to talk about an oil line from Mereenie. It was obvious that wires had been crossed. Tuxworth said, 'Didn't AGL talk to you?' No, I hadn't heard from Maurie Williams the current general manager, whom I knew quite well from the Moomba days. Everingham jumped up. 'Look, when you've got your ducks in a row, let me know,' and left. Tuxworth turned to me and exclaimed, 'Are you trying to wreck the project?' and abruptly turned on his heal. Trevor and I stared at each other and I shook my head. It's different up here.

I went back to the motel and called Maurie Williams, but he was out. Shortly afterwards, Maurie called back, very agitated. 'The minister's upset, and I apologise for not putting you in the loop. We'll just have to wear it for the moment.' I called Graeme Lewis and explained the meeting outcome. He said I should call Neville Walker, a leading businessman and close friend of the chief minister.

Neville and I arranged to have lunch at Charlie's Greek cafe, nearby. He headed Henry Walker, the largest corporation in the Territory. It had started in the construction business and broadened to property development, fishing, a large Toyota dealership and its own airline, Air North. Neville backgrounded me on the political scene in the Territory. He said in truth he was not very close to Tuxworth, whom he didn't seem to like at all. The energy minister and the chief minister had both come from Tennant Creek, where Tuxworth ran a bottling company and Everingham a legal practice. He suggested that he could put a consortium together to build a gas pipeline. I said, 'AGL seems to have an agreement with the energy minister, and we have a close association with AGL.' The development of a coal-fired power station was the chief minister's dream. He had been talking to Bjelke-Petersen about providing coal from the Bowen basin. It would involve lots of jobs and provide a boost for the Territory. He was not in favour of gas, as it seemed to be more expensive and didn't involve very many jobs. I returned to Sydney wondering what the next move would be. AGL was the key, as it could finance such a project.

I attended an oil and gas exploration conference in Darwin about a month later where I met the head of the Energy Department, Ted Campbell, who was an enthusiastic proponent of development. We got on well and I brought up the gas pipeline proposal. He was upset that the gas producers would not establish enough reserves to finance a pipeline. I had been speaking to the producers, particularly Bevan Warris at PanContinental Petroleum, who believed there was no market and not much support for gas. Over lunch we three had a chance to chat and I mentioned earlier conversations. I said we could do some study work showing the viability of the project and if the government could provide a window and a guarantee of a contract if the reserves were proven, then maybe we could put the project together. Ted said he would take it to the minister and see if we could get three or six months deferral on the coal-fired power station. It looked promising.

Back in Sydney, I received a call from AGL saying the energy minister had been given a proposal by the chief minister involving Henry Walker and that Williams Bros-CMPS and AGL were mentioned. I said I had no knowledge of it, and that Neville Walker had no right to put a deal like that to his friend the chief minister. Maurie replied, 'Well, the damage is done, and Tuxworth is very upset.' I wondered what I should do next, as it seemed that at every turn I was upsetting the minister.

Tuxworth came out with his own plan, in which he had put together six companies to own and operate the project. It would be led by Westpac bank, with AGL, Moonie Oil, CSR, Boral and the Northern Territory government in support. However, we still had to get the reserves and put together a competent feasibility study that would give the project a firm base. I thought it was most unusual for government to take this initiative but had no option but to fit in.

Around this time I ran into CSR deputy chairman Jack Campbell in the Qantas Club. I mentioned we might be working together on the pipeline, as CSR was included in the consortium. He exploded. 'I wouldn't put two bob into that deal! Those cowboys will get our cooperation over my dead body.' He was still shouting as he left the lounge to catch his plane.

There was a perception that gas as a fuel would be more expensive than coal, so I thought hard about a totally integrated plant where the cost of the power station would be included in the overall economics. Basically, gas-fired power is much cheaper than coal-fired power because of the cheaper turbines. In fact, if you look at the power station as a site with a long tail for the gas pipeline, in the analysis its capital cost is cheaper than that of a coal-fired power station. On that basis, the gas price is the price from the producer, not including the transportation cost, as this would be part of the power station cost. The fuel is cheaper, capital cost cheaper and the operating costs are cheaper: we have a winner on all levels.

Around that time French oil company Elf contacted me to suggest that gas from a discovery offshore would be closer and more appropriate. I asked what the cost of an operating platform would be, to produce the gas. He gave me a ballpark figure which was more than the total cost of the gas pipeline. It was eliminated as a possibility immediately, without even considering the cost of the marine pipeline required.

John Butters became NTGas manager, and he employed us to do the study work. I don't think he told Tuxworth, the energy minister. However, he said we would have to compete for the main contract if the project became viable. NTGas was looking at a new financing vehicle: a leveraged lease. Such a scheme was unusual in our business, notwithstanding the fact that the size of the transaction would make it the biggest ever in Australia. Things were looking promising; everybody was happy with the studies, and we were getting a good response from the producers' exploration efforts. However, the fields we originally expected to be producing turned out not to be suitable; Palm Valley would initially be used.

Over the next few months, we did more intensive work on the land access issues as the federal government was in a major dispute with the Northern Territory government over Aboriginal land rights. Energy Department head Ted Campbell proved invaluable in helping us with this work; in fact, he was the best government representative I have worked with. That year the annual pipeline conference was held in Alice Springs. At the conference, they had a tennis tournament which

I had won regularly. Ted came to the meetings and then played tennis. I had no problem beating him and, in fact, winning the tournament again, so he decided to take lessons and improve his game for the next year. Our matches became an ongoing battle over many years, and we became very good friends.

Bechtel, a major engineering company worldwide, was our major competitor. We had kept Bechtel out of Australia for pipeline work since winning the Moomba–Sydney pipeline more than a decade earlier. The company put a lot of effort into their bid to win the project, as it saw it as a way of gaining an entrée to Australia. John Butters told me not to take the bidding process lightly and to put in a fully researched bid.

During our first review with the client, I learned that our price was almost double that of Bechtel. Butters told me the other consortium members were attracted to the Bechtel bid. At our next major interview, I asked the client team to examine the range of services being proposed. Unfortunately, the CSR people on the panel were not familiar with pipeline technology and didn't understand the complexity of the project. They asked if we could reduce our price; I countered by asking which services they preferred not to have. As we went through each part of the bid, they decided that our proposal was more than competent.

Later I spoke to John Butters and suggested that in

the final meeting the key representatives from each company which would be working on the project should present themselves to be quizzed by the deciding committee. I knew Bechtel would have problems with this, because it was just before Christmas and mobilising a team at that time from overseas would be hard. I didn't have a problem, as our team was on the ground and confident to do a job in the Northern Territory.

I was right: Bechtel brought a team, but only the lead man spoke as the others had no experience in Australia. Our team performed admirably as all knew the project well. We were looking good. Immediately after new year, I was asked to attend another meeting in Sydney. The committee couldn't make a decision and wanted more information. We waited several weeks; still no decision. The delay was worrying as the decision was clear and I began to wonder if there was another plan. CSR was my concern as it had little experience with pipelines and possibly had hatched a new plan.

More time passed and I became despondent. Finally, I was asked to attend a meeting at the office of CSR, and was left outside the meeting for an hour. I sat there nervously thinking up reasons why I was in the corridor. Had they cancelled the project? Had we done something wrong? This project represented the entire future of hundreds of staff. We had invented the project and ignorant people were set on destroying it.

Eventually, I was asked in. There were eight people around a table; I was invited to sit at the end. I recognised most of the people from the various companies in the consortium. One executive, John Willis, cleared his throat and addressed me. 'We like your bid and would like to start work immediately, but we're about a month late. I know it's not your problem, but we somehow have to make it up as the finance has now been secured.' I stared at him for a few seconds and glanced around the table. There was no emotion on their faces. I said only, 'Thank you, we will begin this afternoon.' Willis smiled and asked if they could help with anything, maybe an upfront payment to assist. This was unusual, but everything seemed unusual. 'Yes, that would be helpful,' I stuttered. 'We could manage $2 million by the end of the week,' John volunteered. I was stunned. I thanked them again and excused myself. I went out into the corridor, sat down and stared into the middle distance. This was the biggest project I had personally won and I was very pleased, but the churning in my stomach had made me sick, and I went home.

Later I called the office and told our publicity officer Kay Turnbull the good news. We needed to mobilise a team immediately, and the race was on. We had set ambitious targets again, and everybody wanted to replicate the success in Queensland. But planning was the key, and I expected there would be many hurdles including placating the Aboriginal traditional owners of the land. I arranged a meeting with Ted Campbell in Darwin and his colleagues alleviated many of my concerns. Bruce Winterford, our land manager, had come up with a plan to talk to all the traditional owners along the route and bypass the land councils who were politically driven. This was an ambitious plan, and there could be trouble if the land councils got wind of it and objected. It had to be done quickly, and we mobilised a large team to tackle the task of contacting the traditional owners, stating our case and paying compensation.

Within six weeks we had agreements with all major traditional owners. We took this to the government and asked how we should manage the next steps. Ted Campbell mobilised his team, and we put our report together with the environmental issues for government approval. This took a further six weeks. The land councils reacted angrily and demanded a say. Ted responded that the traditional owners had made their decision and negotiations were finished. We had strong support from the major contractors, and of course Tubemakers was very keen to provide the pipe. I managed to get my old friend from Tulsa, the Canadian Bob Perry, to come on board as construction manager. We then got Bob Young back as one of the supervisors, along with Ron Black, who became a great mate of Bob Perry.

The project attracted international attention. Alan Newham joined up with the Koreans, who were still trying to break in. Saipem, the Italians who had performed so well on the Moomba–Sydney project were keen to make a bid. The leading Australians were there too. The work was divided into four sections, with the northern section subject to the worst weather and landscape. Newham won this and immediately ran into problems: it had not surveyed the right of way closely enough and needed more resources than expected. We had other problems with the black soil plains as the ground moves after rains and cracks when it is dry. The cast country, made out of limestone is difficult due to concealed caves leached out of limestone threatening the pipeline stability. Ground-penetrating radar helped with advance indications of cavities. A multitude of technical problems needed to be solved in record time to meet the tight schedule we had set ourselves. Our team was world-class, and I relied on their skill.

Meanwhile I had a business to run. I was trying to find better ways to build the business and when the government advertised a Build, Own, Operate and Transfer (BOOT) contract for a gas pipeline to Alice Springs from Palm Valley I arranged a bid which required financing. I felt we could deliver it and make money, but it was high risk and something the company had never done. Henry Herron of Westgarth Baldick was our corporate lawyer and advised me to put in a qualified bid, 'an invitation to treat'. He felt that we had not fully understood the risks and these could be eked out during the negotiation period. I reluctantly agreed, and the government threw out our proposal as it was 'non-conforming'. The contract was awarded to a trucking company which subsequently went broke. Eventually TNT won the contract on much less attractive terms, did a poor job as its survey easement did not match the pipe location, and still made good money. I eventually discovered that our bid would have won the contract had it not been qualified. It was a valuable, if painful, lesson.

I noticed several companies were exploring for oil in the Carnarvon Basin in Western Australia. They had spent tens of millions of dollars, and were planning to spend much more. They had no plans for transporting the oil to market if they ever found it. I thought I could start a company, the Broome Oil Pipeline, and do the initial survey and environmental work to be granted a government licence. If oil was found, we would be a natural to build the pipeline, with minimal risk. I set up the company and sold 80% of the shares to three companies: Moonie Oil, and two investors. I then raised the capital to do the initial work and waited for an oil discovery. It was a brilliant plan, but CMPS had no idea of how it worked. I took Ted Peacock to dinner with the Moonie Oil managers. He thought we were looking for a job. 'No Ted, we're the sellers' – a new experience for him. The company lasted a decade, but oil was never found.

Our publicist Kay Turnbull was a balloonist, a very good one. She was the president of the national association and had competed well in the world championships in Europe. Kay had joined the group to try to tell 'our story' in a coherent way. We were achieving wonderful successes with our work, but the world at large was unaware. Engineers generally take a back seat, and it is the clients who trumpet project success with little reference to us. CMPS questioned my plan to create publicity, but I pressed on into uncharted waters. Kay suggested we prepare entries for the National Engineering Awards, and were honoured with a 'Project of the Year' certificate by the ACEA (Association of Consulting Engineers Australia), for the Jackson to Moonie project. It was a great start. Kay suggested we take out full-page advertisements in the *Financial Review*, highlighting our work on this project. This was radical, as the Engineering Institution and the ACEA frowned on overt advertising, particularly in the national press. I thought if we did it subtly and focused on one point it might work, and we went ahead.

It caused a storm. Santos management told us we needed its permission to tell our story in the media, because we mentioned the Jackson to Moonie pipeline. I responded by saying the pipeline was secondary and the main point of the ads was how we had responded

ACEA award, QLD pipeline

to a technical problem. Santos didn't press the point. We had broken the ice. I had numerous calls praising the campaign, although I was aware that the legitimacy of the campaign was being discussed in the Institution and the ACEA. Regardless, we published five more ads and received no negative comments. Kay reported that our visibility in the oil and gas industry had soared. Over the following years we won many awards due to our excellent work, aided and abetted by the innovative presentations Kay prepared: success breeds success. Kay won plaudits in the Pipeline Industry Association and played a key role in its annual conference. Our staff became proud that their work was being recognised in the media. This new endeavour complemented the main business of delivering engineering and projects for our clients.

My old friends at Santos, John Squarek and Tony Wright, had left to form their own company, PMA, with John McKee, who was the MD, buying exploration permits from Western Mining. It was front page news as basically Santos's top four executives had left, making the chairman Alex Carmichael look silly. Carmichael managed to thwart the deal by convincing Western Mining to not follow through with the sale, leaving PMA in a hole. I asked John Squarek if it might be good to link our companies, as reservoir capability would help our growth and vertically integrate our skill set. They agreed as they needed money and I acquired 80% of

PMA, leaving the two Johns and Tony some equity.

Unfortunately, it quickly became evident the trio didn't want to be consultants and that we had little in common. John McKee left to become the director general of SECWA (the State Energy Commission of Western Australia). I now considered PMA a dud purchase. It was embarrassing, but I had few options. I was in the habit of going to the APPEA conferences to keep in touch with the exploration industry, as I felt the conference provided an early warning system for projects. A prominent explorationist was Peter Jamieson, who had started a new company, ORCA, with leases in the Alice Springs area. I was having coffee when he passed in a hurry. 'Hi,' I called. 'Too busy, catch you this evening,' he responded, and rushed off. A lot of the geologists used the conference to do 'farm-ins' (where new investors are found to fund the next round of drilling), and this clearly was Peter's mission.

Twenty minutes later, I was about to leave when Peter came rushing back. 'I need to talk to you. I understand you own most of PMA.' 'I do.' 'Well, I've been talking to them, and we have an interest in buying them. They'd be a ready-made management team for us, plus they have an extensive library of geotech data.' I said we had only had them for four to five months, and PMA was a key part of our future plans. Peter would not be dissuaded, and I asked if he had a price in mind. He

On the road to Darwin with Bob Perry

AMADEUS BASIN — DARWIN GAS PIPELINE
$380 MILLION LEVERAGED LEASE

The Government of the Northern Territory of Australia
Northern Territory Gas Pty. Limited
Australia and New Zealand Banking Group Limited
and National Australia Bank Limited
have pleasure in inviting

Mr Graham D Campbell

to attend the Signing Ceremony for financing of the
Gas Pipeline from the Amadeus Basin to Darwin.
To be held in the Function Room, Chan Building,
from 9.00 am to 1.00 pm Friday 28th June, 1985
followed by Dinner at Le St. Tropez Restaurant commencing at 7.30 p.m.

TO CONFIRM   DRESS TERRITORY RIG

Leveraged lease

hesitated and gave me a number. I said if he doubled it he had a deal. He said he'd get back to me. Later that afternoon I saw him in the bar, and he called me aside. 'I have to get one last director to agree. Are you still willing to go ahead?' 'Yes, but I need to know tonight.' 'OK,' he said. At the conference dinner, he confirmed it was a deal. I was over the moon; I felt I had got out of jail.

A few days later I had the purchase documents and took them to my board, as the deal represented a lot of money, over $3 million. The CMPS board agreed to the sale, but I knew the board members didn't understand the significance of the deal. I felt that PMA management could otherwise just walk out the door and abandon our company: they were just employees and I would be left with a geotech library.

The following week the sale was front page in the *Financial Review*. PMA joins ORCA – big coup. We were not mentioned in the article, which went on to say that the PMA guys had secured big option deals worth over $100 million as they put a high value on ORCA. That night in the CMPS boardroom, the directors were furious with me. Based on the article, we had lost millions!

I corrected their misperception. I said we had made a capital profit of 500% in five months. We had unloaded a lot of risk and our money was in the bank. The numbers in the *Financial Review* were speculation. Eric Mansfield would not be moved and asked Ted to look into whether I had fully informed the board. The investigation was dropped in a few days, but I had learned some valuable lessons. I had realised the board had little understanding of how speculative oil companies operate and dealing in equity, actual or perceived was foreign to them. Within two years, ORCA had gone broke and the PMA boys were looking for a new plan.

My life was taking many twists and turns. Ted Peacock arranged a meeting with Dr Peter Miller and me, to discuss Peter's role in FIDIC, the global consulting engineering organisation. Peter had been the president of the ACEA, and had gone on to run the world organisation. He had offered me a job after I had accepted with CMPS, but this wasn't discussed. UNESCO was holding a conference in Jakarta and FIDIC had been invited to provide a representative skilled in major transmission pipeline development. Peter hoped I would be FIDIC's representative. Ted felt it would promote the company, and I agreed to go. That was the extent of my briefing.

Jakarta was as steamy as ever. I caught up with our operations before heading for the conference hotel, the Wisma Warung, one with which I was unfamiliar. The meeting wasn't far across the square. I was back where I had started 15 years ago, on my way to Sulawesi.

I arrived at the conference early, around 9.30am, to learn the agenda, but nobody was there. The room was enormous, set up like the UN, with curved tables covered in green velvet arcing into a podium. I found a seat in the middle and waited for something to happen. At about 10.30, delegates started to file in and find seats. They were of all nationalities and many seemed to know each other. Several Chinese sat around me and I introduced myself. Finally, the front bench was filled and the chairman brought the meeting to order. He gave a long introduction which mentioned pipelines a couple of times, which reassured me that I was in the right place.

However, much of what the chairman said didn't make sense to me at all. One of the delegates rose and the chairman proclaimed, 'The chair recognises Egypt' – very impressive, I thought. A speech about development in Egypt followed, but nothing about pipelines. Speeches about development in various other countries continued, all with no mention of pipelines, till just before lunch at 1. I was mystified and decided to participate by raising my hand. 'The chair recognises China,' announced the chairman.' I was mystified. 'The chair recognises China,' he repeated. It suddenly hit me: I *was* in China, or at least I was seated with the Chinese delegates. I had not seen the sign saying 'China' in the section where I had plonked myself down. I rose from my seat and gave a short talk on pipeline development issues.

We broke for lunch and I collared the chairman. I told him I wasn't from China, but represented FIDIC. He smiled. 'I had a feeling you weren't Chinese. Your place is over there, on the side, with the International Bar Association (IBA) representative.'

After lunch, I introduced myself to the lawyer with whom I was sharing a table and asked if he had been to one of these UNESCO conferences before. 'Grahame, we're here for four days. It takes time to get to the subject. All the representatives are sent by their government as a reward. None of them will have much interest in the topic. They'll make speeches about whatever they know,' he said. 'This meeting isn't to progress knowledge on pipelines, but to promote diplomacy and goodwill.' It was a bit deflating to think I had three more days of this. The conference had a grand dinner and afterwards I called some business acquaintances to catch up on our corporate issues.

The following day at the conference delegates from a few more countries rose and spoke. Again, I felt the need to register my presence. 'The chair recognises FIDIC.' I smiled, a little taken aback, stood and expanded on my comments of the previous day, trying to put some flavour into the issues of third-world land use and community engagement. At afternoon tea, a member of the secretariat asked me to write a summary of the conference proceedings. 'You seem to be the only person here who knows anything about pipelines. Would it be possible to get a statement related to the subject of the meeting?' I told him I'd try. The next day dragged on, and I concentrated on drafting a broad statement of the issues that developing countries needed to consider if they wanted a successful pipeline project. I handed over the handwritten notes and went off to another dinner.

After dinner, the chairman approached me warmly. 'I think you've saved our bacon. We've typed it up and, if you agree, we'll issue it as the congress outcome.' I read it through, corrected a couple of mistakes and passed it back. The following morning it was distributed. At lunch, the chairman asked for a vote on the communiqué and received a unanimous acceptance and a round of applause. That was it, and we all left in good spirits.

I returned to Australia, nonplussed: so *that's* how the UN runs. Two months later I received a letter from FIDIC headquarters, thanking me for the excellent feedback on the congress. The writer of the letter added that FIDIC wanted to expand its 'Red Book', the international contract document to include a section on pipelines, covering the unique nature of the contracting environment. I was invited to chair a committee to conclude such an assignment. I was reassured that my committee would be appointed, and I would only have to chair a couple of meetings before the annual conference in Vienna, where I could present my findings. This sounded like a lot of work, but really all I needed to do was take our standard contract terms and massage the language to suit the 'Red Book' style.

My committee co-members were from Denmark, Holland and England. I circulated a draft and waited for a response. Six weeks later I had their comments and we were almost done. I looked forward to Vienna. ACEA is a national association of the partners of firms affiliated; I was not a member. The opening cocktail party was held in the palace where the OPEC meetings occurred; it was very grand. Margaret and I joined the throng, which resembled the UN; there were fine African and Indian ladies wearing their very best. I was accosted by an Australian. 'Dale McBean,' he said, then added accusingly, 'I don't know you. Where are you from?' 'CMPS.' 'Well, why don't you join us?' I said I would shortly after I finished the conversation I was having with an engineer from Tanzania.

Before I could move on, McBean was back. 'I understand you're chairing a subcommittee.' His tone had changed completely; it seemed that it was now his problem rather than mine that he didn't know me. I noticed Peter Miller had joined McBean's group, and I went over. Peter warmly greeted us. 'Grahame, so glad to see you and Margaret! The executive is so pleased with your work. We're looking forward to your presentation on Wednesday.' He introduced us to the other Australians. The conference was the grandest occasion I had ever attended, and I was warming to the accolades, in spite of the fact that I hadn't seemed to have done much. It was my first exposure to ACEA, but not the last.

During the 1980s, the consulting business had changed dramatically. The traditional areas of building and infrastructure were under threat from foreign competition, and margins had been slashed. Integrated services were attractive to clients, but the risks were higher. The foreign contractors were willing to take construction risk on occasions, which we never would do. Davy in South Australia had won the Redcliffe project at minimal profit, hoping to make money with the variations, but the Fluor import, Brad Kern, had minimised that. When they went to commission the plant, they found all the valves – about 3,000 – were unsuitable for cryogenic service. It was a major blow and delayed the start-up by about six months. When they finally got going, the plant had to shut due to a build-up of tars in the vessels. It was process technology 101, and directly related to mixing the gas liquids with the crude oil in Moomba – exactly what I had told them not to do, for other reasons. Shortly after that, Davy went bust on another project in the North Sea for Exxon. A salutatory lesson for our industry.

Meanwhile, the Darwin project was reaching a climax, and we were setting new world records again. The construction was completed in 14 months for the 1,600km. I was proud. It had been the first project I had experienced in which everybody pulled together, and money was made all round. Shortly after commissioning, CSR sold its interest for $25 million, having contributed no capital under the leverage lease arrangements. CSR had taken the risk on the downside, but our management skills had negated that. I didn't ever see Jack Campbell again.

I had taken an interest in the Australian Pipeline Industry Association (APIA). It was a broad group covering owners, contractors, engineers and suppliers. I joined the organising committee and finally was elected president for three years. It took time out of my schedule but gave me an excellent networking base.

We had hit a new high with the success of the Darwin pipeline, but the relentless commercial imperative of finding new projects was always bearing down. Family life was good, and the boys were playing football and doing well at school. Margaret enjoyed the life in Sydney, and we regularly travelled to Armidale to share holidays with the cousins. Her brother and sister had families there. The boys enjoyed the rural environment.

Darwin gets gas. Alan Newham, Mark Twycross, Graham Tait and KK Lee

27. Conquering the PNG Highlands: 1985

We were on a high, but as always we had to find the next big project to keep the business ticking over, and were continually speculating on where development would occur. Papua New Guinea was intriguing. While Oil Search had been exploring for 50 years with no success, Gulf Oil and others were becoming more excited about the prospectivity and had made small discoveries in the highlands. Our question was 'how will you get the oil out' if found. Geologists never think of this, but it was our business. I asked our engineers and surveyors to run some scenarios. We spent a couple of months examining the seismic issues, jungles and sea port possibilities. Eventually, I put a report together and had it printed in the *Oil & Gas Journal*. I had done another paper for the journal on the Wollongong pipeline problems studying unstable slopes for pipelines, and the editors were happy to accept my paper on New Guinea.

At about this time, Chevron Oil bought Gulf Oil and started looking at export strategies. Chevron, which had been impressed by the PNG article, invited us to go to California to discuss our work. This led to a commission to expand our studies and finally do a full-blown feasibility report. We had our new project! I was unaware that Steve Bechtel was on the board of Chevron – Bechtel was our main competition. Even so, it seemed that Bechtel was unaware of our deepening position until we were totally embedded in the development. It asked Chevron to dismiss us, on the grounds that it had the skills to do the work and would provide a more integrated service, close to the head office in California. Chevron declined and set up headquarters in Brisbane, near our office. The project would prove to be the biggest challenge in Chevron's history.

Meanwhile, our relationship with Williams Bros was falling apart. I was talking to a colleague Tom Labiosa in Houston about support for bids in Indonesia when he told me he was no longer Williams Bros' Houston chief and didn't even work for the company anymore. It had just gone 5pm his time, and he had received a note from Larry Fisher saying that the entire marine division had been terminated. I asked Tom what he would do. 'I have no plans. This has come out of the blue.' Impulsively, I said I would rehire the whole group and they could all work for CMPS. 'Really?' 'Yes, consider yourself hired.' The next day I received a call from Larry. 'You have no permission to do this!' he exclaimed. 'I order you to rescind your offer!' I said I didn't work for him, and he could bring it up at the next joint venture committee meeting.

I called Ted Peacock and told him we had a Houston office, fully staffed and ready to go. He invited me to lunch, as he always did in a crisis. 'Do you know what you're doing?' he asked. 'Yes,' I said, 'I'm getting on with business. The PNG project will be the marine division's first big job.'

Williams Bros Engineering Company was in crisis. I'd heard that US Filter had on-sold it to Ashland Oil and Al Dorman had been appointed the new chief. It had been integrated with the other groups and had been finally subsumed into a new entity that had been spun out of Ashland Oil. Ashland had acquired US Filter, and subsequently got into problems over an Iranian oil shipment (which, basically, they didn't pay for). Ashland on-sold the oil and washed the funds through a platinum mine in east Africa. It took the US government ten years to unravel the fraud. An Ashland refinery also spilled 750,000 gallons of oil into the Monongahela River in West Virginia. The oil spill flowed to Pittsburgh where it threatened water supplies. All this resulted in sackings, fines and a restructure.

The engineering companies were spun out as an employee buyout. Al Dorman stayed on as the chief and he set about reshaping the future for the aggregation of firms. It would be run out of Los Angeles; years later it would be renamed AECOM. I asked Ted to call Dorman and put him on notice that we needed to recalibrate our relationship. Ted hated this type of confrontation, but I was determined. A month later Dorman arrived, without Larry Fisher, who had himself been terminated. It was clear to me that my group in Houston was not strong enough to do the PNG marine pipeline work, as it had expanded to more than $1 billion of investment, and I had started talking to RJ Brown, a leading marine *pipeline* specialist. Said Khan, the RJ Brown boss in Singapore, was keen to form a joint venture, but we had to clear it with WB. I hit it off really well with Al Dorman, and we discussed my philosophy of expansion. He agreed to the new joint venture, and I was free to form RJ Brown-CMPS. My new group in Houston would work on the offshore delivery platform in the gulf. Chevron accepted the new arrangements and we had a strong base to attack the market.

Meanwhile, CMPS also had a new crisis, with the resignation of managing director David Evans. Ted Peacock retook the role along with his chairman's role. The oil and gas business and Queensland under Kevin Napier were carrying the company. Ted took the view that the business was cyclical and the others would eventually come good. Kevin agreed with me that major surgery was justified, and we had many talks in Brisbane. I was spending time there as the state government considered stepping into a fight between the gas producers over pricing of gas into Gladstone, a major industrial area. We were hoping to be appointed the managers for the natural gas transmission and distribution system. During my presidency of APIA we hosted the minister for mines and energy, Brian Austin at our association dinner in Brisbane. He was new to the job and surprisingly announced that the Queensland government would build the pipeline and the producers would use it. All the industry representatives were there to hear him. The key ones, including the minister himself, were at my table. CSR bristled at this and refused to negotiate. I smiled and remembered the Jackson project. To illustrate who was in control the minister mentioned he was also the minister for the arts and that CSR would sponsor the Queensland Ballet and Moonie Oil could contribute to the Art Gallery. The chat around the table stopped. The CSR representative left. 'Prickly chap' was the minister's only comment. Sometime after, the minister experienced some turbulence and was sent to gaol. In the interim, we managed to win the government contract to build the State Gas Pipeline. I was very pleased as work was scarce.

Peacock called me to lunch at the club. He had decided to appoint a new managing director and retire as chairman He told me I was in the running and asked how I felt about that. It didn't surprise me and after a moment I told him I was happy where I was. I was wedded to the oil and gas business, and my time in Melbourne a decade earlier had confirmed that. He didn't press the point.

Meanwhile, I needed to organise our Kutubu oil pipeline project. Bob Perry, who had delivered the Darwin pipeline, signed on as our PNG construction manager. He had another string to his bow, in that he had been a pilot in the Canadian air force and in the Cold War had flown NATO missions in Europe. I always felt safe when he was in the plane with me. We flew to Port Moresby for a closer look at the project, for it had progressed to approval for development. A route had been established to the south coast. A major problem emerged regarding the traverse of the marshy river delta area. Near the coast, putting the pipeline in the Kikori river for 30km would be easier than trying to negotiate the marshes. This had never been considered before. Exxon had tried to do an exploratory oil well in the area earlier, had spent $25 million trying to form a solid base to drill, and then abandoned the exercise. We learned a lot from this.

Bob and I flew to Kikori, in the river delta, and found everything inundated. We landed at Delta camp in driving rain. It was run by an eccentric Australian who had been there for decades, trading with the locals. We went to his operations to introduce ourselves and were taken back in time 50 years. The compound was nondescript and set adjacent to the river, which was fast-flowing from the torrential rain. A series of rambling buildings housed his office and warehouses. In the dim light, he sat at his desk with a .45 Colt in easy reach, looking like

Humphrey Bogart in *The African Queen*. There was an iron grill behind his seat to protect him from the river access, where customers pulled up their boats. I learned later he was the agent for the ANZ Bank and his various businesses had made him a multimillionaire. His kids from three wives were educated in Swiss finishing schools, which seemed incongruous given our present surroundings. He was most welcoming and spent some time describing the local environment. He warned us to not underestimate the locals and to deal with them carefully. They seemed primitive but had a well-developed business sense. Thanking him we crossed to our camp a kilometre away, it had 30cm of water pooled across it. I stood on a veranda with Jeff Shepherd, the McConnell Dowel construction manager, and looked out at the scene. The river, our main transport access, was raging. 'Things will get better,' he assured me with his usual optimism. I noted an overtone of frustration in his voice. Jeff had taken on the toughest job of his career but was up for the challenge.

Our first flight upriver was to see the survey crews in action. We flew in an old Hughes helicopter, with a big bubble in the front. There were no doors. Puzzlingly, the pilot explained the absence of doors by saying we had no windscreen wipers. When we flew into a storm, his ability to determine where we were in the mountainous terrain was hampered by the chopper's aforementioned lack of wipers. He needed to swing out to see.

Somehow, we located the survey platform and set down in thick jungle on a structure of heavy bamboo. The jungle canopy seemed a hundred metres above our heads. We climbed into the terrain below, but never actually hit the ground as the tree roots were several metres in the air, like writhing giant snakes. Everything was wet and slimy, with the most amazing beetles scuttling around. One I saw was brown and black with luminous blue boots. After an hour and a half, we stopped to take stock. We had come about 200m. There was no sign of the survey crew. 'Where are they?' I asked. 'Maybe another 300m,' Bob said. I started to worry about getting out before dark. We decided to go back, and I asked what happened if the surveyors got stuck. I wouldn't fancy spending the night here, even on the chopper platform. It gave me a warm feeling towards them and the job they were doing. I also wondered about the construction difficulties. We had been submerged in an otherworld, with only a small amount of light filtering through the canopy.

There were around thirty choppers operating on the project, with no weather forecasts or detailed flight plans. Flights were monitored based on destination and estimated duration. The following day we planned to go to Kutubu at the other end of the line. Bob and I regarded our new chopper, a type I'd never seen. It was a

'Squirrel', made by the French. I joked to the pilot that we must have windscreen wipers as the doors were still there. He looked at me, knotting his brow. Bob checked the instruments as usual, for this time we had a long journey ahead. The pilot took this opportunity to announce he had just arrived in PNG from the Antarctic and any help on directions we could give him would be welcome. Bob became the co-pilot. 'We follow the river upstream until the valley disappears into a cliff,' he told the pilot, 'and then you hover up to find another stream heading in a similar direction.'

Kikori Junction was supposed to be our first port of call, but the villagers were fighting among themselves, and we were told not to land. We circled and saw the locals throwing spears. It was hard to say if we were the target. We flew on to the second station to check our camp, which had been washed out, forcing our team into the trees for safety. They were safe, but we needed to re-establish on higher ground. As we circled, I recognised some faces from Tennant Creek in the Northern Territory.

We relied on the rivers to transport our supplies into the interior. Until the road was constructed it would be our only artery. Floods were common, and the torrent was difficult to navigate. As we flew north for the final leg, the gorge narrowed alarmingly. From our vantage point a few hundred metres above the river, I found the scene very beautiful. We came upon a blank cliff with the river pouring from a hole in the wall. I was mesmerised. We circled until Bob told the pilot to rise up into the fog formed by the waterfall, saying, 'At some point we'll break into clear air.' Wow … when we broke free we all breathed again. The chopper swung to the left and followed the ridges to some clearings, and I sighted a flare from a small camp. We had arrived. Lake Kutubu began to emerge beyond the jungle in the brilliant sunlight; a large pool resting on an ancient volcano. It is surrounded by pleasant rolling hills in a cool environment. Signs of agriculture formed a necklace at the edge of the water.

The main crude oil stabilisation plant was serviced by flow lines from several discovery wells, which stretched tens of kilometres in different directions. There was a large camp to house the 1,000-or-so workers. The airstrip which allowed heavy equipment to be flown in would be a major asset for our contractors. Bob and I toured the area and talked to the managers to get a feel for the problems they anticipated. PNG is subject to attack by the 'rascals' – local gangs whose activities include extortion and murder. Kutubu was too remote at this stage but security was alert to the potential in the future. Port Moresby was under siege from them; it had turned the city into one of the most dangerous in the world. PNG is a difficult place to work. The tribal tensions exist at a very local level. Fights break out constantly for no apparent reason keeping our people on their toes. Later in the day, we managed to join a crew change over flight direct to Port Moresby to join the commercial flight back to Brisbane. It had been a revelation to see the progress that had been made in such a short time.

Back in Sydney, CMPS was still mired in trouble. Over lunch, Ted Peacock wanted to talk to me again about the future. He asked what would induce me to seek the top job of managing director. I told him straight that his handling of the process had been poor, and David Evans had never had a chance to succeed. David couldn't solve the problems Peacock had created as every effort to change would be questioned. I said if ever I did take the job I would terminate the majority of the board to make a fresh start. Ted was taken aback by this. I said that CMPS had suffered ten years of neglect, and he should accept that his management was largely the problem. After another bottle of red, Ted admitted having made some mistakes, but said there was a broad base for me to build on if I wanted to accept the challenge. I figured that I had two options: put my hand up for the job or find a bigger job in the oil and gas industry somewhere else. I needed to think about it.

WB-CMPS was No.1 in pipelines in Australia, probably in the world, but were small players in production systems. At a conference I had met John Morhall, a senior manager with Kellogg, which was a big player in oil and gas production around the world, Morhall was based in Singapore. Kevin Napier in Brisbane recommended I speak to him as he was being transferred back to head office in the USA and didn't want to go. John had been the key man in winning the North West Shelf LNG plant engineering contract. We talked, and I offered him a job in Sydney in the management team. He accepted and brought a new flavour to our client profile. He was also a prime candidate for my job if I decided to take Ted's offer.

I felt comfortable holding two large contracts, in PNG and Queensland. The future looked strong, but our joint venture with Williams Bros was not helping. I decided that we needed stronger partners in oil and gas, as did John Morhall, and we signalled a termination of the joint venture. It had been nearly 20 years, a journey that had once invested the partners with warm friendships. But now the players had changed and the shared vision had evaporated. Over six years I had built a business of which I was very proud. The team was the best in the country and could compete on the world stage.

I called Ted and said that after much consideration I felt I could take on CMPS, as the oil and gas business had a solid future and Kevin Napier was strong in Queensland. Ted initiated a process to hand over the leadership.

Jack May, my successor in Melbourne, was promoted by Eric Mansfield as an alternative candidate, so the CMPS board had a choice. I was fine with that, as I had other options and would leave if not selected. I spoke to Ted again over another long lunch and reiterated my position that radical surgery would ensue if I was elected by the board. He advised me to do it gradually, so as not to create a collapse.

A couple of weeks later Ted called to advise that I was the new CEO and managing director. He had appointed Eric Mansfield to succeed him as chairman. Ted asked if we could have regular meetings so he could provide some guidance. I made it clear I wanted no help and he could retire full time. I never saw him again.

Part VII
The engineering business
1987

28. CMPS

The worst year of my life, again...

This was a strange period for me. I knew what I had to do, but I had a steep learning curve to climb. My first month in charge was spent going through the accounts and trying to imagine what business structure would work for 'the new CMPS'. I spoke with all the senior executives and head office staff and tried to find a core team to nut out a future. The main problem was a bloated middle management of 'associates', who felt entitled. The executive board members felt they had a privileged position, too. I felt I had to create a structure and then try to fit people into the roles, regardless of the history. I avoided socialising with executives and staff, to keep my mind clear. Head office was the big problem; I decided to terminate all positions other than in finance which was essential. That was easy, and it cut costs immediately.

The next part was tough; I had to evaluate about thirty subsections of the group that had not performed for ages, property services, architecture and the like which had popped up at various times. I needed to understand if these groups were badly led, or not really our business. I interviewed the head and second in command of each group, and made a decision on their future. This was painful and difficult, as I had known a lot of the managers for decades. It was not easy to make logical judgements, and I largely relied on gut feel. I needed to create a company that was focused and collegiate. I felt resource development and infrastructure were the core activities.

Finally, I had to deal with the board. I had spoken with each of them to assess their support. The biggest problem was Eric Mansfield, whom Ted had installed as chairman in his final weeks. Eric was the company's lead marketing manager, 'the public face of the company', but I couldn't find any projects in which he had been a key influence. He had also employed me all those years ago. I asked him to come to my office on the morning of our board meeting. He sat opposite me with an expectant expression. Without preamble I said, 'I have no role for you in my executive team.' He stared at me impassively and straightened up. 'You can't sack me. I am the chairman.' I paused, then said, 'You will still be the chairman, just a non-executive chairman. I'm not talking about your board role.' Eric sat quivering, then rose and with no further comment left the room. I stared out of the window until my secretary entered with the board papers. She looked at me. 'Are you alright?' 'Not really,' I replied. 'I don't think it will be a good meeting.' An hour later, thirty minutes before the board meeting, Eric returned to my office and submitted his resignation. I accepted it and he left the building. At the meeting, Bob Morgan was elected as the new chairman. When I didn't offer board member Jack May, who had lost to me in the CEO contest, a key management role, he resigned. Frank O'Brien, another board member, was running a subsidiary company, Integral Fibre Systems, which I had decided to sell because of its high risk profile. Frank was happy for it to be sold, but wanted to remain on the board. I explained he was part of the Integral Fibre Systems package and could not remain. It was a hard meeting and a hard week, and I wondered what was being said about me in the corridors. Kevin Napier, our Brisbane manager, took me aside 'Grahame, I support what you are doing. I have fought head office for a decade and built a business from scratch. It's a cultural thing. The old partners feel they are ahead of the pack, but they are comparing themselves to their peers. There is a whole new set of competitors whom they don't see; they have a contractor pedigree.' I was reminded of Nairn's comments about contractors in Melbourne decades before; the elitist attitude.

Consulting engineering was going through a major change. The ACEA was their industry association. Terms of engagement, fee structures and an ethics standard reinforced their independence from contractors and suppliers. The original partnership structures had morphed into corporate arrangements to satisfy personal risk issues and insurance problems. However, all this was becoming out of step with industry. Resource and infrastructure companies were being offered new alternatives. Construction companies and equipment suppliers were attempting to take the lead role in projects and the traditional clients were attracted to the apparent lower risk. 'If your designs are competent why don't you take the construction risk?' we were asked. This forced us to work in a secondary role with no value attached to our 'independence'. Large foreign contractors were offering attractive packages involving 'complete service' arrangements, and we had no financial strength to combat the attack. Lawyers were pushing contracts that seemed to remove risk from the owners with fixed price where the design had not been developed sufficiently. This polarised the situation with a rise in litigation as projects unravelled during design development. Over many years, delayed work and bankruptcies evolved until better understanding of the problem occurred.

After slimming down the operations with many of the subdivisions gone, I gathered the top twenty managers and gave my view of the future. There was spirited debate largely coming from the Oil & Gas division which held the project management skills and the Queensland division which was strong in mining and infrastructure. Their lead inspired the other locations to emulate the success. Key staff were relocated to support the new enthusiasm, and I waited to see the results.

The new structure would focus the corporate effort, but I was determined to change our relationship with the market. Taking equity positions in projects would allow us to dismount the treadmill of continually diminishing man hour margins but expose us to higher risks. My experience with the Broome Oil Pipeline and the Palm Valley Gas pipeline had shown me the way. I had watched the investors in the Darwin pipeline make huge profits off the back of our ideas, and although we had done well financially, it was small compared to the owners' returns. All of these thoughts were at odds with the ACEA members' concept of their work. A conflict of interest could not be avoided, they cried! My exposure overseas, and particularly to Williams Brothers, made me realise I had to compete with Bechtel, Fluor and Kellogg, to name a few, if I was to stay in business.

I was attracted to the strategy of a competitor, Australian but not a member of ACEA. Minproc Engineering had developed a new design for the development of small gold mines. It stripped the construction down to the minimum recognising that the resource would last less than ten years and hence the plant life should match that. They aligned themselves with a bank that was funding these projects and convinced them to only lend if Minproc was the developer. This led to the development of seventy-odd plants and a bonanza for Minproc. I thought these strategies were brilliant. The bank was happy as it knew the product was competent and the mine developer was given a complete package. Bob Wilde, the CEO, then negotiated to acquire a suite of major mining assets from a liquidator on the basis that they manage these mines and eventually acquire the equity. The deal eventually fell over as the mines could not be brought to profitability. However, this caused a backlash among the larger mining operators who saw Minproc as a competitor and would not hire them for their traditional engineering services. It was clear I needed to tread warily.

Indonesia is a huge market, and we had a good oil and gas business established. All areas of business in the country are divided into various influence zones. Wealthy Indonesians control each of these areas. I had hired John Caporn to take us into the property development area. He had worked in government for John Button, the Australian federal industry minister. Bakrie Brothers was the largest *bumiputera* company in Indonesia, and a protected species. President Suharto gave Bakri Brothers many privileges, but the company continually tripped up. Aburizal Bakrie was the boss until Suharto made him step down from the public company in favour of Tanri Abeng, who had run the Bintang brewery and other successful businesses. However, Bakrie had private family interests which still operated separately. Caporn had negotiated a deal for engineering Aburizal's new urban apartment complex. There were thirty-two towers, each thirty-nine storeys, housing around 4,000 apartments. A shopping centre, sports fields and parks made it a totally integrated living space in the heart of the city of Jakarta. He financed it by selling off the plan before anything started. It all sold in one day – obviously too cheaply from the response. There were many site problems, including drainage and a large cemetery which had to be moved. We needed to fly in around a hundred designers and draughtsmen, whom we housed nearby in a gymnasium across the road from the immigration department. I worried about breaches of the visa rules and we kept a low profile. It was difficult work as the client kept changing the overall design parameters with no understanding of the impact on our work. Culturally we were consistently challenged to 'keep up' and learn the 'Asian way'. Every visit I challenged our commercial position as we were slow to get paid and were exposed to the maximum risk.

Shortly after this, John landed another development in the foothills going towards Bandung. It was called Royal Sentul, an upmarket residential suburb comprising several golf courses and a polo field. The earthworks for the access road was a major job in itself. Our client was a Chinese family, the Riadys, who owned the Lippo Group. They had emigrated from Fujian province in China and made a fortune in banking and major developments. Lippo had developed the old Kemayoran Airport site as an integrated suburban and shopping complex and also had another large development around golf courses on the west side of Jakarta. We were appointed to provide engineering for this, and our profile was soaring.

Finally, renowned Australian architect Philip Cox invited us to join him in a bid for the 40ha site opposite the Hilton in downtown Jakarta. The project was essentially to conceptualise a new CBD for Jakarta. Cox would lay out the town plan and we would design the roads, water supply, sewerage system and power supply. I thought Australians were on the nose for Indonesian government jobs, as the two nations were having diplomatic fights over border issues. The site was owned by the Army Pension Fund controlled by President Suharto. We won the contract, but in joint venture with a Japanese group. This was to access cheap Japanese government funding – an arrangement we would often see in regional decisions. Australia had no equivalent of the concept. We had had a similar project in Singapore decades ago working with the World Bank and the Singapore government. The project was massive; it was larger than building the Perth CBD in Australia and was an attempt by the Indonesian government to rival Singapore as a business hub for Asia. All in all, we had far more work than we could finance, and cash flow was critical. Indonesia was similar to Malaysia, where paying the engineer was low on the list of priorities. I instructed our managers to keep within a maximum payables limit and if we exceeded, to stop work. This was difficult for engineers, as they revelled in the work. Nothing in Australia came close to these opportunities. We had a tiger by the tail.

Indonesia hosted our company's largest projects, I travelled there many times trying to keep the cash flow moving. We were winning plaudits with Canberra for our export drive, but I needed to revisit the core business.

Our regional structure needed to be more integrated to capture the skills more broadly. I spoke to the industry leaders and with their assistance reorganised the company into seven customer sector groups. This was part of a matrix organisation that recognised the regional structure as the P&L (profit and loss) keepers but kept the customer groups our main focus. The senior team needed to be collegiate to make this work, and communication was the key. This put a lot of pressure on me to keep everybody focused.

There was more work to be done. I was still searching for ways to engage the staff. CMPS shareholdings had been confined to the top fifty or so people. I was hoping to have all employees be shareholders. The tax system allowed staff to acquire $1,000 worth of shares tax-free annually. We activated a program to allow this to happen. Also, I was keen to get our young achievers to participate in special training arrangements which would prepare them for management roles. I wanted everybody to believe they personally could stimulate change and innovation.

I was trying to find a business along the lines of Minproc's goldmines to accelerate growth. While on one of my trips to Tulsa, Morgan Greenwood, who had been the president of Resource Sciences Corporation under David Williams, had introduced me to Rick Lafferty. Rick was a grandson of a famous Wall Street banker who went broke in the crash of '29. Rick worked with Williams Technologies in Tulsa, a spin-off from David Williams's empire that he had sold when he was stricken with cancer. Rick was working with the Rentech Corporation, who had developed a plant which converted natural gas to diesel fuel. I encouraged Rick to come to Sydney to expand on his ideas for the Australian energy industry. I was attracted to the concept of utilising small gas fields remote from infrastructure. Rick said the gas conversion plant could be truck-mounted, and convert natural gas to diesel fuel with the so-called Rentech process. It was a Fisher-Tropsch adaption with a new iron catalyst. Germany had developed the process to convert coal to liquid transport fuels during the Second World War. My objective was to build own and operate several of these plants in remote locations where diesel would sell at a premium. Australia had many small gas fields suitable for this technology. Rentech were completing a plant in Pueblo, Colorado, and I was welcome to visit. It was important to see a working plant and I fitted in a visit to Pueblo on my next US trip. We arrived in a snowstorm, but it was clear that the gas conversion plant wouldn't fit on a truck, or a fleet of trucks for that matter. It was funded by the city to run the bus fleet, and was supposedly fed methane from a nearby rubbish tip. It all sounded utopian. I met the construction manager, who gave me a litany of problems, chiefly that no gas had come out of the rubbish tip, so they were forced to use expensive natural gas. Also, some of the units didn't work and were being modified. Denis Jacobsen, the inventor, explained that government intervention had caused all the problems and I shouldn't be put off. Well, I was put off. I told Rick Lafferty that we needed a realistic business plan that would make sense in Australia. There was a lot more work to do. I hadn't found my 'goldmine'!

Opportunities were emerging all around. A railway from Alice Springs to Darwin was being revived. Our successful pipeline following the same route might be interesting for the promoters. During a trip to Darwin, I played tennis in the Sunday midday sun with Ted Campbell. Afterwards, we sat chatting about the future of the Territory over a few schooners. I had won the game and was feeling on top of the world. The following morning I met with the railway proponents and suddenly felt a large clamp across my shoulders. I was semi-paralysed.

Pueblo Rentech plant with Steve Hollis and Rick Lafferty

An ambulance was called, and I ended up in Darwin hospital for three days having tests and being under observation. I wondered how this could happen to a fit, smart person. I recounted the previous day's events and my lifestyle over the prior year. Maybe I wasn't as bulletproof, or as smart as I thought. But no enzymes were found in my blood. I told myself that I hadn't had a heart attack, but realised what I'd suffered was something close. Back in Sydney, the specialist prescribed an angiogram and balloon widening of my arteries was performed. The Chairman of RailNorth did award us the feasibility study for the rail proposal, so the trip was a success. I was as good as new.

I was also feeling good about the reorganisation of CMPS, and I started to change my role in the organisation. We were in the top group of engineering consulting companies in Australia but still had little standing in the commercial world. I was invited to join the Asia Australia Council, which was led by Steven Fitzgerald and based at the University of New South Wales. I also became a member of the Pacific Basin Economic Council (PBEC), which was a business version of APEC. Senior business and political leaders were involved. My presidency of APIA involved travel around Australia; I could combine this with visits to our offices in each state. I was leaving the running of the business to the senior management, which I had structured into a matrix organisation, as mentioned earlier.

I hadn't abandoned my love of music. By chance, I discovered that Bob LaRue had returned to Australia after working for Roy Huffington for many years. He and his wife Paula lived close by, and I was able to play some jazz informally at their parties. Paula had toured the USA with her sister before her marriage. Her sister Julie had introduced us in Houston all those years ago. Julie had also returned to Australia but lived in Cairns in North Queensland. Bob was now working with Australian oil exploration companies, and we spent many hours discussing the future of the industry.

29. We crack the private road business: 1988

My equity dream comes true.

I had a stroke of luck. When walking around Chatswood one lunchtime, I ran into Alan Livingstone, an old friend from the railways. He had been a year behind me in the trainee program. We had recently met at a cocktail party in the city. I'd had no idea he was based in Chatswood. We had lunch and he told me the story of the Abigroup. They had expanded into many areas, including owning car parks and developing major infrastructure for the government; largely dams and highways. Once listed on the stock exchange they came to the attention of Lee Ming Tee, a Malaysian Chinese noted for his manoeuvring on the stock market. He eventually bought a controlling interest and Jim and Alan were out of a job, although with plenty of money.

Alan was dabbling in investments, and we talked about infrastructure developments. He was the person I needed to launch us into privatised infrastructure. I invited him to join the firm as NSW manager, to learn the ropes. He said, 'I don't know anything about running a consulting engineering business.' I replied, 'I'm looking for a manager who understands the infrastructure business.' Understanding the commercial reality of a contractor was his real skill. This was an interim appointment until we could identify our infrastructure 'target'. Alan eventually accepted, and we set about looking for the prize. After my trial efforts with pipelines in the Northern Territory and Western Australia, we needed to find a project where we weren't competing with our traditional clients. Our focus would come down to privatised infrastructure (roads, rail, water systems, etc.).

We didn't have to wait long. The new Liberal NSW government announced a plan for private toll roads around Sydney. The first was a tender to develop the M4 motorway running east–west through the western suburbs. This was our chance, and Statewide Roads (SWR) was formed as the company to develop the road. Alan became the managing director. However, my enthusiasm was dampened at our next CMPS board meeting. The chairman, Bob Morgan, was concerned about the liabilities the SWR project would attract and wanted to minimise the risk to the operating company. I explained that there would be no parent guarantees and that the new company would seek no support from CMPS. Bob questioned the impact the project might have on our professional independence and our reputation. I explained we were not competing with our clients and that the competition came from construction contractors.

The meeting brought to a head undercurrents created by my new style of leadership and direction. I held my ground. CMPS would provide services at normal rates, and the company would sell equity to pay for the bid, which could amount to $1 million – well above our normal costs. Alan Livingstone was able to find investors, and we went ahead. It was important to create a credible board for SWR and Bruce Loder, a former commissioner for main roads, was recruited, along with accountant Bill Widen. Nick Young, our in-house lawyer and admin chief, was invited to join Alan and me. I assumed the role of chairman.

Kevin Napier in Brisbane was a champion. He had built the biggest engineering business in Queensland with mining and infrastructure projects. Kevin's team had successfully managed the development of two toll roads for the government there. This experience would be the bedrock of efforts to build credibility for our bid. CMPS had the in-house skills to put the bid together, and we felt we could devise our own finance plan. Our strategy was for SWR to put a construction management team together and avoid the prime contractor cost. Also, we would have the banks in competition to provide the debt to finance the project. These two decisions would be pivotal to keeping our costs low and avoiding large fees charged by merchant banks. Alan recruited key managers from his former construction associates and created a small, effective team to deliver the project. To put it in financial terms we collateralised all the small contractor balance sheets to spread the risk and satisfy the financiers on completion guarantees.

Eventually, the CBA bank made us an offer that was beyond our wildest dreams. All was in place to submit the bid. A serious question was how the government would evaluate the offers as there were no precedents. The development would generate spin-off benefits for business adjacent to the road; should we factor this in? No, we decided to include a service centre with a petrol station and fast food franchises only. The toll plaza location was important, as we tolled in both directions; it was an open system. The plaza also needed to be in an area where noise could be contained. Only one location, east of Parramatta, seemed to fit the bill. All of the pieces were in place, and our bid was submitted.

Success with the toll road would change everything. Never had an engineering company in the world owned and operated such an asset. I asked Alan how he expected the process to unfold. He said we should expect to wait a while for the politics to be developed. Our main advantage was the simplicity of the bid, 'time and toll'. It would all fit on one page. How long did we want to charge tolls before we gave it back to the government and what was the toll per vehicle? Our risk was construction time and cost. Of course, attracting traffic was key, but we felt that a road in the most travelled corridor in Australia was a good bet. This was underpinned by extensive traffic studies by independent experts. Our several-week wait was an anxious period for me. Alan was quietly confident for reasons I didn't understand. Finally, he called to say we had been invited to attend a clarification meeting at the main roads offices. This was wonderful. We were competitive!

Detailed discussions ensued with the authorities. We had concluded that the road could be built in two years and at a cost of about half of what the Department of Main Roads had estimated. It was a brave challenge, but we felt we could do it. Interest rates were high and represented a significant long-term cost to the project. At about 17%, they were expected to fall over the next couple of years, but nobody could guarantee that.

The SWR board met to review our position. Our design was checked again, and costs were confirmed. About thirty subcontractors were quizzed about their teams and availability. We rechecked the assumptions on utility relocation and other external issues that might cause problems. Our drainage design was a major area for concern. The erection of sound barriers and landscaping needed to be agreed through several local council areas.

After a tense wait, we were called in for final discussions. Alan answered their questions as best as he could, and we waited for more weeks. Finally, we were announced as the preferred bidder. We all let out a collective sigh of relief. It was a huge hurdle to cross, but we had some hard work still to do. The financial packaging details and the contract agreement needed to be finalised. Our arrangements with the Commonwealth Bank allowed for them to provide 100% of the debt in exchange for a 12.5% preference share. We were required to provide no more equity. Blake Dawson Waldron was the law firm that the DMR retained, and the flamboyant Terry Burke was its lead lawyer. I was a director of the Macro Engineering Society at Sydney University, where Terry was also a director, and we planned to go to a world conference in Barcelona.

After I had delivered my paper at the conference, I received a message that my father had died from bowel cancer. I was aware that he was sick but unaware that he was near death. The flight back was sad. Both my parents had died while I was on the other side of the world. The death of a parent is always a time to reflect on one's choice of lifestyle and balance. I had always tried to keep family, work, music and tennis in my life but my last few years had been dominated by work. I enjoyed the challenge and was always competitive. My relationship with my father had been distant, although with his grandchildren he had come to life. He liked spending time with them, and they were all remembered in his will with a nest egg to help buy a home when the time came.

Back at work, the SWR board met to review our position with the roads authority. Various government agencies needed to sign off on the details of the road design and the bank confirmed our loan arrangements. Statewide Roads had overcome all the questions posed by the legal reviews. A week later we were advised that Premier Nick Greiner was ready to sign a contract. Alan and his team had achieved a major coup. However, a huge job lay in front of them to deliver on the promises we had made. The greatest day in the 75-year history of CMPS was upon us.

Unfortunately, most people in the company had no idea of the importance of this win. In a strange way, it attacked the basis on which the company had been founded. The independent 'consulting engineer' providing dispassionate advice to clients had become the major shareholder in a toll road. We had crossed a boundary, in a sense, but the journey had started much earlier. Our main competitors were international contractors who were hard-headed businesses. The idea of professional independence was not part of their history. My forays into advertising a few years earlier had highlighted the divergence. I still believed our strength lay in our professionalism and fought hard to convince our clients that their welfare was our principal objective.

30. CMPS grows in different ways: 1991

I finally get my independent board.

CMPS was growing steadily, and I was intent on making it a dominant force in the industry. Acquisitions were rare; however, Tony Denham – the chief of Macdonald Wagner, a major competitor – called me one day and wanted an urgent meeting. 'We are in trouble,' he said. 'Would you consider a merger?' I felt our businesses overlapped too much, and I declined, but Tony's proposal inspired me to see what made sense in the marketplace.

If we were going to provide a complete service, our two main deficiencies were water and power engineering. Our joint venture with Gilbert Commonwealth in the US had not progressed, and I put a small group together to study the opportunities. Sinclair Knight Merz (SKM) emerged as the best option. I knew Jack Knight from tennis, and we chatted. He suggested a merger broker to help nut out the agenda we needed to evolve a suitable structure. After months of discussion, it was agreed that Jack and I would meet the broker in Honolulu for a few days of final meetings. Privately the broker suggested to me that Jack had cultural issues that might make the merger difficult. I tried to eke these out, but Jack was finding problems rather than solutions.

SKM had about twenty-three partners. After a series of meetings the large majority voted in favour of the merger, but Jack used his veto to kill the deal. Years later he told me it was the worst decision he ever made. However, we had acquired a lot of knowledge through this process and were not done yet. Another water group, Scott and Furphy (S&F), appeared and were keen to merge. With our recent experience, it was done relatively quickly and became my opportunity to do a further major restructure. We were now CMPS&F.

With the new structure, I wanted to create a board of largely independent directors with a broad range of skills. Bob Morgan had no understanding of the SWR freeway initiative and had forced me to divest more than half the equity to pay for the bid. He wanted zero exposure for the consulting business. Initially, I was happy, as it represented the company's largest risk in its 70-year history. It was only after we emerged as the preferred bidder that I realised the value of the forgone equity. I asked Bob to step down to allow me to appoint a non-executive board.

Most engineering companies in Australia had little credibility as managers. CMPS&F was one of the few that did, but my experience in Melbourne with the newsprint mill taught me we had no standing in the merchant banking world, where project finance was managed. If we were to maintain a lead in the project field we needed finance skills. With the help of Sir Eric McClintock, the former Williams Bros chairman in Australia, and his connection with the O'Connell Street Associates, I was able to talk to Ian Stanwell, the former head of AMP. Ian had no idea of our business, but he was well respected. He accepted the position of chairman.

I had identified several potential independent board members and things came together. Tony Shepherd had left Transfield and started his own advisory business and was keen to join. Tony and I had worked together in the early 1970s on the Moomba– Sydney natural gas pipeline. He was a key member of the Pipeline Authority at that time. More recently he had been instrumental in the massive Sydney Harbour Tunnel project for Transfield. Ian Stanwell was ready, as was Russ Ingersoll, a Scott and Furphy director who had been head of the Board of Works in Melbourne. Alan Livingstone had moved on to run SWR and was keen to join: my board was set.

I became aware of a general stirring of interest in my restructuring of the company among the service industries. All the legal and accounting firms were partnerships, as CMPS had been. Even when I became CEO in 1987, CMPS had continued to act as a partnership with its management thinking. The separation of management, board and shareholding roles had not occurred. I attended several lunches where the main topic was corporatisation. Lawyers and accountants wanted to expand their services into the project development advice domain where they may acquire equity as part of the commercial equation. Their push included South-East Asia and my experience there interested them. They found there were legal and legislative hurdles which were largely insurmountable. I became familiar with their strategies and realised the threat to my aspirations.

The burgeoning environmental business was seen by the legal profession as its domain. The issues were legal and not about the ecology. On many occasions mining and manufacturing companies had devolved their environmental problems to legal firms to manage, with expensive outcomes.

The accountants were equally pushing for management roles in non-traditional areas and at one stage were hiring more graduate engineers than the engineering firms. A turf war was being fought by all the professions to dominate the management role for development. The pendulum would swing wildly over the next decade culminating in the demise of Arthur Anderson, an accounting firm which had moved into legal services and management consulting. All of this was grist for the mill as we fought to win a place in the development landscape.

I was on target to achieve most of the goals I had set

myself – setting up a dominant company in the region with good management skills and a capacity to raise finance if required. We had a growing order book and a program to train the next group of managers.

The M4 motorway was taking shape and running ahead of schedule. Interest rates were falling, and the value of the project was climbing quickly. The NSW government issued tenders for two more road developments, the M5 and the Bulahdelah bypass north of Newcastle. After we prepared expensive tenders and were named the preferred tenderer, the government changed its mind on the bypass. The M5 development was delayed and finally given to Leighton on a much-changed specification. It was clear the government processes did not conform to good practice. This situation was exacerbated later, when the M2 was bid and the only two conforming bids were ignored, one of which was ours. We gave up at that stage. The NSW government was in disarray and Opposition leader Bob Carr was running for office on a platform of removing the tolls on the motorways.

We opened the M4 motorway nine months early, to great acclaim. Premier Nick Greiner and the roads minister, Wal Murray, attended the opening; a new chapter in privatised infrastructure was emerging. Shortly afterwards, the Sydney Harbour Tunnel and the monorail started operations in private hands. The media still

SWR M4 Motorway opening with Wal Murray and Nick Greiner

didn't understand the benefits we had created and focused on the imposition of tolls as their main story. Private gain ahead of public good seemed to be the headline. I was learning that politics is about perception and facts were incidental. When we were interviewed by the media at the opening reporters accused us of encouraging people to use their cars at the expense of public transport. I pointed out that buses were not barred from motorways, and commuters would have a quicker transit time. This seemed to get lost in the torrent of simplistic sound bites. When a few media people asked why the project had been so successful, I observed that we were a small and united team focused on a simple premise: nobody was paid a fee or a dividend until we generated revenue and at such a time the shareholders would be first in line. We had used no financial advisor and had no head contractor. The in-house team provided those services.

Shortly afterwards, after a hard slog, the Kutubu oil project was completed in Papua New Guinea in mid-1992, and I was invited to the opening in the highlands. It was a colourful event, with performances by many sing-sing groups, dressed to the hilt in tribal costume and carried spears, machetes and bows and arrows. The management had arranged a show chronicling the legends associated with the volcano and the lake formation. It was spectacular and concluded with the volcano realistically erupting, so realistic, in fact, that half the audience rushed into the bush thinking the next war had started. I was very proud of this project as we had won the engineering and management role by anticipating the market. Again our team had overcome huge technical problems in a very remote part of the world.

Part VIII
Politics and boards
1996

31. I spread my political wings

The Asia Australia Council was a good forum in which to discover the political connections with business. The council held an annual conference in various centres throughout Asia. I attended one in Macau; I had never been there before. We met in the Westin Hotel, at one end of the island. I had a chance to walk around the old sector and enjoy the Portuguese architecture and food. It was so different to Hong Kong.

The conference was filled with intrigue. I sat next to a Filipino gentleman who explained that he helped the president on various matters. He didn't elaborate. His name was Jose Almonte. Over the course of the meetings, we listened to political discussions on regional issues. On the final night, there was a dinner and the Australian contingent gathered in the disco for a get-together. I was chatting with Ian 'Sinkers' Sinclair, the former leader of the National Party, when a group entered in a party mood. Cheryl Kernot, the head of the Australian Democrats party, wanted to dance, but her group preferred to drink. She spied us and made a beeline. 'Christ, she's trouble,' Ian mumbled. Cheryl ignored him and grabbed my hand and we headed for the floor. I escaped after a couple of songs. She would find a partner in federal attorney-general Gareth Evans. Paul

Keating was off by himself sulking; he had recently lost the election. Alexander Downer, the foreign minister, was entertaining the main group at the bar. The whole political spectrum was there. Ian gave me his views on the assembled characters with entertaining stories.

In the morning, I was returning to Hong Kong on the ferry when I saw Jose Almonte struggling with his bag near the gangway. I gave him a hand, and we sat together on the way back, reflecting on the meeting. I listened intently as he gave me his summary. He offered a perspective that I hadn't contemplated. 'Grahame, regional cooperation needs to be improved to maximise our regional strengths. We look to the major powers for direction; this is old-world thinking. We need to strengthen our trading ties, which improves political understanding. We don't need Europe and the USA telling us the future. We will determine that ourselves.' On arrival, he was met by several large security men in traditional shirts and the obligatory dark glasses. As they led him to the stretch limo, he turned and asked if I needed a ride. I accepted, and he was dropped off first. 'Use the car for as long as you like. Look me up in Manila if you come by. I'd love to catch up.' With that, he disappeared into the hotel. I was dropped at my hotel and was glad to be rid of the car, as it looked 'Mafia'.

The following year, the PBEC met in Manila and I resolved to go, just to follow up on Jose's invitation. Fidel

Ramos was the president and Jose was his right-hand man. Jose had become famous as the contact between the USA and the Viet Cong during the Vietnam War. His diplomatic skills were legendary, as were his powers in the Philippines during Ramos's presidency; they had been lifelong friends. I arranged a meeting in Manila and we exchanged gifts. He gave me an engraved cigar box signed by Ramos, and I gave him some Australian stamps. He claimed he had delayed his meeting with Dr Mahathir from Malaysia to take tea with me. He may have been having me on, who knows? Our discussion expanded on his comments in Macau; he was pleased I was with the PBEC meeting as it mirrored his views.

PBEC was the business version of APEC (Asia Pacific Economic Cooperation). I became a member of the Australian council, as it gave me another window on our South-East Asian business. PBEC had quarterly meetings and a big annual get-together at places around the Pacific.

At the following meeting in Singapore, I arrived at one of their cocktail parties to find almost no people there. Waiters with trays of drinks were flanking the entrance. Just beyond them, a diminutive Japanese was standing by himself, so I went over after securing a drink. 'Hi, I'm Grahame Campbell. Seems like we're it,' I said, as I looked around the empty room. 'Ha, pleased to meet you. My name is Alberto Fujimori. I'm the president of Peru.' I was taken aback; he was Japanese. 'How are things going?' I asked. 'Are you enjoying the conference?' I then noticed, by a pot plant, a security guard in a black jumpsuit carrying an uzi paying close attention to us. Said the president, 'It's important for Peru to engage with Asia. I am here to explain Peru to the meeting and sell our mineral wealth to the new markets over here. Have you visited Peru, Mr Campbell?' 'No, but I'd love to go when I get a chance.' CMPS&F had not looked at South America. The language and cultural barriers had seemed too high for us to sell our services, but the Canadian success there showed it was not mission impossible, and, after all, Peru's mineral wealth mirrored Australia's.

I found the PBEC forum excellent for networking. The delegates were senior business figures from the region. I became very friendly with Chote Sophonpanich, who was a director of the Bangkok Bank, which his father had founded. It was the largest financial institution in Thailand. Chote was a keen tennis player and we played several times in different cities. Hanoi was memorable. Chote had told me the chief justice of Hong Kong and the Telstra boss in Vietnam were up for a game with us. It was incredibly hot in Hanoi, and I had lost my sandshoes. On the Sunday morning, we found shoes in a section of town which seemed to sell nothing else. On our walk back to the hotel we encountered bicycle races around the lake. We watched from the shade of a temporary grandstand. After each race, a brass band struck up and the officials handed out a prize. We seemed to be in the VIP section, as we were brought refreshments, but no one challenged us. An ambulance followed the riders around and a carnival atmosphere prevailed. It was hilarious, a Peter Sellers movie; Chote and I enjoyed it immensely.

A diminutive man, Chote, as well being a director of the largest bank in Thailand, was also on the board of an oil exploration company and a petrochemical company. After our game, we four had lunch and arranged to go to the Hanoi Jazz Club in the evening, as Chote loved jazz too. Later, after dinner, John Hewson, the federal Opposition leader in Australia, joined us, but was more interested in pub crawling, although a few hours later he returned, declaring that we were in the best place after all.

In an extraordinary coincidence, I ran into Chote in a restaurant in suburban Houston, Texas, on a Sunday night a couple of weeks after our Hanoi meeting. He had a joint venture with Union Texas Oil and was with their directors. I was with my old friend Robert Edwardes, who was by now with Exxon. He was the engineering manager for the giant Indonesian Natuna gas field under development in the South China Sea. Exxon's main sales target was Thailand, but the Thais were not keen to buy the gas. Jokingly, I told Robert, 'Chote can sort

Tennis in Hanoi with the chief justice of Hong Kong and Chote Sophanpanish

it out,' and I went over to say hi to him. Chote was so surprised to see me. 'Grahame, you get around! Meet my friends, the Union Texas board' When I raised the question of Natuna gas I was surprised to find he was fully informed and he told me the gas quality was poor – too much CO_2 – and couldn't be integrated into their distribution system. I shared this with Robert; he rolled his eyes. Exxon knew this but hadn't found a solution.

All of these contacts were well and good, but converting them to business deals was another thing. Presidents and prime ministers were not going to become our clients. However, I was getting a good education on how 'the big end of town' saw the world. Our capacity for risk was limited. American delegates generally were members of financial institutions and only recognised American firms for big developments. Michael Folie, my university thesis supervisor, who was now with Shell Oil, helped quite a bit. He was a fan of PBEC and involved me in his discussions with delegates. I found the topics interesting but sometimes it was hard to know if it was a good use of my time; time management is always in the back of your mind, so swanning around the world while trying to run the company caused me to pause often and question my decisions.

CMPS&F were engaged in thousands of projects, from concepts to maintaining work that we had completed. This complexity required major upgrades to our management, accounting systems and staff training. The internet was becoming available and to be competitive we needed to offer the latest tools to our clients. I enjoyed the challenge of business which played to my competitive nature. The CMPS&F matrix structure was working well, and we were developing centres of excellence in the various offices. By 1994, we had expanded to twenty-three offices, seven of them international. We operated five joint ventures and had technical agreements with dozens of companies. CMPS&F had a leading role in our industry, but I knew we could grow the project management aspect and develop a more dominant position over the construction companies. However, I had a narrow support from my management team, and this had been diluted by the acquisition of Scott and Furphy. I hadn't realised how traditional they were; they felt very uncomfortable in the management role. Because things were going well, I faced a strong groundswell to stay as we were, but I was determined that we would not 'come back to the pack'.

My thesis work was the cornerstone of my thinking. The integration of the design development with the construction processes maximised innovation. If you lock in price certainty early to minimise risk, you kill innovation. If the development is fairly standard, then fixed pricing may work. However, new technology will suffer if it is bound by traditional contracting. I had learned from the Americans that EPCM (engineering, procurement and construction management) allowed development to be progressed through stages without commitment to a final price. The commercial decisions could be delayed until the design was fixed.

Australian engineering companies failed to understand this as they missed the importance of project structuring and procurement alternatives. This is where the real risk analysis provides clear strategies.

I looked at opportunities in Asia but found the risk profiles too high. Our nemeses were always the construction contractors. We had better project management skills, but they had deeper pockets to finance the expensive and time-consuming bids. Inevitably, we were consigned to the engineer's role. It was a dilemma that I never really solved, as time was on the contractors' side and they gradually strengthened their management skills. I realised I was trying to graft a project management culture from the oil and gas business onto our other customer groups, with strong resistance from within. These issues were debated at the annual conference, and it was clear I was in the minority in pressing the management role. What to do? Get new managers? I was finding it hard to maintain my enthusiasm, but I kept searching for new opportunities.

The board was very supportive, but I needed to keep it fresh. Tony Shepherd had decided to return to an executive role in Transfield, which necessitated a replacement. Nick Greiner had resigned as NSW premier, and I became aware that he was looking to become involved in directorships of companies. He had been through an ICAC inquiry and had appealed the outcome. He had been charged with misusing his position as premier to facilitate an appointment. We decided to offer Nick a board position before the result of the court proceedings, which finally ruled in his favour. His knowledge of government was invaluable, particularly as regards infrastructure development. Nick accepted, and I had a new dimension for my thinking about the future. Almost immediately Nick suggested that we talk to the Victorian government about a major new toll road from the airport in Melbourne around the western side of the city; CityLink. It had been around for a while but become a political football. The new premier, Jeff Kennett, wanted it built and was seeking help from Greiner.

I saw an opportunity to solve my problem. Tony Shepherd had developed a strong position with CityLink, and an integration of our skills would create the team to deliver the project. After several discussions Transfield and ourselves were appointed as the managing contractor; our first major win in Melbourne.

My journey from Kyeemagh had been long and random. I had been trained as an engineer and got off to a shaky start as my music aspirations waxed and waned. I had never given up on music, and it remained an important part of my life. As a family man, I'd had to provide and establish a home. At each point in my development, I was conscious of the learning process and the need to build on opportunities that presented themselves. Engineering as a career was not a technical journey but a learning curve involving cultural, social and management situations. At each turn in the evolution of my thinking, I had to make judgements based on my aggregated experience. Generally, these were leaps of faith which I was happy to take; if I was wrong, I could correct my path, knowing that I was still learning. I had strayed far from the traditional concept of an engineer, but I was always happy to be confronted with each problem as it evolved.

I keep reflecting on what *is* the traditional concept of an engineer. Most of the public know that buildings and bridges involve engineering. Also, machinery and the electricity that drives it have engineers at their core. Adding science, architecture and metallurgy muddied the mix. Introduce procurement, contracts and inspection; then most people have little understanding of the processes. I think semantics start to win the day as putting labels on jobs is not very useful. Projects are delivered by teams that have leaders and specialists from a wide spectrum of skills. Whether these are engineering skills becomes a less important question. The training of the team members and their ability to solve problems as they emerge becomes dominant. A broad questioning of the issues by the team members in a collegiate fashion will produce a better solution.

32. The board years

In 1994, in my seventh year as managing director, I was trying to find an exit from the role and consider a new career path. I had achieved my two main objectives, and the company was travelling well. I had targeted three likely successors for my job, but they all resided in other capital cities. The ideal candidate would have to live in Sydney and share my view of the future. We had established our company's point of difference in the market with our commercial approach to project development; that is, having a strong risk approach to contracting that allowed all forms of engagement from the earliest stages of a concept. The evolution of the project would be flexible, according to emerging circumstances. Workshopping embedded maximum innovation.

As I put pressure on the three contenders for my job it became apparent they were not keen to relocate and step up to the new challenges. This had never been an issue for me. They were 'fat and happy' where they were. It was a huge disappointment. I had been running WB-CMPS and CMPS for more than 15 years, pretty much solo. I had some close friends and many business acquaintances. Being the CEO can be a lonely role, and none of my close friends were working with me.

Suddenly a new dimension for my thinking emerged. I was invited to join the board of EFIC, the federal government insurance and finance group. I asked my board if it would be appropriate. I was chairman of SWR and CEO of CMPS&F, but felt the exposure would be good for the company and I could handle the workload. EFIC invested in overseas infrastructure that was not attractive for normal finance. The EFIC board approved all project investment, so I had a window on a wide variety of projects. The board members were a diverse set of individuals. At my first meeting, I was surprised to catch up with Michael Folie, my thesis supervisor, a good friend since he had joined Shell Oil from the university. He was also attending his first meeting. Another existing member was Andrew 'my friends don't call me Twiggy,' Forrest, a stockbroker who had ambitions in mineral development. Andrew was the most enthusiastic promoter I had ever met. He tackled every topic with direct, strong statements. You were never in doubt of his position. This was in spite of a speech impediment which he had largely overcome. As I got to know Andrew he warmed to the idea that I could help him with his fledgling company Anaconda Nickel. He invited me to join his board, but I explained I had a company to run and wasn't available. Also on the board was Catherine Livingstone, who went on to run Cochlear, the hearing aid pioneer, and then chair the CSIRO. Various government department heads served also to involve government policy in our deliberations. All of this was new and stimulating territory for me.

EFIC proved to be an eye-opener. I had been struggling to build engineering businesses in Australia and SE Asia for 15 years which required absolute focus. I was now exposed to a government entity lending hundreds of millions to regional governments with suspect managements and objectives. It was a fine balancing act to help developing communities with infrastructure supported by Australian firms providing expertise. The smell of corruption was always present. In debating the merits of the proposals, I became aware of the political pressures that were applied on all sides. I thoroughly enjoyed my two-year appointment.

My dilemma was to find an exit path from CMPS&F. It was now two years since I had started the process to find my successor. The CMPS&F shareholders were itching to achieve better dividends and return to a more traditional agenda. However, all internal potential appointees seemed to favour a conservative future. I wanted to leave the group on the track I had set; I resisted their demands and kept steering for growth, especially with an expanded project management business. The success of SWR financially overwhelmed the performance of the consulting business and I searched for other commercial opportunities.

My success in broadening the shareholder base was

beginning to bite back; we had about 400 shareholders and rising. Middle management wanted stability, and I was facing an uprising. I had been in the job nine years and my resolve to fight was waning. I decided to look outside for a younger commercial replacement for myself. Russ Ingersoll, a director and recruitment consultant, suggested John Cooper, who had run Concrete Constructions. We investigated the claims of several other candidates, but settled on John, with his reputation for hard-nosed management. The plan was for me to become deputy chairman, as Ian Stanwell was comfortable as the chairman. My career as a full-time executive was over at 53.

I was then able to accept Andrew Forrest's offer to join Anaconda Nickel's board and consider a career as a professional board member. Essentially, I had four jobs. Life was good, and I had time to think more broadly. I was a director on the Asia Australia Council and the Pacific Basin Economic Council and found I had access to a wide variety of senior executives. CMPS&F won Exporter of the Year, and Prime Minister Paul Keating congratulated me on our international success.

I was invited to become president of ACEA, the peak consulting engineering association. It would take a couple of years to progress through their system joining sub-committees and state positions, but I was happy to give something back to the industry. There was some resistance from the smaller firms, which had been involved in committee work over several years and saw me as a 'Johnny come lately'. They also questioned where I had taken CMPS&F, which went to the core of what members of the association believed was acceptable behaviour. The majority of members did not believe project management was the role of consulting engineers. I hoped to prove them wrong!

I recognised that the association was very conservative and in need of a big shake-up, as the large firms were considering leaving due to the association's agenda being skewed to small firm needs. Costs were rising, and services weren't being delivered. Dick Kell, the current president, steered me through the rumblings and I finally followed him into the chair. I was determined to make the association more relevant to the current world of development. Meanwhile, Cooper was reshaping CMPS&F and had hired a new finance chief, Rodney Smythe, from Allen, Allen and Hemsley, a major law firm. I had been aiming to get our reporting functions to a point where we could list on the stock market. Rodney was ideal to carry this forward, as it instilled discipline into our administrative staff.

After a decade of good health, I started to feel some of the symptoms of my 'heart attack' of a decade ago. It was generally in the morning when I walked around Greenwich. I would have to sit for a few minutes to lower my blood pressure. I felt I could manage it but deep down knew I needed to get it checked out. After Christmas, I told the local doctor my symptoms. She called an ambulance. I was in Royal North Shore Hospital half an hour later. Several days later I was in the recovery ward after a quadruple bypass. A couple of months' rehab and I was feeling strong, but it hit home that I was now fifty-six and my lifestyle had to change. I wanted new challenges, but I had to pace myself.

Anaconda Nickel

Anaconda Nickel was proving the most challenging of my board positions. Andrew Forrest had assembled a group that worked well under chairman Alan 'Coogs' Coogan, who had successfully developed Nabalco, a large alumina project at Gove in the Northern Territory. We met in an office in Bligh Street in Sydney with $5 million and a good idea. Andrew had purchased two leases from an explorer, Peter Salter, and we set about developing a dry laterite nickel mine. Two other mines were 'on foot', Bulong by Resolute and Cawse by Centaur. We needed to decide on a technology route and a strategy. Credibility was critical to success. Andrew had done well to assemble Norm Fussell, ex-Thiess and MIM, Michael Masterman from McKinsey's and John Down, former coordinator general in the Queensland government. My contribution was to advise Andrew on engineering strategies and contracting options. I apprised him of my Huffco experience, where a small core management team had put together a billion-dollar enterprise. Also, the concept of outsourcing services, that is, BOO (Build, own, operate) contracting could reduce the capital investment. Both of these ideas became part of the bedrock of the development. BHP Engineering performed the feasibility study, which allowed Andrew to raise $50 million from Glencore to take us through the next stages to commitment.

Glencore introduced two new directors, Michael O'Keeffe, a Glencore executive, and Chris Linnegar, a former director of Societe Generale. Chris resigned soon after as he felt compromised by being in two camps, although he rejoined the board after the financing issues were settled. Andrew was constantly at loggerheads with Michael over Glencore's divergent objectives.

Glencore wanted a more traditional project development. A critical decision was taken to double the size of the plant, to gain scale efficiencies. This would prove to be a winner and take us past the other two plants, which eventually failed. The decision to buy sulphur and make sulphuric acid was also a key point, as 70% of our power requirements would come from burning sulphur. The autoclaves (for the high-pressure acid leach process) would be the largest in the world and reminded me of submarines. Coincidentally, my friend Hans Ohff was CEO of the Submarine Corporation, and I arranged for Andrew to meet him in Adelaide, where we inspected the new subs for the Australian Navy. This also proved a winner, as a contract for the autoclaves was concluded and Hans took considerable financial risk starting work before we had full financing. Andrew was then able to convince other large suppliers such as ABB, Linde and Monsanto to advance negotiations for the 100 megawatts power station, seven gas plants and the acid plant, respectively. Brambles agreed to a BOO arrangement for the supply of calcite for the process, eliminating capital in that area. The gas plants were similarly contracted.

Suddenly, a crisis. Andrew advised that Glencore had moved to reclaim its loan. Glencore knew the company was headed for financial close and gave it an ultimatum to repay the loan in six weeks or they would 'take over' through a massive dilution of the shares. This despite Michael O'Keeffe, the Glencore nominee, sitting on the board. It emerged that JP Morgan was acting for both sides, which caused major concern. Andrew was about to fly to Zug in Switzerland to see Marc Rich, the founder of Glencore, who had left in acrimonious circumstances and had subsequently sold his interest in Glencore. Alan 'Coogs' Coogan, the chairman, called the board together for an update conference call. Andrew surprised the board by revealing he had enticed Rich to take a position against the chairman's advice. The chairman forbade Andrew to continue the discussions, saying, 'We shouldn't be dealing with someone of Rich's reputation, a person pursued by the US government for a range of offences.' Andrew replied, 'That's all very well, Alan. If you can get the AMP Society to supply equity to us by Friday, I won't deal with him. Who in the world would dislike Glencore the most?' Hence his approach to Marc Rich. The board realised the threat and the risks and discussed a strategy to find the capital to fund the project. The board was divided into three groups and despatched the Europe, Asia and North America to pitch for a financial package to keep the company whole.

Marc Rich came in with the equity the week after Glencore threatened the takeover. The M. Rich funds (funnelled through Pension Funds in Switzerland) supplied the equity that Anaconda needed to achieve the 'Green Field' or new junk bond raising in NYC weeks later. Andrew had hit the jackpot with a junk bond deal which bypassed the whole project financing industry and set new standards. It was so successful that Glencore used the same package to deliver its share. Project financing in Australia was changed forever.

Andrew made the board work hard, really functioning as a part of his management team. Next, we needed a major contractor to deliver an operating plant. After expressions of interest, Andrew focused on Fluor, which was less than enthusiastic, until it realised we had the finance and then warmed up. An EPCM contract was negotiated. At the final stages of the negotiations, Fluor offered to convert to an EPC (engineering, procurement and construction) contract, for an extra $50 million. This was a great deal for us, as we had eliminated the construction cost risk for a nominal amount. Andrew also convinced Lloyds to provide completion insurance for $250 million. This was unprecedented in the industry. We had Sherritt Gordon contracted for the technology, as it was operating a similar plant in Cuba. Sherritt Gordon was paid partly in equity. Andrew was a great user of equity for which most people would pay cash. We didn't have much cash, and a feature of our board meetings was that we checked our liquidity as the first item of the agenda. As soon as we had a cash injection, Andrew would spend it.

I attended several meetings in Melbourne at Fluor's offices when the main design development was occurring. Andrew had emphasised to me that we had to get the capital cost under a billion dollars as it couldn't be financed above the magic number. He was using McKinsey's, Michael Mastermans' old firm, to recommend cuts to the project equipment. This was driving Fluor's engineers crazy. On paper, the cuts could work, but good engineering practice dictated that the sixteen plants comprising the whole enterprise needed some 'breathing space' or under normal operating conditions there would be some 'give and take'. Andrew ignored the advice, and the costs came in under budget. These cuts would come back to haunt us. In record time, we were ready to break ground and create the first mine and processing plant in the world to produce LME grade nickel at the mine mouth. The project would create many world firsts along the way to the first nickel briquettes.

RGC

My board life was accelerating. I was invited to join the RGC (Renison Goldfields Consolidated) board in 1996, not long after I had accepted the Anaconda appointment. Mark Bethwaite was the CEO and Tony Cotton the chairman. I had lunch with them at the Royal Sydney Yacht Squadron and asked if my Anaconda role was a conflict. They saw no problem, and I accepted the directorship offer.

RGC was a much more mature enterprise than Anaconda. Board meetings were quite formal, and my biggest problem was remembering the names of all the mines that we operated. The core business was mineral sands, and the company ranked first and second in the world for zircon and titanium dioxide production, respectively. Additionally, we had a controlling interest in Goldfields and extensive tin operations in Indonesia and Tasmania. The history of the company had begun with the copper, lead, zinc operations on the west coast of Tasmania. These had been largely sold off, but the operations reminded me of my start as an engineer, when I joined CMPS so long ago in 1968. Some copper-gold mines west of Townsville in Queensland were still operating, but with small returns.

My first board meeting reunited me with Peter Mason, a Sydney Boys High student; it was his first board meeting too. The initial months were spent in orientation, with trips to the operations and learning the corporate structures. RGC had five public companies, with varying ownerships, the result of acquisitions over years. It was expensive to administer.

At my second board meeting, the main discussion was around a mine development in Virginia in the USA. Mark Bethwaite, the CEO, asked me to look at the reports in detail, to see if I could see why things were not progressing well. It took no time to identify a problem with management. The mine engineering was being run out of Toronto, and the design was constantly being changed – in small ways, but contributing to instability. I recommended a different strategy. The senior decision-makers needed to be at the site with direct and close communication with RGC and the contract engineers. However the damage was done, and the project was late and over budget.

On another front, Mark was keen to acquire a new operation in Peru to mine gold and copper. It was an ambitious project for us, as Canadian company Barrick Mines had spent $50 million on the operation before abandoning it. I suggested an independent appraisal by a consultant, Neil Cusworth, who I had worked with at Anaconda. He had worked on the MIM project in the Argentine and knew South America well. Cusworth's report was scathing. The feasibility study had opted for second-hand equipment to cut costs, and the transport and export facilities were not fully explained. The board voted not to proceed. This put Mark in an exposed position, as the company had too much overhead and poor returns on many of the operations.

The major shareholder was applying pressure, and it was clear to Peter and me that a major shake-up was on the cards. At the end of the year, the management held its annual review and strategy meetings at Manly. The board joined the final executive meeting and a dinner at the Manly Pacific hotel. Afterwards, Peter and I found ourselves in the bar pondering the earlier discussion. It was clear management was not pulling together. The staff Christmas function a few weeks later in The Rocks crystallised the issue. The CFO confided to several board members at the function that the senior management team had lost confidence in CEO Mark Bethwaite, who was sailing in Turkey over the holiday period. I was shocked. The chairman, Tony Cotton, canvassed the board members and concluded that Mark should be terminated on his return.

I quizzed Tony on how he had reached his conclusion, and he explained that he had spoken to all Mark's direct reports and had received a unanimous response that they had lost confidence in Mark's ability to lead the group. Tony told Mark of the board's decision and became the interim CEO until another could be found. The search for a new CEO was compromised by Hanson, the major shareholder with over 40% of the shares, announcing it wanted to sell its holding, which put the company in play. This was a difficult time for the board, as the company needed a new vision. We identified a strong candidate, Vince Gauci, for CEO, but had to advise him that the job may be short-lived because the company might be sold. Vince accepted our advice and went on to lead MIM successfully. One wonders where the future would have taken us if Vince had been given a chance. Shortly after this, Westralian Sands entered negotiations to form a merger and several months later Iluka Resources was born.

CMPS&F

Amid this diverse activity, the CMPS&F chairman, Ian Stanwell and I were invited to a meeting at Macquarie Bank to be introduced to executives from Setaroute, a French toll road company. I was familiar with the group as it attended the International Bridge, Tunnel and Turnpike Association (IBTTA) conferences around the world. Alan Livingstone and I had been to New Orleans, Paris, Rome and Nova Scotia to keep across toll road developments. The Setaroute people explained they were building a global network of engineering companies and wanted to acquire CMPS&F as the Asia/Pacific link. It already had European and North American companies in the group. Ian and I retired to a vacant meeting room. I advised him that we were not for sale, but would cooperate on projects where it made sense. He agreed, and we rejoined the others. Ian put our position and discussed a wide range of possibilities. We agreed to talk again.

A week later the chairman received a cash offer of $30 a share from Setaroute to buy the whole of CMPS&F, fifteen times our auditor's valuation. I was stunned. Ernst & Young, our auditor, valued the company at about $2 a share. I felt it was worth about $10. The offer could not be ignored, and there were no caveats. The offer didn't include our equity in the M4 motorway, as this was held separately as 'B' shares. I was the largest shareholder and was ambivalent, but I knew the other shareholders would find the offer very attractive in spite of their altruistic engineering ideals. It would create a large number of instant millionaires.

In fairly quick time the deal was done. Cooper didn't want any help from me. I severed all ties with a company I had been associated with for nearly 30 years. Cooper seemed to have convinced the French owners that he could run the ship without external guidance. There was no board. CMPS&F was renamed EGIS by the new owners and within several years had collapsed to be a small operation that was finally sold off to a local competitor when Setaroute lost interest in engineering. Eighty years of engineering history vanished! I didn't feel badly about this as the shareholders had been richly rewarded but I had not achieved my ultimate goal. This was to be achieved in a totally unexpected way.

Worley

Shortly after we had concluded the CMPS&F sale, John Grill called to chat. 'What are you up to, now you've sold the engineering company?' I replied tongue-in-cheek, 'Sailing my boat and putting my feet up.' John paused, then said, 'Why don't you give us a hand, I'd like to pick your brains?' He had built up Worley, an oil and gas engineering business that had grown out of work on the Bass Strait Esso operations. John had worked for Esso as a structural engineer and Worley had expanded when he hired Peter Meurs to include 'mech and elec' services. John and I had cooperated in Indonesia for a period, so I understood his business style. He asked if I would join his advisory board, to help guide development of the firm along the lines I had taken with CMPS&F. I said I'd love the challenge. It would allow me to realise my dream of an engineering company taking a leading role in development.

Worley had grown by a series of joint ventures with companies and individuals. It opportunistically exploited opportunities that presented themselves along the way. There was little structure, and local managers were given free rein to develop business. This led to many successes and some failures. After a decade of hurly-burly, a period of consolidation was required to align equity interests and coordinate the work of the entrepreneurial engineers in the field. With the myriad joint ventures in Asia, it was a monumental job to unravel equity entitlements for an ongoing operation. John was adept at managing the personalities, but we needed stronger financial management to get the company to be a credible reporting unit. There were many small entities whose performance was erratic. Every reporting period the 'dogs' would emerge, along with the stars. It was the nature of the beast when you were testing new fields. A key person in settling the business plan was Robert Bruce, who ran an annual strategy session for the senior managers, emphasising a focus on realistic but challenging targets. The 'hedgehog' became the totem, hedgehogs being known for their careful, steady progress. Better reporting and accounting systems were implemented to inform the top team. All of this needed to be done without compromising the unique style of the group. It was not easy, and John did a masterful job steering the ship.

John had formed an equities group similar to mine at CMPS&F, to look at creating assets. The first venture was a gas pipeline from Kambalda to Esperance in Western Australia, to provide gas for a new power station to service the area. It was a bold move along the lines of the M4 motorway and stretched Worley's management skills. I visited the site to advise on contractor management as we had not provided a timely survey for the route location. Worley developed another power station in the north of WA, but the appetite for these projects diminished as we approached an IPO (initial public offering). The restructure and alignment with equity interests had been achieved, and a new CFO installed.

Being a non-executive board member can have its challenges. You are exposed to initiatives at board meetings, and you try to help with advice. Sometimes it becomes necessary to go beyond the advisory role and participate with management in the development. I realised my connections in the USA could be critical for one such initiative. Peter Meurs, John Grill's senior manager, lived in Perth and became excited by a concept developed by I&E systems, a Worley joint venture. Dermot Kennedy, an Irishman, was the inventor. He was a passionate advocate and believed unwaveringly in its success. The idea was to eliminate electrical and control system drawings and replace them with diagrams describing the functions at the nodes of the devices. Under the existing system, 25% of the as-built drawings had errors. This was because the design cycle had the I&E work at the end of the line and subject to numerous modifications which were often not recorded in the drawing system. During commissioning, field operators would affect changes to get the plant working and fail to update the as-built drawings. DAD (Drawings are Dead), the new idea, used a protocol which guaranteed 100% accuracy and promised to revolutionise the industry. The difficulty was to overcome history; everybody in the world was trained in the old system. However, Woodside Petroleum embraced the idea and it seemed that this success would eventually lead us to conquer the world.

I had established a bond with SAIC, a company in California, during the development of the SWR tollway in Sydney. A subsidiary had provided the toll equipment, and they exposed me to their other hi-tech operations in La Jolla, near San Diego. SAIC was affiliated with the University of Southern California and the Scripps Institute. Its chief operating officer, John Glancy, was keen to commercialise the many inventions the company had evolved with their military contracts for the US government. Its main management meeting was held quarterly, with around 500 of the top team attending. (SAIC had about 40,000 people working around the world, principally in the US.) The meeting was held over three days and included three or four presentations. The main purpose was networking and small discussion groups. I was asked to make a presentation on the Australian opportunities and revelled in the networking. One afternoon, one of their senior managers spent several hours flipping through hundreds of ideas that had been studied over the years, generally for military applications. My mind buzzed with how we could use these in our work.

John arranged a dinner with former Admiral Bill Owens and himself at a beachside restaurant. Bill had been No.2 in the US joint chiefs of staff; he had run the Navy. I raised the subject of DAD and John immediately thought of motor cars. One of his jobs was chairing a company that acted as a buying agency for the top five vehicle manufacturers. The wiring of cars and trucks was a haphazard process, and DAD might simplify it. I discussed this with Peter Meurs, and he arranged for himself, Dermot and me to visit California. All went well until we had dinner in San Diego's Old Town and Dermot had too much to drink. John had incorporated a company to act as our joint operating base, and Dermot became suspicious that he was being railroaded, and demanded $1 billion for the use of his invention. We tried to reason with him that we could all make a lot of money if we took it slowly and let our equity grow with success. Dermot became more aggressive and drunk, and the dinner was a shambles.

In the morning, John called to suggest that we delay decisions until Dermot had settled on his position. The rest of the trip was not much better, as at each meeting Dermot was paranoid that people were trying to steal his work. We went to Walnut Creek, near San Francisco, to meet with companies that might be interested in working with us. Each meeting started brightly, but slowly went downhill as Dermot became uncooperative. I discussed the outlook with John Glancy when I returned to Australia and apologised for wasting his time. We remained good friends. A potential multibillion-dollar enterprise had been trashed. I relayed my experience to the Worley board and reflected on my board work. I was finding that the lot of a director could be very frustrating after having spent so many years as a chief executive.

ACEA

All my theory on time management went out the window when I assumed the role of president of the Association of Consulting Engineers Australia. The CEO was discovered to be an alcoholic who went missing on many occasions. I was forced to dismiss him and temporarily fill the role myself. The ACEA had twelve head office staff. I interviewed all the staff to find out what they did. By lunch, two staffers had handed in their resignations. By Wednesday, I had a good idea of the operations and sat with three of the seniors and mapped out an agenda. 'Who are we? What are we?' and so on. By Friday, we had six staff left. My first thought was to halve the membership fees and reconstruct the services to focus on a defined set of issues. My second thought was to take the operations into the digital age and communicate only by email. There was a strong resistance to this as a minority of small members were not on the internet. We finally appointed a new CEO, Therese Charles and I gave her a strong base on which to build the new association.

My two-year term as president of the ACEA was enjoyable, as I had completely turned the organisation around so that it was useful for the broad membership. I kept asking the question, 'Why are we here?' to focus the staff on providing services the members were asking for. The most important was to be an effective lobbyist to government on poor practices in engaging engineering services. Everybody wanted innovation. Government processes effectively killed it. Buying engineering services on price was the problem.

The presidency involved travel to all Australian states to chair local meetings and share the national agenda. It was an opportunity for me to expand the members' thinking about project management and encourage them to take a more senior role in their projects. It was a difficult sell as most firms were only comfortable with the engineering role. However the larger firms were keen, and progress was made. However, it was hard to describe project delivery strategies when most of the audience had never been involved. After two years of the presidency, it was my greatest disappointment.

Worley

Meanwhile, Worley started acquiring companies to expand the portfolio, and John Grill decided Toussaint & Richardson would be a good entry point to the minerals processing industry. T&R had a good track record in the alumina business. Worley was getting ready to list, and my experience with CMPS&F was useful as we had reached that same point about the time the French turned up. I was appointed to chair the due diligence committee, and UBS was appointed the financial advisor. It was a torturous process, and Freehills did a good job with the legals. A new board of independent directors needed to be assembled, and some senior executives in the group rebelled on being excluded, which put a lot of stress on John Grill to manage the expectations of his top team. Russell Staley was a key member and decided to quit when he was not included in the new board. This was a blow to both the management and the culture of the group. Russell exemplified the direct and responsive style to clients that had become the hallmark of the company. John needed his best bedside manner to limit the damage, but Russell Staley did not change his mind. John Schubert, the former boss of Esso Australia, became chairman and the float was successful.

Worley was in a dynamic phase, and we started negotiations to acquire Parsons Corp in the US, a group about twice our size. Andrew Wood was the arranger and success would propel the group into the top tier internationally. Again, I was appointed to chair the due diligence committee, and I realised there were some historical links. Parsons had acquired Gilbert Commonwealth, the power group I had joint ventured with at CMPS&F. Also, when Parsons exited the Australian market I had taken over its files and continued the business, albeit in a reduced form. Parsons Corporation had been spun out of the Ralph M Parsons company, and comprised its oil and gas, power and petrochemical businesses. Parsons Corporation owed a large debt to the self-owned pension fund, and this had constrained its ability to expand. The major obstacle was an asbestos liability that Ralph M had assumed, but if it disappeared, Worley might be exposed. Parsons had large provisions on projects in Eastern Europe and the Middle East. Also, arrangements in Saudi Arabia were messy. We worked through these problems and eventually raised the money to conclude the deal, again with the help of UBS. The company was on a roll, and the stock price was surging.

SWR

SWR was turning into a great success, and we were pursued by Macquarie Bank to sell our interest. The sharp reduction in the interest rates and the new NSW Labor Government's need to deliver on its election promises was giving us new opportunities. Premier Bob Carr declared that all users of the M4 and M5 would have their tolls refunded. This created a surge of traffic. Politically, this did not placate voters, so he announced a $100 million boost for road development in the western suburbs. We received the money to add another lane in each direction to our system – more traffic through the toll booths. We had sold the franchise for a super petrol and fast food centre on the M4 to Caltex and McDonalds.

This provided another source of revenue. The asset in which we had invested $1 million was now worth nearly $300 million. Alan Livingstone and I sat down to contemplate the future. 'Grahame it's been an interesting journey. CMPS&F have come and gone; it's probably time to leave private roads to the politicians and the financiers. I'm very proud of what we have achieved'. I looked at Alan and said 'we achieved more than expected with your small, highly focused team.' We remain good friends. Macquarie finally acquired SWR and another chapter in my life closed. Engineers had captured the full value of their work for the first time.

Anaconda Nickel

Anaconda Nickel was ramping up quickly. Andrew's relations with Glencore continued to be poor, and he needed new equity players to counter their position. Anglo American was introduced to the project and Andrew convinced them to invest about $400 million. We had expanded our exploration permits to cover a large part of Western Australia. This allowed Andrew to develop his Three Nickel Plant strategy, along with a series of infrastructure initiatives for water, gas and sulphur supply. The Murrin Murrin project was in full swing, and Fluor had decided to 'self-perform' most of the work. This proved to be a mistake. Several contractors were willing to provide very competitive prices for the bulk of the work, but Dick Wright wanted to expand his business and direct hire. They had a fixed-price contract and it became wobbly. Fluor worldwide was experiencing problems and had sustained big losses in South America. They had appointed a new global boss, Jim Stein, an ex-Shell manager. Andrew discovered they had procurement problems with the internals for the autoclaves; they were complicated fabrications in titanium, requiring specialised skill. Fluor declared a three-month delay. Andrew immediately flew to northern Italy to talk to the fabricators, some of whom didn't speak English. He explained the importance of their work and the need to get the output to Australia. They responded that Fluor had not supplied the raw materials under the contract; when they received them, they would start work immediately.

Andrew invited them to the opening ceremony at his expense and then called Jim Stein to arrange a meeting. Jim was to be in San Francisco the following day, and Andrew arranged to meet him there. He then called me to ask if I could attend the meeting. I was not in Sydney, but with the dateline allowing me to arrive before I left I could make it. Andrew and I met first, in the Fairmont Hotel on Nob Hill. He was accompanied by his secretary, Albert, who seemed to always be with him on these trips. We had dinner, and I was briefed on the issues. Later, we drafted two letters that he hoped

Anaconda nickel plant

Jim Stein would sign, to emphasise the importance of the project within Fluor's organisation. This continued till the early hours of the morning, with Albert typing the changes as we went.

After breakfast, we went to a meeting room in the hotel to await the Fluor team. Jim was accompanied by their global construction manager and the regional chief.

After introductions, Andrew gave an impassioned speech about the laterite nickel industry and his goal to build several plants. He said he hoped that Fluor would be his partner for all this. He produced a schedule devised by Fluor on a sheet of paper and theatrically threw it across the table; it looped around and landed near Jim. It showed the project was three months behind schedule. 'Whoever produced this should be shot,' declared Andrew. 'I've been to Italy and we are now back on target to complete the project on time. Jim, with your drive and my assistance we can create a new world for project delivery in major mining development.' Jim Stein, taken aback, stared at Andrew then glanced at his colleagues. I don't think he had ever been exposed to this attack before. Before Jim could respond, Andrew produced two letters. 'Jim, I'd like you and me to sign these as a signal to our organisations that this is the start of a great phase in mineral development for the world.' They essentially signalled to all that this was the most important project in Fluor's portfolio and it was to be given the highest priority. They paused to read the letters, one to the project staff and one to Fluor staff generally. A chastened Jim thanked Andrew for expediting the project and pledged the full force of Fluor's resources to deliver the project. He asked if we'd had legal review of the letters. 'Jim, Grahame and I drafted these last night and Albert typed them then. I want us to bind together and surprise the world.' I thought he was going to launch into another speech. Jim's advisors were saying, 'Don't sign!, we need a legal check,' as he put his signature to the paper with a flourish. He stood and reached over for Andrew's hand. After handshakes all round Jim invited us for lunch.

Later Andrew invited me to a Japanese restaurant for sashimi to wait on a guest who had flown in from Calgary. He said, 'I want you to meet Tim Burns from Canadian consulting engineering company Hatch. Hatch may be able to help us with engineering the next plant. They have new autoclave technology.' We three had a spirited discussion and after Burns had gone Andrew asked what I had thought. I said, 'We need to get this one built and see how it performs before we launch into new technology.' Andrew said, 'Grahame, you are always looking at the obvious. I want to build a much bigger future.' I smiled to myself. It had become no secret to me that Andrew's and my priorities were quite different. I flew back to Australia the next morning, while Andrew flew to London.

A major port strike disrupted equipment delivery, and Andrew was dockside doing deals with the unions to release our plant. This was to have repercussions later, when he reneged on agreements he had made at the dock. Union bastardry disrupted the building site when they put maggots in the food in the main canteen. As we approached construction completion, a series of failures by Fluor emphasised the fragile nature of our relationship. Fluor struggled to manage the site, which had sixteen individual plants trying to complete simultaneously.

Andrew's early cuts to the plant design began to bite as the commissioning process staggered forward with little give in the interfaces between the operating units. The autoclaves worked well, but the pressure-relief vessels were designed 'upside down', as it was discovered. Fluor had used an alumina plant configuration and not followed the Sherritt Gordon design. This delayed the final commissioning and cost Fluor $100 million to correct. Serious problems emerged with the concentrators and their agitators. Michael Masterman, our ex-McKinsey executive director, was sent to the site to engineer a hundred-day turnaround. Andrew brought in key experts from around the world to help, but the shareholders were restive. Glencore and Anglo were discussing a new approach. Andrew had tried to keep them at arm's length, but James Campbell, an Anglo American executive, came onto the board and was recruiting key execs from his African operations to cast their eyes over the proceedings.

Andrew decided to change the board composition and asked John Down and me to step down, in favour of Rodney Adler and John Morrison. I was initially peeved, but realised that the end game was in progress and the two large shareholders were determining the future in private meetings in London and Zug. It had been a wild ride and I had learned much about board responsibilities. My idyllic view of time management with boards was shot. Anaconda had averaged a meeting a week either on the phone or face-to-face in Western Australia. The meeting time was small compared to the travel and preparation time. Each board had a budget and strategy session which took the best part of a week annually. International visits could consume a week each. However, the intellectual stimulation was intoxicating.

USC

My presidency of the ACEA was at an end when another opportunity arose. Ralph Pickering, whom I knew through a mutual friend, called and wondered if I could help his 'born again' tech wreck, Utility Services Corporation (USC). I still had the SWR and RGC boards.

I'd met Geoff Lord, the chairman, many years before when he ran Elders Resources. Ralph, Geoff and I had dinner, and I agreed to join the board. They had bought the Melbourne Metropolitan Board of Works IT group and restructured several companies to form a services company for utilities and an IT services group mainly focused on telecommunications. It was a brave idea, and I had background on the utilities side to offer some suggestions.

The first AGM was rowdy, as a number of long-time shareholders voiced their disapproval of the performance of the company. They were especially upset that the directors were to be rewarded with share options, to be voted on at the meeting. The chairman had structured board fees to be paid in options because of a lack of cash. The meeting heard some heated comments and then Geoff started negotiating the terms of the options. I was appalled, and wondered if I should be there. Finally, a deal was done, and he turned to the board with, 'I'm sure my board will agree with me on this…' There was silence. I raised my hand. 'I came onto this board to make a difference. I will be paid nothing if the share price doesn't triple on the stock market. If the shareholders don't like this, then I'm happy to go.' There was some rustling in the audience. 'In the interests of board solidarity I'll agree to the new arrangements, but reserve the right to resign if I feel the company is not supported by the majority of the shareholders.' There was a round of applause. The meeting concluded and Geoff came over to apologise. 'Geoff, I'm serious, you can't do this.' 'Grahame, thank you for your comments. You turned the meeting around.'

I needed to take stock of my workload and decided to not expand my portfolio further. Although I was working hard, the more mature directorships took less time, although each went through crisis periods and Anaconda and USC held meetings interstate necessitating extra days of travel. USC was a difficult board, as the executive chairman attracted ASIC attention, generated from his history with Elders and John Elliott's leadership. The high-profile Elliott had been investigated by the National Crime Authority and in another development convicted of trading while insolvent and finally bankrupted. They were corporate raiders and had intervened in the Robert Holmes a Court attempt to take over BHP. USC was expanding rapidly and needed fresh equity. When Geoff suggested the board underwrite a deeply-discounted rights issue at no cost to the company, it seemed a cost-effective way to raise capital from the shareholders. A shareholder would be crazy not to take up the offer, and there would be little for the underwriters to pick up. The ASX endorsed the scheme and we went ahead. Then ASIC decided we had misused our directors' powers, and we were investigated. It came to nothing but was an unsettling experience. USC was becoming more IT-oriented and when it completed a reverse takeover of the distressed Davnet it was an opportunity for me to exit gracefully. It can be tricky leaving the board of a listed company, as it attracts attention. I was happy that the stock had multiplied by a factor of ten and I had become a significant shareholder.

Iluka

Iluka became the new name for the merged entities of RGC and Westralian Sands. Ken Court became the new chairman for an interim period in which RGC resolved some loose ends, and I was the only sustaining RGC director to join the new board with the other Westralian directors. I had been travelling to Perth for board meetings for many years for Anaconda, so the Iluka meetings were just an extension of that. My relationship with the new CEO, Malcolm MacPherson, was strained from the start. I needed to sign off the annual accounts for RGC and Malcolm thought I should just sign whatever was put in front of me. I refused and our relationship never really recovered. MacPherson had a very narrow corporate view, having run a business confined to the south-west of Western Australia. He now had to deal with operations across Australia, Indonesia and the USA. This, in my view, proved beyond him. With the removal of the Sydney head office the company thrived in the early days; however, the short-term vision quickly began to bite.

Indonesia was the first casualty. In the post-Suharto era, managing the various arms of government was difficult. Our local managing director had done a superb job of building the business, including the development of a smelter for $2 million. We had two major dredges operating over the main ore bodies, but there were 6,000 illegal miners on the leases who were producing more mineral from our tailings than our operations, at a lower cost. Their production appeared at our smelter gate cheaper than ours. This was both a threat and an opportunity. The downside was the environmental clean-up that resulted from their work. The business was the jewel in the crown of RGC, but Malcolm had no ability to work with this situation and set about finding a buyer.

The US operations were doing poorly because the DuPont legacy contracts were loss-makers. The development of new deposits in Florida and Georgia needed careful management. Again, Malcolm struggled to cope. The board was aware of the problems but loath to make changes. We were directionless. A change in chairman stirred things up, and Ian Mackensie took the reins. I shared my thoughts about who should be the CEO and eventually discussed with Dick Tastula, one of my co-board members, the possibility of his filling the top job till we could find a replacement for Malcolm. During our next board meeting, which was attended by the chief of Egon Zehnder, an executive search firm, the chairman suggested we couldn't sack Malcolm until we had a replacement. I looked at Dick and said we had a temporary replacement in Dick Tastula; he had run Barrick Gold in Australia and could easily hold the fort. The chairman paused, asked Dick if he would accept, and with his nod the board unanimously endorsed the move. The chairman left the room to tell Malcolm he was out and we had a new lease of life.

The process of finding a new permanent CEO was difficult, as the search firm produced a mediocre crop of applicants. The leading candidate after several rounds was Mike Folwell, who had a recent history at Pioneer Services, where John Schubert was the CEO. I called John to ask his opinion, and he was relatively negative. He said he had five regional reports and Mike Folwell had the biggest region, but the worst standing. I relayed this back to the board and was rebuked by the search firm. I responded that I felt it was my duty and did not accept the rebuke. The board finally accepted Folwell's nomination and we had a new CEO. This proved to be a mistake; these decisions can take years to rectify.

Iluka was in a volatile transition stage as the WA mines were almost depleted and the new exploration discoveries were in Victoria and South Australia. Technology was a difficult question, as patent fights with

Rio Tinto were an ongoing impediment. Low-grade ilmenite had formerly been seen as a waste product, but various technologies were emerging to upgrade the material to a synthetic rutile. Mike rushed into a new development on the back of a preliminary feasibility study. The study quoted a $30 million capex (capital expenditure), which I thought could blow out to $100 million. When I opposed the deal, Mike bristled, accusing me of attacking him. The board formed a subcommittee of two (Dick Tastula and me) to seek further information. It took just one day to discover there wasn't much support at the operating level, and the project was dropped by management. Mike was a great user of McKinsey-style consultants. The overhead shot up. We had the opportunity to buy a large resource in Victoria and the die was cast. The future lay in the eastern states.

Jacinth-Ambrosia was discovered in remote South Australia and held a large reserve of zircon. The cost of providing infrastructure initially made the development unattractive and an innovative plan to utilise the plants in Narngulu, near Geraldton in Western Australia, was examined. It took several years and a change of leadership to solve the puzzle.

A bigger problem emerged around the process of delivering the reserves in Victoria. The management was keen to award an EPC contract for the Hamilton processing facility to Downer EDI, which was focused on the mechanical issues. I felt the planning process was rushed, and tried to inject other contracting strategies. It was clear management would not back off, and I was isolated at the board table as other board members felt it was up to management to decide the contracting strategy. A contract was signed which on first review revealed the major flaw. The foundations for several parts of the plant were not on a fixed-price basis. It was do and charge. I asked why. 'We couldn't finalise the design due to vibration issues with the machinery. But it only represents a minor component,' was management's comment.

The $7 million allowance blew out to $32 million with a six-month delay, and we had hardly started. Don Morley, a fellow director, and I went to the site to discuss progress in early March to find almost no progress after five months of the contract. Downer was a large contractor originally from New Zealand. It had grown quickly by acquisition, and its ownership had gradually swung to Chinese equity. The integration of the business units was poor, particularly with the mining-related groups. The contract was led by the WA-acquired group JR Engineering, led by Joe Ricciardo. He had little alignment with the parent company and had built his success with West Australian–related projects. The unions in Victoria ate him up. Roach Mining was the umbrella company, but could not control or manage the numerous Downer entities involved in the work.

I called my friend Hans Ohff, who had left the Submarine corporation and taken several directorships, to ask if he could come to the site to offer advice. Hans agreed, but met the boss of John Holland at the airport and found out that Holland was doing fabrication work for the project; as he was a director of Holland, he had a conflict. He spent a day on-site and reported that there was no chance the project could be completed with the current management. Bill Bissett, our operations manager, had commented that there were seven cranes on-site as evidence of progress. Hans countered that none of them was working! The key point Hans made was that there was no project manager. He found a potential executive for the role, but Downer declined to hire him; Holland eventually took him on as its Victorian state manager.

At a board meeting, I stated that Iluka was two generations behind best practice with its project delivery concepts, and the board members nodded sagely, but there was no discussion. The chairman then moved on to the next item: gender equality in the company. The future of the company depended on effective capital management for the major transition to the eastern states. I felt despondent as the board, and particularly the chairman, did not think the role of the board was to tell management how to deliver projects. I believed our future would be bleak until we changed the CEO. Gradually, other deficiencies in the management emerged, and there was a push for change from the other board members.

Director Bob Every finally identified David Robb as a potential CEO. David had been unsuccessful in the race to head Wesfarmers after the retirement of Michael Chaney. Bob was a director there. David was loath to join; he looked at the books and thought we were a basket case. After many discussions, primarily with Ian Mackensie, and a mathematical analysis of the pros and cons, David felt he could make a difference and with a Perth base and an increasingly awkward situation at Wesfarmers he started out on the long journey to repair the damage inflicted by the previous incumbents. We were trying to find a way to develop the zircon-rich finds in South Australia. I had some useful meetings with David and with Hans Umlauf, the new development manager, and the company leapt into best practice with an alliance contracting strategy for the Jacinth development in South Australia, the next major project for Iluka after the debacle of the Hamilton work. Parsons Brinckerhoff was appointed the alliance partner, and I went to Adelaide to discuss with all the senior staff their roles in the alliance process. Some of the board members visited the site to experience the remoteness and scale of the project. It was most satisfying to watch the work unfold and note the successful commissioning, under budget and on time. I was very proud. It had taken almost a decade to get Iluka to this point.

33. Reflections

All of my board roles had exposed me to the whole gamut of corporate experience. My great regret was that I did not have much support for the project outcomes which was my passion. Directors largely were accountants and lawyers who concentrated on corporate governance and finance issues, their comfort zone. They felt project delivery was a management problem. Risk avoidance generally led to contracts that were more expensive and finally litigious.

In 2000, I had been elected an honorary fellow of the Institution of Engineers and also elected a life member of the ACEA. It's nice to be recognised by your peers, but I was keen to find new challenges. I had reconnected with the Centre for Independent Studies, run by Greg Lindsay, and started attending its meetings and annual conference. This stimulated an interest in political ideas, and I began reading books by philosophers and political analysts. My son Miles, who had developed a strong interest in electronic systems and started his own business training teachers in high schools, exposed me to the entrepreneurs in the new digital age. He suggested I read up on the new theories related to the impact of the internet and new approaches to social connectivity. PJ O'Rourke, David Stove, James Lovelock and Jared Diamond reshaped my view of the world. I was trying to find a deeper philosophy behind the world I had experienced, hoping to replace the world of engineering and directorships with new and equally stimulating worlds.

The major casualty in my life was my marriage to Margaret. During the tough times when I was setting the new directions for CMPS in 1987, we separated and divorced. It was largely my fault and the children suffered. Thankfully today we see each other regularly at family functions.

My love affair with music could now blossom, and I started a series of musical *soirees* at my home in Cottage Point, north of Sydney. I had become friends with Steve Clisby, who was helping me acquire the music software that I was using to compose and record musical pieces. I had set up at home a small recording facility that allowed digital and analogue music to be mixed. With a keyboard, I recorded drum and bass tracks that could then be overlaid with my saxophone and clarinet solos. It was a lot of fun, but technically challenging for me. Steve was a singer and musician from Los Angeles, who had spent 20 years in Europe and recently come to Sydney. We shared similar tastes, and he brought his band to Cottage Point, where I had a grand piano to round out the equipment.

Paula LaRue and I had been playing for years at private parties with her friends. At one time the ABC decided to do a TV piece on my work at CMPS&F and asked if I could play the clarinet on camera to compliment the show. I immediately asked Paula to help, and she arranged to have Wayne Ford play bass to round out our small band. I was thrilled with the outcome. We decided to work together on a number of songs, and an opportunity to play for Alan Newham my old colleague from Newham Techint at his Christmas party gave us a chance to show off our wares. Alan and Vicky, his wife, were happy and we were invited back for many years – our only steady gig! At Paula's birthday party during this period, I was reunited with Julie, her sister, and we struck up a friendship that has blossomed. Our love of music has brought us full circle from our chance meeting in Houston in 1979.

By now three of my children had married, and seven grandchildren were swelling the numbers at family events. My peripatetic life, it seemed, had imbued them with a travel bug. My eldest son David lives in Vietnam with his wife Phuong and their children, Quang and Naomi. My daughter Corinne resides in Dubai with her husband Clint and their children Lily, Lucy and Darby. My second son Miles lives in Sydney with his wife Lanie and their children Finn and Henry. My sister Andrea spends most of her time with her kids and grandkids and lives in the same apartment complex as my former wife Margaret, and they are good friends.

I am developing a love of photography and the bush, particularly around the waterways where I sail regularly. I keep in contact with my engineering colleagues, and we swap stories, but I am always looking for new ideas to research. I am healthy and am spoiled for options with hobbies and travel. My partner, Julie, and I have spent time together in India, Egypt, Nigeria, South Africa, all of South East Asia, Portugal, USA, Costa Rica, Oman, France and Mexico in recent times experiencing 'cultural immersion' as I call it, exposing ourselves to new ideas and cultures.

The philosophy of engineering is always in the back of my mind as I search for a better understanding of how we build and live in our world. Our society structures a path for the individual. You attend school and maybe university before joining the workforce. Assuming you are healthy and gregarious the path is well defined. Initially life experience is defined by the local community which eventually gives way to a larger community as we travel, read and meet others. My experience came from farm stays, hitch-hiking and the music business among many others. Pivotal for me were my master's studies which recalibrated my undergraduate experience. It took me into the Oil & Gas world of fast moving project development. Having experienced travel in Asia, the Middle East, North America and the Caribbean I started to understand the cultural impact of resource development. As I reached my final challenge as an executive, I was exposed to the world of political and financial pressures. My path could not have proceeded without the help of many mentors and life experiences. Keeping an open mind under sometimes extreme pressure is essential. A bit of luck doesn't go astray either.

A local band performance

With Steve Clisby

Desert island clarinet

www.ingramcontent.com/pod-product-compliance
Lightning Source LLC
Chambersburg PA
CBHW021112300426
44113CB00006B/123

About the Author

Pastor Jay Offer is a native of Washington D.C. He is currently the founding pastor of Harvest Crusade Ministries in Glen Burnie, Maryland. From an early age he gave his life to the Lord and immediately began service in the church. First he began playing the bongos as a six year old for the youth choir of Mt. Calvary Baptist Church in the suburbs of Washington D. C. Eventually he became a choir director at the age of 17 then moving to the Interdenominational Church of God, also in the Washington D. C. suburbs, as a musician.

Pastor Offer entered the U.S. Army as a broadcaster traveling to Asia and back earning awards for his work as a broadcast journalist. After a short stint in the private sector he eventually settled into law enforcement and moved to Baltimore. At the New Bethlehem Free Will Baptist Church he began to flourish in ministry. He served as a minister of Music for 21 years. In that timeframe he was elevated to a Deacon then a lay minister. After being ordained he was called to plant Harvest Crusade Ministries just outside of Baltimore.

Pastor Offer has had a burning passion for the people of God all of his life. His calling to teach, preach and be an instrument of healing is evident in his ministry. It is also evident in his community involvement. He doesn't care where the call is, if he is needed to minister, even in the ministry of presence he goes willingly. The Sanctification Walk was born out of the urging of the Holy Spirit to equip God's people to first live in His will. In these 21 days of prayer and fasting, he brings illustrations of our duty to God and how His favor is released upon the people. Pastor has written numerous songs, produced and performed on various recordings. This marks his first endeavor into the world of writing books.

www.ingramcontent.com/pod-product-compliance
Lightning Source LLC
Chambersburg PA
CBHW070612300426
44113CB00010B/1497